A HISTORY OF FAKE THINGS ON THE INTERNET

A HISTORY

of

FAKE THINGS

on the

INTERNET

WALTER J. SCHEIRER

STANFORD UNIVERSITY PRESS
Stanford, California

Stanford University Press
Stanford, California

Printed in the United States of America on acid-free, archival-quality paper

Library of Congress Cataloging-in-Publication Data
Names: Scheirer, Walter J., author.
Title: A history of fake things on the Internet / Walter J. Scheirer.
Description: Stanford, California : Stanford University Press, 2023. | Includes
    bibliographical references and index.
Identifiers: LCCN 2023017876 (print) | LCCN 2023017877 (ebook) |
    ISBN 9781503632882 (cloth) | ISBN 9781503637047 (ebook)
Subjects: LCSH: Internet—Social aspects—History. | Disinformation—
    History. | Online manipulation—History. | Deception—History.
Classification: LCC HM851 .S2485 2023 (print) | LCC HM851 (ebook) |
    DDC 302.23/1—dc23/eng/20230424
LC record available at https://lccn.loc.gov/2023017876
LC ebook record available at https://lccn.loc.gov/2023017877

Cover design: Lindy Kasler
Cover art: Stocksy and Shutterstock

To hackers everywhere

CONTENTS

CONTENTS

PREFACE

Observations from the Internet's Trenches

Close to the year-end holidays in 2011, I found myself on a flight to São Paulo with a carry-on bag loaded with brand-new, unboxed Apple products. It was my first time serving as a mule of any sort, and naturally I was a little nervous about what would happen when I arrived at Guarulhos International Airport. I was going to Brazil to deliver a series of lectures on machine learning, as well as to spend some time with a close friend and his family. In fact, the idea for me to smuggle thousands of dollars' worth of merchandise had been my friend's—thanks to the heavy import duties imposed by the Brazilian government, foreign electronics bought within the country were fantastically expensive. By making the purchase in the US, I'd be helping him save thousands of *reais* on his Christmas shopping. "If they pull you aside at the airport, just tell them that everything is your personal property," he told me. No problem.

The period in which this happened is significant. It was shortly after the introduction of the iPhone 3G and the iPad. These two products in particular made the Internet easily accessible to nontechnical users for the first time, and the entire world took notice. Tremendous desire for smartphones and tablets was expressed by consumers across all demographics—something that the tech market had never before experienced—not even during the dot-com boom of the late 1990s. And it was only after the Internet could be carried around by all users at all times that its full potential was realized.

Disembarking from the plane after landing at Guarulhos, I attempted to look as casual as possible while passing through customs. Naturally, an officer rushed over and pulled me aside as soon as I entered the screening area. Even with my tenuous grasp of Portuguese, I gathered from the stern order I received that my bag would have to be searched. After eyeing all of the luggage on my flight that was bursting at the seams with newly purchased goods from America, I knew that I would not be alone in receiving this special treatment. As I put my bag onto the belt of the X-ray machine, I heard a thunderous crash as an enormous suitcase fell off of a cart pushed by the couple behind me. Clothes, souvenirs, edible tidbits, and other assorted items they had collected during their travels scattered everywhere. A squad of officers ran over to investigate, and much shouting ensued. A stroke of luck in my favor! During the pandemonium, the X-ray operator had not paid any attention to my bag as it passed through the machine. I grabbed it on the other side and swiftly walked away while the chaos behind me continued. I shook my head as I exited the airport and hopped on a bus—saved by a typically Brazilian airport experience.

After we all had a good laugh over what had happened to me at the airport, my Brazilian hosts got right to work setting up their new gear. Holding his iPhone in my direction, my friend's brother-in-law exclaimed with a big grin on his face: "Look, *Facebook*." "Hmmm . . . ," I thought, "I wonder where this will lead?" At that time, I had been familiar with Facebook as a social-media platform that connected students and alumni from particular colleges, most typically those who were tech-savvy. It had only recently started to attract a broader base of users who realized that with a smartphone, its camera, and myriad apps they could produce their own content and reach a global audience of millions. I had a feeling that things on the Internet were about to change dramatically. I knew that dubious news sources were popping up on the web that reported on unvetted content posted to social media—the more sensational the better. This type of reporting stirred passions and led to aggressive online arguments. But I also knew about all of the creative ways technology was being used to reinvent storytelling. Some of the best parts of the Internet were forming as different people encountered each other for the first time. Watching these volatile elements mix would be interesting, to say the least.

While 2016 and the years that followed have seemed like a new horror to many, it was all old hat to me. My Brazilian friends and I would exchange messages of solidarity during what would be very turbulent periods in the politics of our respective countries. Donald Trump's rise in America would be paralleled by Jair Bolsonaro's in Brazil. Both were billed as authoritarian strongmen, with their oppositions alleging that they posed a clear threat to democracy and the international order that had held sway since the end of the Second World War. In practice, Trump and Bolsonaro functioned as virtual politicians, emphasizing their interaction with information networks more than their traditional policymaking. The COVID-19 pandemic response in America and Brazil is testament to this, informed as it was by a politics that blurred the line between online and offline life, to sometimes strange effect. America and Brazil suffered significantly during the pandemic. But to Trump and Bolsonaro, circumstances that could not be thwarted by the Internet didn't really matter to one's political fortunes.

Each man possessed a savvy understanding of contemporary mass media, which allowed for crafting narratives that were devastatingly effective, within their respective electorates and beyond. The Internet was the new frontier, and in some sense, it was the only thing that really mattered to the politics of the moment. The movements that developed around Trump and Bolsonaro exploited social media to promote candidates, mobilize voters, and push agendas that were not constrained by a conventional understanding of reality. By aggressively developing stories around political fantasies, engagement could be maximized with supporters who identified positively with the story lines, as well as with detractors who reacted negatively to the same material.

For example, throughout the course of the pandemic, Trump sought to portray COVID-19 as a mere nuisance by tweeting that the "coronavirus is very much under control in the U.S." (Bump 2021); that America shouldn't "be afraid of Covid" (Kolata and Rabin 2020); and that he was completely "immune" to the coronavirus after contracting it (Smith 2021). This was part of a pattern of Trump crafting controversies that individuals of all political orientations found irresistible to share online. In total, according to the *Washington Post*, Trump made 30,573 false or misleading claims while in office (Kessler et al. 2021)—so many that by the end of his tenure anything he said could be treated as irrelevant to the situation on the ground. In the latter days of his administration, the major social-media companies took the extreme step of banning him from their platforms altogether. Seeming to hold views on the pandemic similar to Trump's, Bolsonaro suggested that Brazil should stop being "a country of sissies" (Londoño et al. 2020), embrace its natural immunity to the coronavirus (Collman 2020), and recognize that its president did not want to hear anymore "whining" about the crisis (Paraguassu and Brito 2021). The Internet just ate this stuff up.

Online falsehoods were not restricted to just speech—a deluge of images and videos supporting alternate political realities turned out to be an even more effective outlet for swaying public opinion. Trump and Bolsonaro beckoned their followers to engage in participatory fakery by creating and sharing political content. If a new piece was exceptionally good, they would often share it with their millions of followers. This scenario spread across the world like wildfire. Ordinary people began to manufacture evidence of political treachery, in large part through fashioning memes—digital content in the form of images or text meant to be remixed and shared by an audience—that were deceitful and laced with violent rhetoric. Successful memes in this vein amplified bad information as they traversed social media.

The implications of participatory fakery can be alarming, to say the least, and warnings against it proliferated. With a highly polarized electorate, could fake information make the difference in a close race? According to a recent report from the Brookings Institution (Galston 2020), it's not hard to imagine that "a well-timed forgery could tip an election." What about the general question of the veracity of information? Do things change with a massive proliferation of falsehoods? WITNESS, a nonprofit that documents human rights abuses and their consequences, has noted that now "pressure will be on human rights, newsgathering and verification organizations to prove that something is true, as well as to prove that something is not falsified" (Witness Media Lab 2021). All of this taken together was hailed as the new era of "fake news." And the entire world could not get enough of it.

Technological developments facilitated the virtual bully pulpit that Trump and his junior partners made their ludicrous proclamations from. Certainly all those new Facebook users creating and sharing fake content were consequential to how the politics unfolded. But behind the scenes, changes were being made to smartphones and their cameras that were even more fundamental to undermining trust in the information that they recorded. Most familiar was the proliferation of smartphone apps designed to alter digital images, sometimes in radical ways, at the request of the user. These so-called filters are now available in Snapchat, Instagram, TikTok, and many other popular platforms. An underappreciated change, however, was that phones began to subtly alter all of the photos their cameras took, to improve the way they looked. The question of what, exactly, improvement might mean aside, this feature brought every single photograph on the Internet into question. The concern raised by the human rights experts at WITNESS is not only about what people are intentionally doing with technology; it applies equally to what technology is silently doing, without our awareness.

Was any of this truly new, though? I had been using a computer since the late 1980s and had been online since the early 1990s. Much of what I have observed since 2016 I had seen before, in other forms. Ordinary people were learning the art of digital fakery, something that was very recognizable to me as a former computer hacker and current media-forensics expert. If truth be told, I originally got into computing through the hacker scene.

In the 1990s hacking was a vibrant underground subculture whose activities were not limited to breaking into computers. Hackers were generally interested in using technology in unanticipated ways—including to change the world, as they saw fit. In this regard, the production of fake digital material delivered via the Internet was a surefire strategy for success. The manipulation of the news media by hackers was routine. And there were plenty of targeted disinformation campaigns against major corporations and world governments. I remember being astonished after first watching this unfold: amateurs on the Internet could force the world's power centers to react to their antics with relatively little effort. While I enjoyed the challenges of the technical aspects of computer hacking, I found these operations with a strong social element the most interesting. Later, while observing the politics of the Trump era, I recalled some of the early cases of digital disinformation that were legendary among hackers but largely unknown to the public. Was there some connection to the participatory fakery of today?

Heading to graduate school right after college, I drifted into research that had a connection to security. With my hacker background, this was a natural fit—I got to think unconventionally from the other side, preventing security breaches instead of causing them. It was at this point that I began working on digital forensics, and I was particularly interested in the examination of multimedia content for evidence of tampering. In the early 2000s, the Internet was still new to most people and mobile computing technology still rudimentary, yet there was growing interest in trading photos and other self-generated content online. It was clear to me that this would be the next big thing. At that time, the research community working on digital forensics was quite small, and rather welcoming of newcomers. Photoshop had been around for a decade at that point, and based on its ever-growing set of features, everyone knew that there was a lot of work ahead of us. The more researchers the merrier. In fact, that's how I met my Brazilian friend. He would later go on to become Latin America's leading media-forensics expert and was even hired by former Brazilian president Dilma Rousseff to demonstrate that photographs linking her to leftist terrorism during Brazil's military dictatorship were fake (Folha de S.Paulo 2009).

My early work in forensics looked at image tampering and camera attribution—the areas that researchers believed would be relevant to legal investigations. In this period, the focus was exclusively on serious criminal activity, particularly terrorism, which was on everyone's mind following the 9/11 attacks. Real cases would periodically emerge, like the allegations against Rousseff, as well as others related to child exploitation, in which a defendant would allege that the evidence against them was fake. But for the most part the research community was just keeping pace with the photographic and image processing technologies that we and our colleagues in the criminal justice system believed would be used by those intending to break the law. During this time, I kept thinking about the hackers who had specialized in disinformation and how they were doing things that pushed technologies in directions that ordinary criminals wouldn't be interested in. I was also intrigued by all the new image-manipulation features appearing in graphic-design technologies—many incorporating powerful artificial intelligence (AI) algorithms. What were artists actually using them for? With the Internet becoming a shared creative space for the world, perhaps these things were related.

Over the next decade, emerging national security concerns mobilized the US government to take more action against the perceived threat of media manipulation. With interest in international terrorism on the decline (though it remained a persistent, albeit limited, threat), policy makers and analysts once again turned their attention to old adversaries. Decades after its conclusion, the federal government still had a mindset shaped by the Cold War. For many years, the training material on photographic deception used within the intelligence community and federal law enforcement agencies largely consisted of old darkroom examples from the Third Reich, the Soviet Union, and Maoist China. Those familiar with this material believed that emerging technologies would lead to a new iteration of traditional *active measures* (Rid 2020)—political warfare exploiting disinformation and propaganda—executed by Iran, Russia, China, and their client states. Given their significant resources, nation-states had the capacity to manipulate information on the Internet far more effectively than individual amateurs. In particular, there were pervasive fears around election integrity—especially after the turbulence of the 2016 election.

Around the time of the election I had started my own laboratory at the University of Notre Dame and was looking for a research project that touched on all of these matters. Fortunately for me, DARPA, the military's advanced research agency, which had funded the creation of the Internet and early work on self-driving cars, had recently announced its media-forensics program (Turek 2022a), the objective being to develop capabilities to detect tampering in web-scale collections of images. The new capabilities were intended to be released not just to the military but also to other government agencies, technology companies, NGOs, and even journalists. This was a fight that required the participation of a broad coalition of partners. Initially, the anxiety was around Photoshop and related image-editing tools. Deepfakes, doctored videos generated by AI, appeared shortly after the program began and raised the stakes considerably. Wanting to contribute, I put in a proposal and was selected for funding. My lab got to work right away.

We knew we were on an important mission, and everyone was eager to contribute. The government provided us with manipulated images, created specifically for the program, that were meant to mimic what was believed to exist in the real world. This was helpful to our research and development, but I was far more interested in the real cases. These, after all, were what we would eventually have to detect. And we could learn something about the context they appeared in, which might be important to understanding what they actually meant. So I tasked my students with finding real instances of altered photos on the Internet. Armed with the latest automatic manipulation detectors and some knowledge of the places where fake content was originating (yes, we had some 4chan enthusiasts in our midst), they set out on their mission. Surely they would return with loads of evidence of Russian active measures. . . .

Over the course of several months, the students hit pay dirt—social media was awash in fake content. But something wasn't adding up—what they brought back to the lab wasn't matched to what the government thought the problem was. There were no deepfakes and very few instances of scenes that were altered in a realistic way so as to deceive the viewer. Nearly all of the manipulated political content was in *meme* form, and it was a lot more creative than we expected. As an expert in media forensics, I had broad working knowledge of the history of photo doctoring, and what we had in front of us looked quite a bit like the long-forgotten manipulations from the darkroom era of photography. The manipulations performed by professional photography studios were nearly always a form of cultural expression, not the traditional political propaganda that was documented in those old books sitting on the shelf at the CIA.

Very much in the spirit of participatory fakery, ordinary people on the Internet were working on political story lines through memes, providing proof that a major media outlet was no longer needed to shape the broader conversation around contemporary events. While there was a lot of violent rhetoric and imagery in what my students had collected, much of it was tongue-in-cheek—more satirical than diabolical. I asked my colleagues about their experience with fake content on the Internet—all conceded that they hadn't run into the active measures that we were all worried about. It was memes all the way down.

And this wasn't exclusively an American phenomenon—we had exported participatory fakery abroad through the meme. Working on a big case study on the integrity of the 2019 Indonesian elections for USAID, my students and I had a further opportunity to examine the nature of the problem. An analysis of two million election-related images that we retrieved from social media seemed to confirm my suspicion: the fakes were once again a far cry from sophisticated disinformation. Assumptions made about who was faking content were also questionable. In the case of Indonesia, Western analysts believed that China, the regional hegemon, was responsible for a large amount of it. But we didn't see much evidence for that. From our perspective, the sources were disparate. While there is often an expectation that right-leaning groups are more apt to generate fake material, the general phenomenon is not associated with only one political alignment. During the course of the Indonesian election, we saw plenty of instances of memes conveying false messages in support of the centrist candidate, President Joko Widodo, just as we did for his challenger, the right-leaning Prabowo Subianto. This was representative of the global election landscape.

Which is not to say that nation-states aren't playing in the realm of political fantasy. But if they aren't following the Cold War playbook, how are they exploiting fake material? Not in the ways that you might think. Wannabe demagogues and spy-thriller plots notwithstanding, the big story can be seen unfolding within the global technology industry itself. At a strategic level, the great powers are seeking technological dominance through aggressive subsidies for their domestic industries, lax regulation, and the exploitation of loopholes in international intellectual property law. And they are most interested in those technologies that facilitate the imaginative aspects of today's Internet: from blazingly fast 5G networks that can deliver even more fake content to users to sophisticated augmented-reality apps that can alter what we see around us on the fly.

A captive global audience locked into a newly indispensable technology, with no alternatives available because of an uncompetitive marketplace, is subject to the whims of the country that developed it. Whoever controls the software and the information networks controls what that audience experiences. The individual user has no choice in the matter, and there is little that other countries can do, save turning off large portions of the Internet—something liberal democracies have been reluctant to do. It's important to recognize, however, that at the same time the development of popular technologies is in part a response to the desires of the domestic market. There is no better example than the economic plan of Xi Jinping, which seeks to captivate the citizens of China with creative technologies while simultaneously exporting them abroad. The execution of Xi's plan is contributing to the construction of a parallel universe on the Internet, inhabited by potent AIs, where nothing is what it seems to be.

Top-down control of information by those in power is an understandable phenomenon—this has always been a problem. But why is there near universal interest in faking everything and anything on the Internet today? This puzzled me, and to help answer the question, I decided to go back to where I first encountered fake digital content, to learn about the motivations and personalities behind the early instances. What I would learn would radically change my perspective on the nature of reality.

Putting my cards on the table: I have always been skeptical of the dire warnings about technologies that somehow steer us away from the truth. I'm an optimistic technologist with a vested interest in supporting creativity as an instrument of human flourishing. Haven't creative art forms like the novel always challenged the truth in some way? Why turn away from new innovations in storytelling simply because they provide an outlet for folks intent on making things up? That feels overly constraining. I like Internet culture, and you probably do too. But I'm also wary of the ways things can go awry. The ethics surrounding the use of new creative technologies is supremely important. Fiction can steer us to dangerous places: sometimes you get to a "Stop the Steal" rally, but most of the time you don't. Knowing this, vigorous support of technological progress is warranted, as long as there is an equally vigorous rejection of any concomitant, parasitic unethical behavior. Throughout this book, we'll scrutinize the ethics of individual incidents where something was faked. As we will see, things aren't nearly as bad as they might seem.

ACKNOWLEDGMENTS

I'm tremendously grateful for the outpouring of support this project received in the midst of a global pandemic. In spite of the crisis, a number of folks were incredibly generous with their time, lending resources, tips, feedback, and a heap of encouragement. First and foremost, I owe a debt of gratitude to Meghan Sullivan, director of the Notre Dame Institute for Advanced Study, who first suggested that I dig into the history of fake things on the Internet through a serious critical inquiry and then (to my surprise) stepped up with a fellowship to give me the room to do it. This book was an outgrowth of the 2020–21 fellowship year at the Institute, which had the very appropriate theme of trust and which put me in dialogue with a group of outstanding scholars and public intellectuals. In particular, Denise Walsh, Hollie Nyseth Brehm, Katlyn Carter, Robert Orsi, Pete Buttigieg, Ted Chiang, and Aaron Michka provided spectacular feedback and guidance as we workshopped different chapters of the book. I couldn't have asked for a better group to be in lockdown with!

Notre Dame as an institution has been phenomenally supportive of interdisciplinary research. Additional thanks must be given to Pat Flynn, former chair of the Department of Computer Science and Engineering, for providing me with further resources and allowing a computer scientist to try his hand at writing a history. I don't think I could have undertaken a project like this anywhere else.

Other scholars provided input on specific topics that helped shape the text of this book. There is a small but mighty community supporting the nascent discipline of "hacker studies": Robert W. Gehl at York University,

Acknowledgments

Sean T. Lawson at the University of Utah, Gabriella Coleman at Harvard University, and Felipe Murillo at Notre Dame all provided essential input on the computer underground. Margaret DeFleur at Louisiana State University was a wonderful tour guide through the discipline of mass communications and shared a very unique first-hand perspective on the hacker scene. On the forensics front, I'm thankful for background knowledge and feedback given by Neil Johnson, formerly of George Mason University, now with Pacific Northwest National Laboratory. The ever-brilliant Maria Ma at Yale University deserves my appreciation for many late-night pandemic Slack chats about ancient memes and modern China. Credit goes to a former postdoc in my laboratory, Michael Yankoski, for making a bunch of helpful suggestions and corrections to my various drafts. Mark McKenna at UCLA, as well as He Jing and Wanjun Sui of Gen Law in Beijing, provided me with expert intellectual property guidance in curating the photos included in this volume. And of course I'd be remiss if I didn't thank the many voices who speak in this book. The conversations I had were fascinating and provocative, and I hope this is reflected in what appears.

Margo Irvin and the team at Stanford University Press have been an absolute pleasure to work with. Three anonymous reviewers deserve credit as well, for spending a great deal of time with earlier drafts of this text. The published version of this book has exceeded expectations in all respects.

A HISTORY OF FAKE THINGS ON THE INTERNET

1

Restyling Reality

WHY IS THERE SO MUCH FAKE STUFF on the Internet? Perhaps it has something to do with a rare civilizational transformation that is taking place right now—a transformation that is challenging our relationship with information in ways that alter the very perception of existence. No longer content to live within the confines of the physical world, the global population moves seamlessly between alternate realities made possible by radical innovations in technology. What began with the campaign to relocate as many aspects of our lives as possible into the smartphone has accelerated during the COVID-19 pandemic, with both work and play for many becoming virtualized. The Internet presently exists as an extension of the world's imagination, its data centers filled to the brim with competing fictions. This has been a boon to creativity, and may be jumpstarting a cultural renaissance like none other. But myriad dangers lurk here as well.

As the popular press reminds us on a daily basis, many bad things are hatched in the darker corners of the Internet. And those bad things are frequently underpinned by the pervasive barrage of falsehoods on social media. This has been singled out as a pivotal problem of our time—usually in alarmist terms. For instance, a recent report published by the Pew Research Center, a nonpartisan American think tank that studies social concerns, likened the Internet to a weapon of mass destruction merely because it is a participatory space. According to the report, "The public can grasp the destructive power of nuclear weapons in a way they will never understand the utterly corrosive power of the internet to civilized society, when there is no reliable mechanism for sorting out what people can believe to be true or false" (Anderson and Rainie 2017).

Blame for this tends to be assigned to specific social technologies and those responsible for creating them. If only we could trust-bust, reform, and regulate our way out of the post-truth stalemate, the global political crisis unfolding around us could be resolved (Zuckerman 2021). Or so the current thinking goes, reinforced by a growing cadre of activists, academics, and policy makers—all echoing a now-familiar narrative constructed from news-media coverage of extraordinary events tied in some way to the Internet. But this line of inquiry betrays a certain naïveté about the online experience. Do all falsehoods necessarily mislead us? Are those who produce false content always malicious? What would happen if media that facilitate the widespread dissemination of fictions were strictly regulated or even banned? Who even has a good grasp of what those media are and how they work?

Thoughtful inquiry into the matter of fake content on the Internet has been rare. There simply hasn't been much interest in the historical development of such content or the social role it has played since the dawn of global information networks in the late 1960s. This is surprising, because at a fundamental level, fake stuff is interesting to everyone and always has been (McLeod 2014). Long considered a locus of rationalism, today's Internet is more often than not pushing against facts and reason as it serves as a conduit through which popular stories move. The Portuguese political scientist Bruno Maçães has argued in his recent book *History Has Begun* that imaginative mythmaking on the Internet is upending society in ways that were inconceivable a generation ago (Maçães 2020a). This, he tells us, is a phenomenon that we should not fear but instead embrace. In his words, "Technology has become the new holy writ, the inexhaustible source of the stories by which we order our lives." Yet there can be no doubt that within these stories there is tension between creative act and malicious deception, especially when both employ the same set of software tools to achieve their ends.

What exactly is going on out there in the digital terra incognita? This is a complex question. But if we could answer it even partially, we would have a better understanding of the economic, political, and social landscape of contemporary life. Instead of bemoaning the present state of affairs, in this book we will track a very different critical course by following

FIGURE 1.1. A window into the turbulent imagination of an artificial intelligence. This scene was automatically generated by the VQGAN + CLIP algorithm (Nerdy Rodent 2021). Courtesy Ahsen Khaliq. Reprinted with permission.

an undercurrent of inventiveness that continues to influence how fake content is created, disseminated, interpreted, and acted upon today. Maçães, one of the few optimistic voices on this matter, is generous with a vision for this new digital landscape but meager with the evidence for what it constitutes and how it came about. Perhaps we can help him out by filling in those crucial details.

With respect to society's perspective on reality today, a brief review of both the distant and the near past is helpful to set the stage for the chapters that follow. While it is undoubtedly tempting to jump right into a discussion of state-generated disinformation, right-wing propaganda, left-wing delusions, and other political material, let us leave these for the moment (we'll come back to them later). Instead, let us consider the ways in which the imagination has directed culture over the centuries. Reality has always been shaped by ideas that are projections of the imagination, an essential aspect of our humanity. The imagination's move into information networks is the product of social trends related to this phenomenon. Because of this, social technologies have had an outsized impact in the past several decades—and they bear a strong resemblance to some of the oldest known communication mediums.

Indispensable Stories from Parallel Timelines

Why, exactly, should we take a closer look at historical instances of fakery? On the surface, the artifacts that have been left behind appear incidental to the potent social trends we're interested in; they're merely the output of some creative process driving those trends. But we don't have direct access to that process. It is impossible to travel back in time to recover the exact social context in which something appeared, and we do not have enough knowledge of the brain to understand the cognitive mechanisms that were invoked in its creation. By looking at the historical evidence, however, we can observe specific patterns recurring over time in what has been handed down to us. Rather crucially, early fictions are directly connected to those social trends that would upend our contemporary life, and so they are important indicators of what was to come. Why have we always been seeking to transcend the confines of the physical world? Because as humans, we can imagine possibilities beyond it. And this takes us into the realm of myth.

Working in the early twentieth century, the French anthropologist Claude Lévi-Strauss considered the question of how significant myths have been to the organization of society. He noticed an uncanny similarity between the myths of different cultures, from the primitive to the modern (Lévi-Strauss 1969). From this basis, Lévi-Strauss argued that an unconscious production of mythologies is an essential aspect of human thought (and perhaps says something about the underlying organization of the human brain). When confronted with a contradiction, a myth provides a simplification by which the mind can resolve it, thus relieving burdensome anxiety in some cases and creating entirely new possibilities for society in others. While one could be duped by this process, the simplification is often a breakthrough in its own right, allowing one to think through complicated situations with newfound clarity. This is what we tend to describe as creativity.

Lévi-Strauss also made a crucial observation about the experience of myths in practice, specifically, that humanity exists in parallel timelines: the physical world (i.e., the historical timeline) and the myth cycle (i.e., a fictional timeline). Mythical thinking, he argued, was in no way inferior to scientific thinking, but served a different yet equally important role in society:

> If our interpretation is correct, we are led toward a completely different view, namely, that the kind of logic which is used by mythical thought is as rigorous as that of modern science, and that the difference lies not in the quality of the intellectual process; but in the nature of the things to which it is applied. This is well in agreement with the situation known to prevail in the field of technology: what makes a steel axe superior to a stone one is not that the first one is better made than the second. They are equally well made, but steel is a different thing than stone. In the same way we may be able to show that the same logical processes are put to use in myth as in science, and that man has always been thinking equally well; the improvement lies, not in an alleged progress of man's conscience, but in the discovery of new things to which it may apply its unchangeable abilities. (Lévi-Strauss 1955)

The phenomenon of mythical thinking extends far beyond a single person dreaming up a myth in isolation. It is a palpable manifestation of a collective unconscious, informed by shared information—all members of a community operate within the same frame of reference (Campbell 2008). A part of the relief one feels when drawing on a myth in their own life is knowing that others are doing the exact same thing, perhaps even sharing in the revision of the same contradictory experience. Similarly, a big idea that transforms society is propelled by a crowd that is simultaneously enthralled by it.

Here we can make a connection to the present by considering the relationship between historical myths and Internet myths as they spawn *memes*. A meme is a cultural artifact that is meant to be transmitted from person to person and that can evolve over time like a biological organism. With the remixing of information in service of this evolution, current circumstances can be integrated into an overarching story and understood within that context. We know the meme today as a bite-size form of storytelling on the Internet, often making use of images or videos, but the general concept describes a highly effective mechanism by which myths of various forms can change and spread over time using any available medium of communication (Dennett 2010).

Current writing on Internet culture dates the genesis of what is now commonly understood to be a meme to the early 2000s, which coincides with the emergence of social networks (Shifman 2013; Mina 2019). But the phenomenon is much older. The evolutionary biologist Richard Dawkins, who originally popularized the notion of the meme in the 1970s, went all the way back to antiquity for his examples of how this process works over long time spans. He astutely argued that the durable meme complex of the philosopher Socrates is still alive and well within our culture, over two millennia after it first appeared (Dawkins 2016). When we look at what came before images and videos on the Internet, we see that historically memes have always encapsulated falsehoods, mythmaking, and culture quite effectively. The only real difference from today is the use of mediums that have long fallen out of favor.

It is, of course, the oral tradition that appeared first. The Homeric poems wove a rich tapestry from ancient Greek mythology and religion and fomented a host of ancient memes. Importantly, there are significant elements of fantasy throughout the stories of *The Iliad* and *The Odyssey*, from the actions of the gods to the circumstances of the Trojan War itself. There is no definitive proof that the war actually occurred, yet many ancient and modern people believed it was a real event, in spite of the lack of evidence (Wood 1998). Further, orality entailed changes to the stories, by virtue of people not having perfect memories. Once an acknowledgment was made that the story would be slightly different from telling to telling, the bard had room for improvisation in the performance.[1] A large portion of the classical canon is based on novel reworkings of Homer, and the bulk of Greek and Roman culture shares some relationship to *The Iliad* and *The Odyssey*, which everyone was familiar with. The denizens of the ancient world weren't just enjoying the Homeric poems as entertainment; they were, in a sense, living them.

Given the primacy of Homer and the low rates of literacy in the ancient world, the study of myth has (not undeservedly) emphasized the oral tradition. However, this overshadows another early development that is more important for our understanding of Internet culture: the use of visual mediums. We are, after all, visual creatures, relying on our sight to navigate any environment we find ourselves in. Thus an exchange of drawings, paintings, and sculptures is arguably a more natural way for people to communicate—and an even better way to immerse oneself in a myth cycle. Art was fairly accessible in antiquity, meaning ordinary people would possess objects that were creative in nature, often depicting familiar characters and scenes from a well-known story. With this development, *The Iliad*, *The Odyssey*, and the general mythological milieu could be transferred as memes via specific visual mediums.

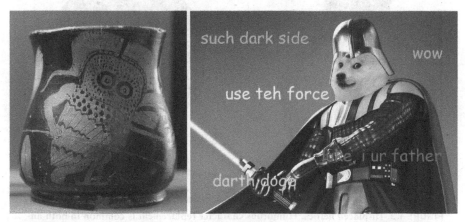

FIGURE 1.2. Anthropomorphic parody, as conveyed via the meme. While the mediums that have conveyed memes have changed over time, the form has not. **Left**: An owl dressed up for war in the guise of Athena; Attic red-figure Anthesteria *oinochoe*, ca. 410–390 BCE. **Right**: Stock meme character and cryptocurrency icon the Doge, dressed up for war in the guise of Darth Vader. Left, © Marie-Lan Nguyen / Wikimedia Commons. Licensed under CC BY 2.5.

Take, for instance, ancient Greek pottery.[2] Vases, bowls, cups, and other household items were frequently decorated in whimsical ways that remixed the classical canon. Pottery became an effective medium for ancient memes because it was in common circulation and could be exchanged far easier than a long poem could be recited from memory. Mass production ensured that the entire population of the Greek world was supplied with the latest iterations of their favorite stories.[3] This wasn't true of what was analogous to visual fine art of the period, which was slower to introduce revisions to the canon and not as accessible to the ordinary person. Remarkably, even in this archaic medium, then, we find strong parallels with content that exists to promote fictions on the Internet today. According to Alexandre Mitchell, a scholar of early forms of visual communication, the painted pot can "tell us something about rules of behaviour, about the differences between the public and the private sphere, about gender difference, ethnicity, politics, beauty and deformity, buying patterns, fashion, perceptions of religion and myth." Notably, humble pieces of pottery conveyed "what people really thought and experienced" (Mitchell 2009).

FIGURE 1.3. Displaced heroes. Humorous character replacement is common in both ancient and modern memes. Mockery of exaggerated portrayals of valor, especially, plays a role in critiques of cultural values. *Left*: A lunatic stock satyr character as the Greek hero Heracles in the Garden of Hesperides; Attic red-figure *oinochoe*, 460 BCE. *Right*: stock meme character Wojak, who represents melancholy, in the guise of Marvel superhero Captain America. Left, © The Trustees of the British Museum. All rights reserved. Reprinted with permission.

Anyone who is familiar with Internet memes knows that there are certain repeating motifs that are formed by drawing from a collection of standard elements. The same is true of the paintings found on Greek pottery. The use of stock characters was common, and this gave artists significant flexibility in treating a familiar scene. Silly anthropomorphized animals and fantastic creatures like satyrs served the same role as the Doge or Wojak in modern memes (figs. 1.2, 1.3)[4]—all could be used as comic stand-ins for gods, heroes, and other more serious figures. Many of the painted settings were drawn from the universe of the Homeric poems, similar to the way the settings used in the memes of today are drawn from a specific pop culture universe like that of *Star Wars* or Marvel Comics. Stock characters and settings were often intertwined with real events like athletic contests or religious festivals, allowing the artist to make commentary on current affairs.

The way in which humor was deployed is significant to our understanding of the mood of a piece (Larkin 2017). Parody emerged as one of the earliest forms of social commentary, offering a humorous alternate reality within an alternate reality. One common form it took was absurdist comedy. For instance, the body parts of depicted figures could be exaggerated to emphasize some trait—something we find in popular Internet tropes like the "big brain," which is used to make ironic statements about

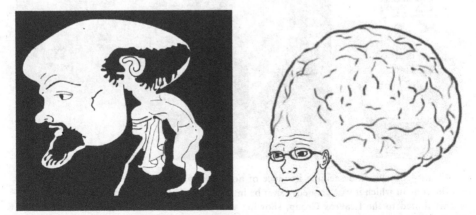

FIGURE 1.4. Ancient and modern big brains. *Left*: Caricatured bystander; an Attic red-figure *askos*, 460–440 BCE. *Right*: The "big brain" meme template. Left, Musée du Louvre, G610; vectorized drawing © Alexandre G. Mitchell (https://www.alexmitchell author.com/). Reprinted with permission.

poor decision making (fig. 1.4). Nonsense writing, particularly confounding to archeologists, was also present in various scenes (Mayor et al. 2014). While many explanations for it exist (e.g., misspelling, meaningless decoration), it can function as an absurdist element, with the context providing clues as to how to interpret the joke. When we consider similar modern instances, like the "meme man" genre of memes,[5] which highlights the absurdities associated with the culture of Wall Street, this makes perfect sense (fig. 1.5). Humor has not changed much over time, and it remains an effective form of criticism within a myth cycle.

While less accessible than visual mediums, ancient long-form writing should not be discounted, as it was a prototype for later writing in periods of higher literacy. The search for historical analogs to what we today call "fake news" has revived debate over the credibility of the Greek writer Herodotus and the tone he set for later writers chronicling significant events (Holland 2017). Peppered throughout his *Histories*, which is widely regarded to be a foundational work of scholarship in the West, are tales that can't possibly be true. For example, embedded in a mostly accurate report on the geography of Persia is the following account of the local insect life:

FIGURE 1.5. When a seeming instance of nonsense writing is viewed from outside of the time in which it was created, can it be interpreted? *Left*: Athenian black-figure *olpe* attributed to the Leagros Group, showing two Amazons with a dog, 525–510 BCE. The text on the pot reads "OHE(Y)N" and "KE(Y)N," which is inscrutable even to the modern viewer with knowledge of the Greek language. *Right*: "Meme Man" meme mocking the culture of Wall Street. One wonders how the text in this meme will be interpreted 2,500 years from now.

In this sandy desert are ants, not as big as dogs but bigger than foxes; the Persian king has some of these, which have been caught there. These ants live underground, digging out the sand in the same way as the ants in Greece, to which they are very similar in shape, and the sand which they carry from the holes is full of gold. (Godley 1920a)

In antiquity, how often were such stories recognized as fake? Were ancient commentators skeptical of their own culture's histories? Writing hundreds of years after Herodotus, Pliny the Elder matter-of-factly reiterated the story of the Persian ants in his own *Natural History* (Bostock 1855). If fact-checking existed in the Mediterranean two thousand years ago, no evidence of it has been handed down to us.

The contemporary explanation for stories like the one about the ants is that in the past people were simply ignorant, living in intellectual darkness until the dawn of the Enlightenment in the late sixteenth century. Scientists are especially prone to promoting this explanation, which itself turns out to be a gross misrepresentation of the way in which information was exchanged and understood for centuries.[6] The ancient reception of historians like Herodotus and Pliny was quite different from the reception of today's scholarly histories. In the Greek world, there was a certain expectation that past events would be blended with elements of myth when recorded, in order to convey the relevant cultural context that wouldn't be directly available in a simple recounting of the original event (Romm 1998). This provided a richer (and in many cases more entertaining) understanding of the event to the person experiencing the retelling. By the editorial standards of today's most serious publishers, such reporting would obviously not pass muster. But it's not unlike what happens in more popular forms of writing that are prevalent on the Internet like tabloid journalism and conspiracy-theory-laden social-media posts.

The evolution of writing eventually led to the invention of the novel. Should we be concerned about that medium in our discussion of the development of fake things? On the one hand, the novel announces itself as a work of fiction—we aren't meant to believe it. Yet on the other hand, the novel is necessarily a manifestation of fakery—the author had to invent the characters and the world in which it takes place. Crucially, the ancient novel also existed within the myth cycle, blending the very same elements that were found in other forms of creative composition like poems and histories. Early examples of the form like the *Metamorphoses* by Apuleius (Adlington and Gaselee 1922) and *Daphnis and Chloe* by Longus (Henderson 2009) also drew on the familiar settings and characters that were available in the catalog of Greco-Roman myth.

To the overly pedantic observer, everything we have discussed thus far should be rejected out of hand if it is being used for more than just entertainment. After all, a reasonable person should not be fooled into thinking that stories with clearly fictional elements like satyrs, heroes, giant ants, and the like are, in any regard, true. This begs the following question: is mythmaking distinct from lying and its more ignominious cousin, bullshitting? The answer is *yes*. According to the philosopher Harry Frankfurt, a lie is an attempt to deceive someone in order to achieve a specific objective in a tactical (i.e., limited) sense, while bullshit is largely vacuous speech that is a manifestation of the utter disregard for truth (Frankfurt 2009). A myth is both contentful and strategic (i.e., global) in its aims. It is the foundation of something large that builds connections between people—something we all strongly desire. Lying and bullshit are associated with the negative behavior of individuals, while myths are the collective expression of an entire community and are meant to be a reflection of the human condition. We cannot live without them.

If the inclination to tell meaningful stories explains why there is so much fake stuff on the Internet, then the situation we find ourselves in is ultimately good. Memes are not lies (they are too creative and typically aren't trying to achieve an immediate, limited objective) nor are they bullshit (they are more information-rich). In general, the bulk of fictional writing on the Internet doesn't conform to either type of problematic content. Instead it supports contemporary myth cycles. That is not to say that myths don't influence behavior in any way. In some cases, that is the intent.

Kembrew McLeod, a professor of communication studies at the University of Iowa, has written extensively about the *prank* as an operationalized form of mythmaking. He defines it with a simple formula: "performance art + satire × media" (McLeod 2014). The performance-art component makes the prank a provocation, sometimes involving direct engagement with an audience in order to get them to do something. In addition, pranks lean heavily on humor, with a satirical component meant to stimulate critical thought. Unlike hoaxes, they are not often malicious in nature.

Historical prankster Jonathan Swift is fondly remembered for pushing the boundaries of what his audiences could tolerate with shocking jokes that possessed some element of ambiguity. For instance, Swift's satirical commentary on the eighteenth century Irish economy in the form of a procannibalism pamphlet titled *A Modest Proposal*, which suggested that the poor of Ireland should sell their children to the rich as food, has triggered recurring moral panic over the course of several centuries. Which, in turn, has made his joke funnier for those in the know, as each misunderstanding further emphasizes the critique Swift was trying to make about the neglect of the poor. The multiplicative media component of McLeod's formula stands out as being particularly important to the success of a prank: technology acts as an accelerant. By the time Swift arrived, the printing press had enabled writers to have a broad and enduring impact.

Already at the dawn of civilization, then, all of the ideas were in place for the construction of the Internet myth engine. Yet it took a couple thousand years to get to where we are now. For much of that time, myth cycles were guarded by the clergy and aristocracy, with things proceeding as they had since antiquity. A sharp separation between lived fictions and observable phenomena began after the Thirty Years' War in Europe, with the newly emergent bourgeoisie's push to marginalize the supernatural, which it alleged was a tool used by clerical elites and the landed gentry to control everyone else (Piketty 2020). The motivation for doing so was just business: the belief that rational markets would increase wealth caused a radical reorganization of society and culture that was, in many ways, completely alien to the ordinary person. The separation would prove to be temporary, however—it's easier to topple a monarch than a fundamental human need (Douthat 2021b). The myth cycles now exist digitally on the Internet, where they are increasingly supported by AI and are more influential than ever.

This convergence of myth and technology had been anticipated in science fiction at the dawn of the Internet era, most notably by the writer William Gibson in his novel *Count Zero* (Gibson 1986). In Gibson's vision of the future, AIs take the form of Haitian voodoo gods in cyberspace in order to interact with people in a more appealing way. In a purely technological setting, it's easy to dismiss the appearance of anything resembling mythical thought if one possesses a purely rational mind. In a sense reminiscent of Lévi-Strauss, one of Gibson's characters discusses the difference between mythical and scientific thinking in the new convergence between religion and technology that is appearing, realizing that one shouldn't be too quick to dismiss apparent impossibilities:

> We may be using different words, but we're talking tech. Maybe we call something Ougou Feray that you might call an icebreaker, you understand? But at the same time, with the same words, we are talking about other things, and that you don't understand. (Murphy 2010)

In the novel, the voodoo spirit Ougou Feray is equated with a fictional computer hacking tool Gibson called an "icebreaker." Both represent the idea of unfettered access: the ability to go where others cannot. Yet in the passage above there is recognition that modes of thought could be radically different from person to person, even when expressed in the same exact language, blurring the separation between the rational and mythical. The early days of the Internet brought Gibson's vision of the future to fruition: digital myth cycles laden with ambiguity.

The Internet Simplifies Reality

In the controversial 2016 BBC documentary *HyperNormalisation*, the filmmaker Adam Curtis suggested that contemporary life has become a never-ending stream of extraordinary events that governments are no longer capable of responding to (Curtis 2016). The reason for this, according to Curtis, is that politicians, business leaders, and technological utopians have conspired to replace the boggling complexities of the real world with a much simpler virtual world, facilitated by revolutionary advances in computing. By retreating to the virtual world, it's possible to escape the everyday trials of terrorism, war, financial collapse, and other catastrophes that regularly plague the globe, without confronting them in any serious way. The film is both compelling and highly entertaining, introducing its audience to an array of eccentric figures, famous and obscure, who have had an outsized influence on the virtualization of life. Critics were mixed in their reactions to the film, in some cases not being able to make sense of the patchwork of concepts presented (Harrison 2016; Jenkins 2016). Given its coverage of everything from UFOs to computer hackers, one couldn't quite blame them. But this reflects the tangled logic of the Internet we now inhabit.

What Curtis is really portraying in *HyperNormalisation* is the resurrection of the myth cycle during a specific period of the twentieth century. The film establishes that the process began during the 1970s and accelerated through the 1990s dot-com boom. What exactly happened in the 1970s to trigger this? Curtis believes that it was the activities of several key politicians of the era, including Henry Kissinger, the US secretary of state, and Hafez Al-Assad, president of Syria. Both injected chaos into the international system, with the consequence of a global pullback from the resulting unmanageable complexities. However, this wasn't the only contributing factor. Contemporaneous trends in technology development were supported by the flight from complexity and related popular demand to return to the livable fictions of earlier centuries. The primary developments coming out of this were new communication mediums.

In the 1960s, sophisticated information networks began to connect to aspects of everyday life that previously had been untouched by computers. This started with the move to digital switching in the telephone network, which streamlined the routing of calls and made it easier to connect computers that could communicate over the phone lines. Demand for more bandwidth led to the development of better networking technologies throughout the 1970s. Ethernet, a high speed local area network (LAN) technology, was invented by Xerox's Palo Alto Research Center in 1973. The TCP/IP protocol suite, the language the Internet speaks to move information from point to point, was created for the Department of Defense's ARPANET (the precursor to the Internet) in the early 1970s (Salus 1995). Bell Labs, the storied innovation hub of the Bell System (Gertner 2012), pioneered a host of Internet technologies in the same decade, including the UNIX operating system (Salus 1994), a server platform that would later make cloud computing possible. All three technologies would become indispensable to the operation of today's Internet.

To savvy product designers at technology companies in the mid-twentieth century, the universal popularity of the phone system hinted at the potential for widespread adoption of computer networks by the general public. The new information networks would be highly interactive, moving more than just audio signals, which made the difference for ushering in drastic societal change. This was very different from print media, radio, and television, which were passively consumed. Information flowed both ways on the nascent Internet. Writers like Gibson noticed that this was happening and imagined how these networks would be used in the future. All signs pointed to a massive disruption in the prevailing social order, with elaborate fictions taking shape within a cyberspace that would be actively experienced.

Even allowing for these two catalysts of virtualization, it's mystifying that a globalized society conditioned by the idea of rational markets was not able to keep humanity's impulse toward myth at bay. Why did that happen? The technology investor Paul Graham has speculated that a refragmentation of society, made possible by networked computers exposing users to the entirety of the world's ideas, drew people away from the homogenized national cultures that had developed after the Second World War as a mechanism of behavioral control (Graham 2016). National television might have brought a country together each evening, but the programming wasn't really engaging to everybody. Similarly, a small number of oligopolistic corporations may have streamlined the structure of the economy, but they limited consumer choice. These systems were developed for efficiency during the war, but they were also a natural extension of the dismantling of the pre-Enlightenment world. From a policy perspective, such a setup stabilized society. Everyone was on common ground and directed away not just from countercultural ideas but also from any vestiges of the old religious and cultural traditions that pushed back against purely scientific explanation of observable phenomena. It turned out that not many people wanted to live that way. As soon as it was possible to fragment into myth-driven tribes again, people jumped at the chance. Early technology platforms supported, and in some cases even encouraged, this.

At the root of this refragmentation isn't the cliché of a lost soul wanting to find their true self. There is a fundamental resistance to the organization of society based on rationality, where individuals are defined only by their role in the economy. The philosopher Byung-Chul Han has posited that the abandonment of myth cycles in favor of markets didn't just limit our choices, it made us very ill (Han 2020). According to Han, depression, attention-deficit hyperactivity disorder, schizophrenia, borderline personality disorder, and other neurological disorders of the day aren't diseases in the traditional sense. Instead, they are the symptoms of excessive striving in a chaotic reality many feel there is no easy escape from. Without a check on excessive initiative, whether through intimate social relationships, religious practice, or other cultural traditions that appear irrational to the market, it's easy to fall prey to behavioral patterns that are harmful. This is exactly what the contemporary economy fosters. As Han has explained, "Where increasing productivity is concerned, no break exists between *Should* and *Can*; continuity prevails." Han's view is no doubt controversial, but it explains much. The move to a simpler, virtualized reality is the treatment many of us are seeking, without even realizing.

One often forgets the sincere optimism of the early days of the Internet, which stemmed from the promise that Han's dilemma and others could be resolved through technology. *HyperNormalisation* explored this idea by invoking the figure of John Perry Barlow, the longtime lyricist for the Grateful Dead and cyberlibertarian extraordinaire, who anticipated the construction of a viable alternative to conventional life, which he too believed had become dominated by work (and bland, passive forms of entertainment). Something had to be done to relieve the resultant alienation. Writing in the 1990s, Barlow proposed that "when we are all together in Cyberspace then we will see what the human spirit, and the basic desire to connect, can create there" (Barlow 2007). His vision was for users of the Internet not just to consume the vast amount of information available but to interact with it by contributing to the burgeoning artistic, political, and social movements assembling there. That optimistic spirit still lives on in some capacity today, in spite of the hand-wringing from political commentators over the alleged destructive nature of participatory media. The realization, however, was far different from what Barlow, a holdover from the 1960s, had hoped for.

To achieve Barlow's vision would require restyling reality in a way that would reverse the forces of alienation present in the physical world. To this end, early Internet users created content by taking something real and changing it at will to satisfy the creator and the community they intended to share it with. This activity would become explosively popular in the smartphone era, but more often than not the products had little to no connection with hippie idealism. The human spirit is gloomy at times, spinning dense webs of frustration and anxiety as reflected in shared multimedia posts. It's surprising, in retrospect, that Barlow did not foresee this, as it had been happening all along in illustration, photography, creative writing, and many other endeavors that would move to the Internet. The key difference was that originally, ordinary people couldn't effectively remix content at scale. With the Internet and accessible software, now they could.

Paradoxically, the simplification of life into virtual reality led to new complexities. Curtis, in his film, points to computer hackers as transcendent figures who, with their ability to move freely through the Internet, were able to detect that new exploitative power structures were taking root there. Chronic problems facing the richest countries were being reduced by corporations and governments to storyboards, to which new plot elements could be added or removed at will. But such virtualized responses did nothing except change perceptions. Over time, hackers learned how to take control of communications mediums and modify the storyboards used in conjunction with them for their own purposes. The simplification strategy was brittle, and the activities of the hackers that exploited this brittleness proved to be a useful prototype for later, less benign, actors. Similarly, Graham's refragmentation hypothesis was originally posed to explain the recent phenomenon of aggressive political polarization, which he attributed to an unanticipated consequence of Internet movements and their own storytelling activities. This is not to say that effective responses can't be mustered from virtual reality. In fact, new ideas there that combine real and creative elements might be key to solving the world's most pressing problems.

A Changing Media Landscape

When Barlow first imagined the possibility of a collectively creative high-tech future, the Internet was, relatively speaking, rather small. It consisted mostly of university and government computers, along with a handful of corporate machines. People would temporarily connect to the network via slow dial-up telephone connections and didn't spend much time using it. According to the United Nations International Telecommunications Union, a mere 2 percent of the globe was connected to the Internet in 1997 (International Telecommunications Union 2007). The sheer scale of the Internet in the present decade is a marvel of human achievement—nothing else in technology comes close to rivaling its capabilities and reach (fig. 1.6). This infrastructure is the cradle of the fake material we are interested in.

The statistics for today's Internet reveal explosive growth in connected devices, computing power, and, most importantly, content. A recent report by the defense technology company Northrop Grumman noted

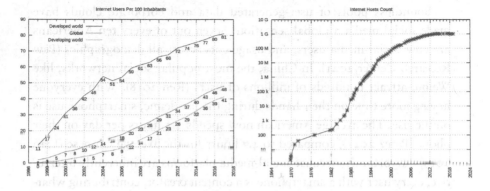

FIGURE 1.6. The Internet has grown drastically in both users and number of connected computers (hosts) since its widespread adoption by the general public in the 1990s. Left, © Jeff Ogden and Jim Scarborough / Wikimedia Commons. Licensed under CC BY-SA 3.0. Right, © Kopiersperre and Ke4roh / Wikimedia Commons. Licensed under CC BY-SA 3.0.

that in 2016 a zettabyte of data, or one trillion gigabytes, was transferred on the Internet for the first time (Bonderud 2020). This reflected a dramatic increase in multimedia content such as the images and videos being posted to social media, as well as the proliferation of networked mobile devices with cameras. By 2022, the number of devices connected to the Internet was predicted to number between 12 and 29 billion (Fadilpašić 2019; Maddox 2018). And many of those devices would be smartphones: in 2020, 3.5 billion smartphones were already in circulation (Newzoo 2020). The cloud provider Domo has estimated that 1.7MB of data is now generated each second for every person on the planet, reflecting pervasive mobile connectivity (Domo 2017).

The enormity of the system of backend servers managing the data flowing to and from all of those phones cannot be neglected. Vast cloud-computing platforms maintained by a handful of large technology companies like Amazon and Google have concentrated the Internet's data into centralized locations, making it easier to manage and exploit (de Leusse and Gahnberg 2019). The exact size of these cloud platforms has never been publicly disclosed, but to anyone using them to host a website or app, their resources appear limitless. According to the *Wall Street Journal*, in 2015 Amazon was adding more computing capacity than it had in all of 2004 *every single day* (McMillan 2015).

Boundless pools of user-generated data and corporate clouds have made social media a global sensation. Seven out of every ten Americans are now social-media users, and usage cuts across all demographics (Pew Research Center 2021). In China, the most popular social networks, like Weibo, attract hundreds of millions of users (Ren 2018). With everyone having more time on their hands during the pandemic, smartphone use is on the rise. The average American now spends 4.2 hours per day on their phone (Perez 2021), compared to 4.7 hours for the average Chinese (Liao 2019). Importantly, because social-media platforms are inherently interactive, every user with a smartphone is a content creator, contributing whatever they want to the universal pool of data on the Internet. Putting these numbers together, that's a lot of capacity and time to work with.

When it comes to the images, videos, and everything else being obsessively shared by users of social media, nearly all of it has been altered in some way, from smartphone cameras silently changing our photos to make us look better to Internet trolls making insidious changes to historical events with Photoshop. This poses a dilemma: if the truthfulness of a great deal of the data found on the Internet is in question, what implications does that have for its subsequent use? Should a photo that is automatically altered by a camera be treated the same way as a photo that is intentionally altered by a skilled human artist? There are no simple answers to such questions. But that hasn't stopped forensic specialists skilled in data analysis from trying to provide some—especially via algorithmic means.

How much of the Internet is fake, anyway? Like the size of the corporate clouds, this is currently unknown. However, the best estimates indicate that less than 60 percent of web traffic is human generated, the bulk of users on various social-media platforms are bots, and the veracity of most of the content people are consuming is in question (Read 2018). Thanks to the open nature of the Internet, any data found there—be it files or collected user behavior—will inevitably be employed elsewhere. Partly this reflects the big-data business plan: users provide data to a company in exchange for being able to use a platform at no cost. All of the text, photos, and videos are then used by the company to enhance its products and improve user experience. That much of the data is not original and has been altered in some way leads to a bizarre outcome: each enhancement pushes us further into a hallucinatory realm. Because the platforms are inherently social, the data is necessarily public, and can thus be used as the raw material for any endeavor by anyone. Enter AI.

Today's AI systems are trained with enormous amounts of data collected from the Internet, and they're demonstrating success in numerous application areas (Zhang et al 2021). How powerful has AI become? There is much fear, uncertainty, and doubt around this question (Ord 2020). AI reached an inflection point in 2012 with the demonstration that *deep learning*, that is, very large artificial neural networks, could be exceptionally effective when the computational power of Graphical Processing Units (GPUs) was combined with public data from the Internet (Metz 2021). In essence, GPUs are compact and inexpensive supercomputers, largely marketed to gamers but useful in other capacities, like AI. A GPU sold in 2021 by NVIDIA, a computer hardware manufacturer, for instance, was about as powerful as a supercomputer from the first decade of the twenty first century (Liu and Walton 2021). GPU hardware is particularly adept at processing large batches of text or image data in parallel, substantially cutting down the time needed to train neural networks. This led to a breakthrough in Stanford University's Imagenet Large Scale Visual Recognition Challenge benchmark in computer vision (Russakovsky et al. 2015), where the task involved having the computer automatically label an image based on what was depicted within it. It also led to the mistaken popular notion that a viable model of general intelligence had been developed by computer scientists.

Deep learning would go on to dominate the fields of computer vision and natural language processing, but it didn't replicate all of the competencies of human intelligence. Computer scientists were creating *perceptual systems*, not cognitive ones—that is to say, systems that replicated parts of human sensory processing like vision and audition, not cognitive facilities like reasoning or consciousness. To make the distinction is not to downplay the achievements of engineering here—what modern deep-learning systems can do is absolutely astounding. In particular, the class of systems known as generative models is most impressive. A generative model is an AI system that is able to synthesize new content based on what it knows about the world (a creative example is shown in fig. 1.1). The notorious deepfake algorithm (Paris and Donovan 2019), which reanimates recorded video of a person, is an example of a generative model, as is the GPT-3 language model from OpenAI (Brown 2020), which is able to write comprehensible passages of text. It is here that we truly see the interplay between the material posted to social media and the neural networks that learn from such data: human and machine generated artifacts are now indistinguishable (Shen et al. 2021). This is arguably the greatest achievement of AI so far, panic about deepfake aside.

Contemporary trends in technology have assembled the global population, troves of multimedia data, overwhelming processing power, and state-of-the-art AI algorithms into an ecosystem that looks uncannily similar to the myth cycle described by Lévi-Strauss. If a realignment of society and myth has indeed taken place on the Internet, it is hardly surprising that madcap meme movements like QAnon (Zuckerman 2019), WallStreetBets (Banerji et al. 2021), and Dogecoin (Ostroff and McCabe 2021) have all become increasingly visible during the most anxiety-ridden period of the twenty-first century. Digital memes have replaced physical memes, meaning any facet of reality, including major news stories, can be reworked on the fly and repackaged for the Internet via human or machine intervention. Contrarian thinkers like Maçães and *New York Times* opinion columnist Ross Douthat have commented on the vast potential of this new instantiation of the myth cycle to break the world out of years of cultural, political, and economic stagnation by presenting alternatives that would ordinarily be unthinkable in an exclusively rational environment.

Douthat in particular has argued for a model of the Internet as a meme incubator. Using the example of Elon Musk's electric car company Tesla, which requires vast amounts of capital to achieve its sci-fi tinged goal of producing an entirely sustainable and autonomous automobile, Douthat has explained that a corporation in the twenty-first century can be a meme, engaging with the Internet in unconventional ways to raise enthusiasm— and subsequently more capital. This, he has said, is representative of how the meme incubator works:

> And it isn't just evidence that fantasy can still, as in days of yore, remake reality; it's proof that under the right circumstances the internet makes it easier for dreams to change reality, by creating a space where a fantasy can live independent of the fundamentals for long enough that the real-world fundamentals bend and change. (Douthat 2021a)

Here again is where the past is diagnostic—this is not a phenomenon new to the Internet. It has been unfolding for many years but is only now reaching fruition. And to understand it brings a certain optimism that otherwise seems impossible in the face of so much negative press surrounding technology at the present moment.

Historical Perspectives on a Contemporary Controversy

So what is this book about? In a nutshell, we will take a deeper look at the technological trends and individual incidents that have shaped the development of labyrinthine alternate realities on the Internet. This inquiry will span from the invention of the camera to current developments in AI. Familiar arguments about the origin and operational purpose of fake content, which tend to filter everything through the lens of contemporary American politics, will be strictly avoided. Instead, the spotlight will be on the history of four influential communities that haven't received much recognition for their contributions to the rekindling of the myth cycles but whose dreams have become reality with startling regularity: computer hackers, digital artists, media-forensics specialists, and AI researchers.

Our explorations will draw on methodologies from a diverse group of disciplines. In an anthropological mode, we will consider reality to be a domain defined by both thought and the world—the latter crossing both physical and virtual spaces (Lévi-Strauss 1981). Thus we will proceed by scrutinizing messages, not the integrity of the medium conveying them. An understanding of how various communications mediums work is still essential though, as one needs to gauge their effectiveness for the task of participatory storytelling. For this we will draw on mass communication theory, which by the mid-twentieth century had largely predicted what would occur on the Internet (McLuhan 1994). Computer science also lends a hand for an informed discussion on the design decisions and technical operation of relevant infrastructure and algorithms. As we will see, even the technical aspects have an exceedingly strong social component, which is often obfuscated by programming languages and engineering lingo (Coleman 2016). And we will stay far away from alarmism, instead seeking pragmatic ways to draw distinctions between instances of fakery that are significant engines of cultural creation and those that pose a threat due to their message (Vallor 2016). When possible, we interrogate the very people involved in a case of interest, instead of merely extrapolating based on whatever they have fabricated. Appropriately to our object of study, at times their words will both clarify and beguile.

Each chapter is presented as a case study of sorts, looking at the roots of a specific technological trend. Thus while the book is organized chronologically, it can still be read in any order without losing too much essential context. Each trend was chosen as a pertinent example of how myths become tied to new mediums of communication. We will learn about hackers who fooled the news media (chapter 2); the history of darkroom and digital photographic manipulation (chapter 3); how stories were told through digital textfiles (chapter 4); the symbiotic development of media forensics and digital photographic manipulation (chapter 5); the origins of shock content (chapter 6); AI systems that make predictions about the far-off future (chapter 7); and the creative spaces of the Internet that are restyling reality today (chapter 8). As we will see, the four communities of interest intersect in surprising ways, demonstrating the fluidity of computer science—an asset that allows the discipline to rapidly parlay serendipitous interactions into innovations.

2

On the Virtual Frontier of the Imagination

WHY IS THERE SUCH PROFOUND MISTRUST of the establishment news media? Potential answers come ready to hand, but occasionally one surfaces from the most unexpected quarter. In this chapter we will reconsider the phenomenon of "fake news" by looking at a remarkable early instance, in which computer hackers exploited both broadcast television and the Internet. A common assumption made by journalists, academics, politicians, and other commentators is that fake news is intentionally designed to undermine the truth as a means to some malicious end and therefore must always be bad. Yet rarely do we find deep investigations into specific cases that include probing the motivations of those involved, the actions behind the scenes, and the outcomes over a long period of time. Such an investigation is presented here, and it reveals fake news to be a powerful medium for myths, especially those created to critique the news media.

A Hacker Called Quentin

In 1992, the newsmagazine television show *Dateline NBC* aired an episode on computer hackers (Dateline 1992), then a novelty in the technology world, which portrayed the supposed motivations and techniques of these brazen young cyberpunks. While the episode had all the trappings of the sensational reporting on hackers then commonplace, it also contained a rather unusual revelation that, if one were paying close attention, was more startling than the accounts of high-stakes intrusions on telecom systems and subsequent legal entanglements that filled most of the airtime.

The opening moments introduced the audience to an anonymous hacker called "Quentin," his voice changed and appearance dramatically obscured with stage lighting to protect his true identity. Billed as a "computer genius who illegally breaks into computers for fun," Quentin expounded on the temptation to make money from his hacking adventures, which included stealing corporate secrets and reading the email of American politicians. In full view of the camera as this was going on, records of UFO activity from Wright-Patterson and Kirtland air force bases scrolled across the glowing screen of Quentin's laptop as NBC correspondent Jon Scott matter-of-factly narrated the findings. Quentin, it turned out, had penetrated secret military computers to uncover evidence of extraterrestrial phenomena. Did *Dateline* really break the story of the century in a long forgotten segment from the nineties? Of course not. But how did a major television network end up airing such a wild tale? What unfolded during the filming of this episode and afterward constitutes one of the most creative acts of deception ever executed on the Internet. And it can help us understand the broader role fake news is playing within our culture now.

To the uninitiated, the world of the computer hacker resembles a collection of clichés drawn from classic science-fiction films like *Wargames* and *The Matrix*, in which the hacker tends to be a brilliant but socially awkward nerd who commits serious crimes online for fun and profit, all while keeping one step ahead of law enforcement. *Dateline*'s portrayal of Quentin very much conforms to this stereotype. And when we think about computer hacking today, it's often within that criminal context: the hacker who has penetrated our personal computer system and is now watching us. Large-scale data breaches, which have directly impacted the lives of millions of people, reinforce this paranoid view. But such motivations are far removed from the underground subculture of interest here. From the 1980s to the early 2000s, an extraordinary group of individuals came together to form a scene that was obsessed with using computer technology in ways that had never been intended.

Who, exactly, were the hackers participating in this scene? This is difficult to ascertain, because in most cases the hackers are pseudonymous presences identified only by handles—the names they used online. In a way remarkably similar to that portrayed in writer Vernor Vinge's seminal cyberpunk story *True Names*, the hackers existed in a virtual reality they established within information networks, and they interacted as characters that were developed around their assumed handles. Originally, this convention was intended to protect those behind the handles, as breaking the law came with the territory. But it added to the mystique of hacking. Mike Schiffman (aka route), a hacker active in the nineties, describes the scene in those days as "a lot like professional wrestling; you have these bombastic personality types that hide not behind flashy costumes, but *nom de plumes*. . . . People were real tough behind the computer."[1]

The use of handles left an opening for speculation around the real identities of the hackers. Were they government agents conducting sophisticated espionage operations or members of organized crime syndicates moving into a new racket? Or maybe they were indeed just a bunch of misfit nerds. When the hacker scene got off the ground in the early 1980s, it attracted a membership that didn't fit neatly into any single category. The cross-pollination of different groups would turn out to be a key element of the scene's success.

First, there were folks drawn from older counterculture movements that had a vested interest in constructing alternatives to a mainstream society they viewed as hopelessly corrupt. Early figures such Robert Osband (aka Cheshire Catalyst) and Chris Tucker (aka Nightstalker), both former yippies, and Bootleg, a rascally outlaw biker, were representative of this type of hacker, who resisted authority through the misuse of information networks that were connecting the globe.[2] They got their start in phone phreaking, the practice of hacking the telephone system, which had been promoted in counterculture literature like Abbie Hoffman's satirical *Steal this Book* in the 1970s.

Second, there were trained engineers with formal technical knowledge and professional experience who wanted to do far more with computers than what they could hope to in their day jobs. Many hailed from the Boston area, with its large cluster of universities, and in the early 1990s they coalesced around storied hacker groups such as the Cult of the Dead Cow and Lopht Heavy Industries.

Third, there were creatives with an interest in computing as a new artistic medium. Lloyd Blankenship (aka The Mentor), a professional role-playing game designer, was the voice of the original hacker generation. He is best remembered for authoring the manifesto *The Conscience of a Hacker* for an early issue of *Phrack* magazine.[3] *Phrack*, the flagship zine (underground magazine) of the scene, originally circulated on bulletin board systems (BBSs). Similar to today's Internet forums, BBSs were multiuser computers run by hobbyists in the 1980s and 1990s that were connected to the telephone system so that other people could dial in and exchange knowledge via messages and files. In writing that was effectively an invitation to the hacking scene, Blankenship described an alternate reality that could alleviate boredom, transcend conventional boundaries, and bring about a transformation of society that he believed was not achievable in the terrestrial world:

> And then it happened . . . a door opened to a world . . . rushing through the phone line like heroin through an addict's veins, an electronic pulse is sent out, a refuge from the day-to-day incompetencies is sought . . . a board is found. (Blankenship 1986)

And finally, there were a whole lot of punk kids. A few old yippies notwithstanding, the hacker scene tilted overwhelmingly young. Teenagers and college students flocked to what they saw as a revolutionary movement that not only scratched their itch for rebellion but also gave them behind-the-scenes access to a host of new technologies that were swiftly transforming the world. Not for everyone, computer hacking did attract a certain personality type: individuals who were curious, compulsive, and most importantly, creative.

However, certain barriers to entry existed. Unsurprisingly, early hackers were overwhelmingly affluent white males who, in many cases thanks to their parents, had access to computers at home (a rarity in the 1980s). This lent a certain macho air to the scene, which was not appreciated by all but did strongly influence what the membership was interested in. The handles, writing, and even software that the hackers produced seemed to be drawn more from gritty Western films than the stiff corporate culture one would have found at a technology company like Hewlett-Packard or IBM.

Before the Internet era, the process by which a new hacker learned about the scene involved a fair bit of luck. More often than not, this was a chance conversation with somebody in the know, the discovery of a hacker zine on a BBS, or an encounter with another hacker on a computer that had been compromised multiple times. Paradoxically, newcomers to the scene were met with both suspicion and openness. The threat of law enforcement always loomed, but fundamentally, this was a social movement intent on growing its community. If one could get past the abrasiveness of the initial contact with other hackers, one would have a wealth of knowledge to share. Hackers have traditionally been allied with the open-source and freedom of speech movements within computing and organized around information dissemination more broadly.

Why is this particular period so special in the development of the culture surrounding technology? In retrospect, it is incredibly surprising that a motley band of kids and a handful of not-so-reliable adults could coordinate to create enduring institutions, including the entire computer-security industry. Amateur hackers were playing with very sophisticated technologies that had previously been the exclusive realm of powerful governments and major corporations. They set up digital infrastructure and their own media, including electronic zines like *Phrack* and print publications like *2600: The Hacker Quarterly*, which had a global readership. They also set up a physical presence in the form of yearly conferences (Summer-Con, HoHoCon, and DEF CON, to name a few) and monthly meet-ups in major cities, such as those sponsored by *2600*. Some of these things persist to this day, having long outlived the original scene.

After certain aspects of the hacking scene became known within the corporate and government worlds—not least, detected intrusions—the response led to serious consequences for those involved. Investigators were baffled in the beginning—why in the world would groups of kids be so invested in attacking computer systems that most people associated with mundane work? It was initially assumed that this had to be related to espionage in some way. Internal security at AT&T, partnered with agents from the FBI, came to this conclusion as early as the mid-1960s while chasing phone phreaks within their network (Lapsley 2014).

Espionage was not entirely out of the question; the early days of the hacking scene coincided with the end of the Cold War and heightened tensions between the United States and the Soviet Union. In 1986, Clifford Stoll, a system administrator at Lawrence Berkeley National Laboratory, uncovered a Soviet-funded plot to access US government computers. The incident led to the arrest of German hacker and KGB asset Markus Hess, but it was an outlier for the time (Stoll 1989). Nevertheless, national security concerns would taint later hacking cases involving American high-school and college students that had absolutely nothing to do with spies. Indeed, it was rather peculiar to assume that the young people being rounded up by federal law enforcement had been recruited by a hostile power. Out in suburbia, in the pre-Internet era, where would they even encounter Soviet intelligence? The hackers recognized this absurdity. It would also get them to think deeply about why the federal government was so sensitive about computer crime and how they could exploit that sentiment in unusual ways to raise their own profiles.

As the hacking scene matured, it challenged the popular notion of what hacking was. Over time, hackers moved progressively into different information networks, constantly pushing deeper into what was uncharted territory for outsiders. Exploration had always been a core activity of the hackers, who, knowing no boundaries, operated as digital frontiersmen. An important but frequently overlooked aspect of the scene followed from this: the hacker's ability to step into a space where others could not go and seed it with new information. Gradually, hackers became content creators (Coleman 2016), enamored with the idea that they could use their newfound command of information networks to control the messages crossing them and influence the reception of those messages by mass audiences.

Adam O'Donnell (aka Javaman), another hacker active in the nineties, believes that futurist motivations helped shape the era: "We fantasized about what the future would look like and tried to bring it about."[4] Contrary to the popular conception of the hacker as an engineer who exclusively uses technical means to achieve their goals, there is a significant creative component to hacking. Through the production of artifacts like textfiles (digital texts circulated as individual files), BBS posts, chat logs, and television appearances, elements of fiction (especially science fiction) could be deployed at will. In O'Donnell's words, "what the hacker scene was doing was part technology, part narrative creation." By the time the *Dateline* episode aired in the early nineties, computer hackers had acquired in-depth technical knowledge, sophisticated infrastructure, and significant experience in manipulating people (Gehl and Lawson 2022). The pieces were in place for them to build structures within their newly acquired digital territory that would support their culture for years to come.

If hackers were behind the *Dateline* story on UFOs, why did they specifically target the news? A thought here is that within the news-media ecosystem, one finds a mass audience consuming messages directly from a media technology—predominantly print in the nineteenth century, radio and television in the twentieth century, and the Internet today. Co-opting any one of those technologies would provide a direct channel to millions. But the human element of news production is a weaker link. It has always been particularly vulnerable to attack by virtue of the way news stories are collected—reporters look for scoops that have mass appeal, above all. The news is, in practice, a system that can be hacked. And the exposure of weaknesses within the news-media ecosystem in the nineteen would have grave consequences later, when trolls, political operatives, and intel ligence services picked up where the original hackers left off. While this raises many questions about the integrity of the media and the trust the public places in it, a more basic question intercedes: What would motivate anyone to leak an outlandish story about UFOs to NBC News?

UFOs Land on the Underground Hacking Scene

Dateline's episode on computer hackers featured two notable individuals from the hacking scene: Adam Grant (aka The Urvile) and Scott Chasin (aka Doc Holiday). Grant had gained notoriety in the early 1990s for his role in hacking computer systems owned by BellSouth, which helped trigger a nationwide crackdown on computer crime by federal law enforcement, dubbed *Operation Sundevil*.[5] He was sentenced to fourteen months in prison on related charges. Chasin had retired from illegal hacking shortly before the episode aired, and was by then on his way to establishing a successful career as a technology entrepreneur by parlaying the skills he had honed in the computer underground. But he would continue to lurk around the hacking scene. A third hacker, Chris Goggans (aka Erik Bloodaxe) had, by his own account, a behind-the-scenes role in the production of the episode.[6] Goggans was a key figure in the underground who had recently assumed the editorship of *Phrack*.

The three were affiliated with a group that called itself the Legion of Doom, after the collective of comic book supervillains from the 1970s featured in the animated series *Challenge of the Superfriends*. Wielding wide influence, the Legion of Doom's activities centered around the development of technical attacks, the dissemination of hacker material through BBSs and early Internet outlets, and the practice of compromising computer systems for the sake of curiosity (and sometimes revenge).[7] All of this

```
==Phrack Magazine==

Volume Four, Issue Forty-Two, File 13 of 14

HoHoCon 1992
Miscellany
```

The hackers were getting nervous. It was understandable. Just a few weeks
before HoHoCon and already two other "get-togethers" had experienced
turbulence from the authorities.

Rumors began to fly that HoHo was to be the next target. Messages bearing
ill-tidings littered the underground. Everyone got worked into a frenzy about
the upcoming busts at HoHoCon. People began to cancel their reservations
while others merely refused to commit one way or the other.

But, amidst all the confusion and hype, many declared "Let them try to
raid us! I'm going anyway!" These were the few, the proud...the stupid.

FIGURE 2.1. The introduction to a *Phrack* report on HoHoCon 1992, written by Chris Goggans.

was coupled with the development of an intricate mythology that shaped the subculture that the group was working to bootstrap with other hackers. Blankenship was also a member, and his textfile *The Conscience of a Hacker* was an early example of how the Legion of Doom was contributing to the cultural canon of the scene. But that was only the beginning.

To what lengths would hackers go to construct a viable mythology? The story of "Quentin" did not abruptly end after the *Dateline* episode aired in the fall of 1992. Speculation grew within the hacker scene around the identity of the anonymous hacker and the veracity of the material that was visible on his screen. If true, it was a stunning revelation. If false, somebody had hacked NBC. Both outcomes would be equally astonishing in the eyes of the computer underground. Shortly before the holidays that year, a swarm of hackers descended upon Houston to attend HoHoCon, an annual conference sponsored by the Cult of the Dead Cow, a hacker collective interested in executing culture jamming campaigns through computer networks.[8] During the conference, Goggans and Chasin took the podium to address the *Dateline* situation. Goggans summarized the talk in a conference report (fig. 2.1) that he published in *Phrack*:

Up next, myself and Chasin. Our topic was a bit obscure and cut deliberately short due to concerns about the nature of our speech. During the
Dateline NBC piece that featured Chasin a piece of information flashed
on the screen that alluded to UFO information stored on military computers. Chasin and I had gained possession of the research database compiled
by the hackers who were looking into this. We discussed their project, the
rumors surrounding their findings and the fear surrounding the project.
Not knowing the true details of this we declined to comment any further, but made the documentation available to anyone who wanted a copy.
(Goggans 1993)

The *Phrack* report included the new documentation on the incident.
The significance of this material appearing in the scene's premier publication cannot be overstated. In the early nineties only a few hundred people
would attend the "cons," which were chaotic yet engrossing events that
attracted the elite of the underground, as well as aspiring hackers eager
to hear what they had to say.[9] A practical constraint on holding physical gatherings was that many of the hackers were just young teenagers,
without the financial means or transportation to travel far from home.
Thus it was common practice to summarize the proceedings of meetings
in textfiles that would be uploaded to BBSs and Internet sites, in order to
update the larger community on the latest technical innovations and social
happenings within the scene.

Goggans and Chasin knew that by revealing their UFO investigations
in *Phrack* they would reach a much larger audience and increase awareness of the *Dateline* disclosures, with the bonus of having the material
archived in perpetuity on the Internet. Started in 1985, *Phrack* was published on an irregular schedule, with each issue containing news from the
scene and a series of technical articles on networks, operating systems,
the phone system, and the intricacies of other more esoteric technologies
that could be explored in unconventional ways. When a new issue appeared, everyone in the know read it. The timing was opportune for a
sensational disclosure in *Phrack*, as the zine had gained legendary status
within the underground after being briefly shut down by the US Secret
Service during *Operation Sundevil* in 1989 and by virtue of its association with a then still unfolding rivalry between the Legion of Doom and
another hacker group calling itself the Masters of Deception (Slatalla and
Quittner 1995).[10]

At the end of the HoHoCon report is a release of additional technical material allegedly recovered from government computer systems. Quentin, it seemed, was not a lone wolf prowling the Internet but the spokesperson for a shadowy syndicate pursuing information on the "greatest cover-up in the history of the world." The preface of the release is intentionally over the top, and it makes reference to turncoat military officials, unexplained disappearances, and secret tests of alien "corona discharge" propulsion technology. But the technical information that follows, in the form of screen captures of command line terminal activity, looks plausible. It was not uncommon to see such juxtapositions in hacker writing, where bravado and hyperbole were intermixed with dumps of real data.

Intriguingly, expanded versions of the material seen on Quentin's screen in the *Dateline* episode are included. The information from the Wright-Patterson and Kirtland bases is shown to be associated with two classified projects called "ALF-1" and "Green Cheese" (figs. 2.2, 2.3). A flurry of Internet network addresses, computer names, personnel lists, and facilities tied to these two projects overwhelms the inexperienced reader but sets up a puzzle for the journeyman hacker. The extensive mapping of government networks that is provided was meant to entice others to join the search for evidence of UFOs. Most remarkable is the accuracy of the associated network addresses, whose ownership by the Department of Defense was real and endures to this day.[11] Data dumps of ambiguous plausibility like this one would become increasingly common as the nineties gave way to the new millennium and hacking and the mythology around it grew in popularity.

The people and places named are more suspicious. In between references to real military installations, figures within the intelligence community, and government contractors, the lists are sprinkled with tidbits that would be familiar to ufologists. Visible in the *Dateline* episode and in the *Phrack* dump are mentions of Paul Bennewitz and Project Beta. Bennewitz was a businessman living in the Albuquerque area not too far from Kirtland Air Force Base. In the late 1970s, he became convinced that lights he would observe in the night sky near the base were of extraterrestrial origin (Barkun 2013).

Over the years, Bennewitz's behavior grew increasingly erratic, and he came to believe that he was receiving transmissions from alien spacecraft and a secret underground facility called "Dulce." In 1988, he wrote

```
----------------------------------------------------------------------

PROJECT ALF-1

A Planetary Effort

TOP SECRET TOP SECRET TOP SECRET TOP SECRET TOP SECRET TOP SECRET
TOP SECRET TOP SECRET TOP SECRET TOP SECRET TOP SECRET TOP SECRET

These are the raw data.  Where comments are appropriate, they
will be included.  The data will be grouped together with dates,
names etc. to make correlations easier.

There are countless references to the aliens, their down space
craft and what the Government is doing with them.
If, as is supposed, the research on the craft and the 'ufonauts'
continues today, then undoubtedly there are computer records, somewhere.

I. Searching the Skies; Tripping the Electronic Fence around the
USA.

US Space Command Space Surveillance Center, Cheyenne Mountain,
Colorado Springs, Box Nine (Electronic Surveillance Room)
```

FIGURE 2.2. PROJECT ALF-1 was disclosed in the *Phrack* report on HoHoCon 1992.

```
----------------------------------------------------------------
                          Project
                     ->Green Cheese<-
                        Data Base
----------------------------------------------------------------
Holloman AFB
     Location: New Mexico.  Preconceived landing 15 years ago.

DDN Locations:
--------------

NET : 132.5.0.0 : HOLLOMAN :

GATEWAY : 26.9.0.74, 132.5.0.1 : HOLLOMAN-GW.AF.MIL : CISCO-MGS :: EGP,IP/GW :
GATEWAY : 26.9.0.74, 132.5.0.1 : HOLLOMAN-GW.AF.MIL : CISCO-MGS :: EGP,IP/GW :

HOST : 26.10.0.74 : HOLLOMAN-TG.AF.MIL : VAX-8650 : VMS : TCP/FTP,TCP/TELNET,TCP
       SMTP :

HOST : 26.6.0.74 : HOLLOMAN-AM1.AF.MIL : WANG-VS100 : VSOS : TCP/TELNET,TCP/FTP,
       TCP/SMTP :

Host: DDNVAX2.6585TG.AF.MIL
      156.6.1.2

----------------------------------------------------------------
```

FIGURE 2.3. Project Green Cheese was also disclosed in the HoHoCon 1992 report, but in more technical terms.

a paper titled "Project Beta," which laid out a plan to mount a defense of humanity by attacking the Dulce base. Shortly after this, his family committed him to a psychiatric facility. Compounding Bennewitz's bizarre activities was an apparent air force disinformation campaign to feed him false material about alien activity as a distraction from the true cause of the phenomena around Kirtland that he was publicizing: classified weapons testing (Rose 2014).[12] This led to accusations of government misconduct, which in turn, continued to feed the conspiracy theory.

The *Phrack* report also contained the following warning to the skeptical reader:

> Believe what you will about the reality of this project. Much will be dismissed as hacker lore, but within the core of every rumor lies a grain of truth.

Much of the writing produced by hackers has this flavor: a blend of technical elements that are real and fantastic elements that push the imagination into the new realm of cyberspace. According to Jason Scott, a historian at the Internet Archive and authority on early online culture, the textfiles produced by the hacker underground function as "cheat codes for life."[13] Like in a video game, possession of the right information grants access to places others cannot go—be it some remote corner of the Internet or one's own imagination. If you combine a bunch of weird ideas circulating in the underground (say exploration of defense networks and space aliens), you get this strange, and quite possibly good, effect. Scott notes that for young hackers at the dawn of the Internet's ascendence, "the textfiles are a very reasonable defense mechanism against the world." Confronted with enormous economic, political, and social change, while at the same time armed with a new communications technology that can reach anyone on earth, they were bound to propagate secret knowledge meant to subvert prevailing institutions. To the individual hacker, collecting textfiles was a means of acquiring this secret knowledge. And the fact that other hackers had access to it bound the community together.

The emergence of textfile trading on computer networks, and the later trading of multimedia content like images and videos when bandwidth increased, was a direct outgrowth of new mass communications technology appearing in the late twentieth century. Why would computer networks become more important to society compared with other information networks like traditional broadcast media? Hackers discovered that they could create and disseminate content to a global audience at will during a transition period when only technically savvy users were connected to computer networks. But the impact self-produced content would have on the formation of culture once everyone was connected was quickly realized. By the early nineties, this process was already well underway. Hackers also realized that they could manipulate both new and traditional media, pulling an audience consuming broadcast content into computer networks by crafting enticing messages that broadcasters could not resist airing. For a certain demographic of young and savvy computer users, hunting for evidence of UFOs on the Internet was not only alluring but also a gateway to a larger underground subculture.

As the media ecosystem started to become more interactive in the 1970s, the communications scholars Sandra Ball-Rokeach and Melvin De-Fleur suggested looking at the "big picture" to understand the interaction between media and their audiences (Ball-Rokeach and DeFleur 1976). As societies become more connected and technology becomes better, media increasingly absorb additional information systems. This means that people become more dependent on the media and that media has more of an effect on their behavior. Communities that latch onto new forms of media seek a better understanding of the world around them, the ability to meaningfully and effectively act within that world, and a mechanism to escape from that world when it becomes overwhelming. As it became easier to escape our immediate surroundings via technology, we began to live large portions of our lives within a media ecosystem, which set the stage for the construction of elaborate alternate realities. The hacker scene was early to manifest this in practice, on the Internet.

Because the interface between the physical and virtual worlds is often cloudy, misunderstandings were bound to occur. Goggans, by his own telling, had already landed in trouble for an earlier ruse in *Phrack*. In the 1989 article "How We Got Rich Through Electronic Funds Transfers" (Goggans 1989),[14] he had spun a tale about two bold hackers whose exploration into the X.25 packet-switching networks used by financial institutions eventually led them to commit felony wire fraud. Similar to the dump of material from projects ALF-1 and Green Cheese, it is a mix of real technical content and silly embellishments, packaged as a get-rich-quick guide for other hackers. Goggans knew how to craft the technical bits in such a way that made them look real, because he had seen similar things while exploring other networks: "The article contained fake X.25 network and Telex terminal information—we'd find stuff like this all of the time when war dialing."[15] A close reading of the article reveals elements of a joke, including the two hackers traveling to Oklahoma City to visit a hall of records to obtain new birth certificates (as if this were possible), a secret Legion of Doom owned HP-3000 minicomputer (then retailing for well over $100,000[16]) located in Turkey, and an unscrupulous accountant trying to pay off a car debt with the stolen funds. Even if one were on the fence about the veracity of the article while reading, the concluding punchline is further justification that this was a piece of satire:

> It's kind of weird having over six-hundred $100 bills in a drawer, though. Too bad we can't earn any interest on it!

Some did not find it funny, however. According to Goggans, one of the banks named in the article was concerned enough to contact federal law enforcement after catching wind of what *Phrack* had been publishing.[17] With the Legion of Doom already on their radar, the Secret Service opened an investigation but quickly determined that the article lacked credibility. Nonetheless, out of duty, they questioned Goggans, with one agent telling him, "We know it's not real." He was off the hook for this escapade. Information asymmetry emerged as a crucial facet of self-published underground material. Goggans had learned an interesting lesson: if fake content could be crafted to look plausible enough to people who were not expert technologists, then groups outside of the hacker underground would pay attention if the message was sensational enough. The *Dateline* episode served as a successful test of this lesson, and the seeds were now planted for a further deception.

"Better, Stronger, Faster"

Skulking in the background of the developing intrigue around the *Dateline* episode was Michael Kubecka (aka Omega), member of the Cult of the Dead Cow and stepson of Melvin DeFleur, who had been thinking about how to operationalize the new ideas about participatory media that he had heard around the dinner table.[18] Emerging from a loose network of underground BBSs in the early 1980s, the Cult of the Dead Cow was a group of textfile purveyors extraordinaire. In a drastic departure from the technical material that was most commonly traded between hackers, they pushed their writing into a space that blended elements of the computers that they inhabited with strikingly imaginative fantasies.[19] Accordingly, journalist Joseph Menn has described the group as the "liberal arts section of the computer underground" (Menn 2020). They were also experimenting with new ways to manipulate communication channels in order to influence people, as reflected in their tongue-in-cheek motto: "Global domination through media saturation."

The Cult of the Dead Cow had achieved renown thanks in part to the innovative promotional strategies formulated by its leader and primary editor, Kevin Wheeler (aka Swamp Rat). Wheeler, who had studied marketing at Texas Tech University, realized that he could overcome the slow propagation of content on BBSs by establishing a network of affiliated boards, which he called "outlets."[20] The outlets would distribute new files as soon as they were released, thus short-circuiting the inefficient process of hackers sharing files on individual boards they dialed into whenever they felt like it. Because of this, Cult of the Dead Cow content was far more prevalent than that of other groups, drawing an enormous readership within the hacking scene. The textfile operation was coupled with conference organizing, and venues like HoHoCon gave the Cult of the Dead Cow a real-world platform for hyping its content. Creative forms of textfile promotion were actively encouraged by the group—especially those that unleashed shock and awe on their audience.

Kubecka had a big plan to launch a textfile in a way that had never been attempted before. With two associates, Michael Seery (aka Reid Fleming) and Dan MacMillan (aka White Knight), he started writing content based on the *Dateline* episode and the groundwork Goggans and Chasin had already laid at HoHoCon 1992 and in *Phrack*. This was to be the definitive data dump of the anonymous group investigating projects ALF-1 and Green Cheese, revealing evidence of a government cover-up so elaborate it would make even the most hardened skeptic think twice. In true hacker spirit, the ultimate objective of this writing project was to outdo Goggans. If the Cult of the Dead Cow could one-up the Legion of Doom's most visible member, bragging rights would ensue. And it would be even more fun if Goggans ended up playing along.

There was a long-standing fascination with fringe content within the hacker scene. Partly this had to do with the age of the average hacker in the early 1990s and the culture they would have been immersed in while growing up. Kubecka and his associates drew creative inspiration from the tabloid news they were exposed to as children: "The three of us who wrote that textfile grew up in the 1970s. There were a lot of strange stories being told back then: cattle mutilations, UFOs, Bigfoot. The textfiles that appeared in the 1980s and 1990s were a stone soup made out of all of this stuff."[21] Indeed, the 1970s were an uncertain time in America. Coming on the heels of the politically turbulent 1960s, they ushered in an era of broad economic decline through deindustrialization and the acceleration of urban decay in major metropolitan areas. The result was an unwinding of the social structures that had provided stability since the end of the Second World War. The rise of a paranoid media culture was merely a reflection of the unease that was in the air at the time. Coupled with this was a deep suspicion of new technologies, eliciting highly visible protests from organizations who already felt under siege in the changing environment.[22] Reflecting on this period, Kubecka emphasized that "as hackers, we had no fear of the digital world. It was a new way to reach a global audience." Thus the hacker could move freely between the paranoid fringe and technical environments, blending the ideas they found interesting as they saw fit.

Why would UFO stories in particular be integrated into hacker culture? The juxtaposition seems odd on its surface. The answer to this question has to do with the military's long standing fascination with UFO lore and its role as a technology leader. A surge of reporting on UFOs has made it seem like the Pentagon has only recently taken a serious interest in unexplained aerial phenomena (Cooper et al. 2019). However, from Allied pilots spotting "foo fighters" in the skies over the European and Pacific theaters during WWII to units stationed at classified test airfields embracing extraterrestrial mascots (Paglen 2010), UFO legends are ingrained into the culture of aviators, sailors, electronic warfare groups, and various sectors of the aerospace industry.[23]

In the Cold War era, defense spending was the primary driver of high-tech innovation, meaning a fusion of military and technology cultures was already underway. The crowning achievement of the military in the world of computing was DARPA's creation of the Internet in the 1960s. As the

Legion of Doom knew, as late as the early 1990s, many of the computers hooked up to the Internet were still government property, and many of the original users were affiliated with the Department of Defense. Thus it should come as no surprise that textfiles on UFOs had been circulating since the dawn of computer networking.[24] This was the environment Kubecka and his friends inhabited, one that could be a wellspring of inspiration for those who could wrap their heads around so many disparate, yet significant, ideas. It was time for them to further develop Quentin's story and do something even more creative than the initial deception. So they spent months writing.

Fast forward to HoHoCon 1993 in Austin, Texas: Goggans and Chasin were back at it. Taking the podium, Chasin asked the audience if they remembered the previous year's talk "about a group of hackers that gave us some information that they found evidence of alien lifeforms," which elicited laughter from the assembled crowd.[25] Yes, a number of folks within the hacker underground were still thinking about this. Goggans then asked the audience if they remembered the *Dateline* episode that inspired the talk: "How many people saw the first *Dateline* that Scott was on? Now, do you remember a sort of shaded figure, Quentin? Do you remember what was going across the screen while he was talking?" Hands went up across the audience. "How many of you saw the *follow-up* piece that they did?" Half of the audience thought they saw this second episode air on NBC. But there was no follow-up piece.

At that point, Goggans and Chasin turned the podium over to Kubecka and MacMillan, who had been standing by to disclose their own information about the now exposed government conspiracy. They began by playing a clip of the supposed second *Dateline* episode as a teaser for what they would talk about next. In advance of the conference, MacMillan had shot a video of his sister dressed as Quentin, her back to the camera, with the textfile he, Seery, and Kubecka had written scrolling across the screen in front of her. Heightening the silliness of the moment, the speakers and conference organizers spent a few minutes fumbling with a malfunctioning television and VCR. Finally, a grainy video played, segueing in the span of about thirty seconds from a video-game ad to the fake *Dateline* clip and then to an infomercial. Apologizing for the poor quality of the footage, MacMillan told the audience, "We weren't able to get a copy of the original tape, we got this from a local guy who was flipping through channels trying to find the hockey game." The crowd continued laughing—even if none of this was true, it was still terribly funny.

After the laughter died down, Kubecka and MacMillan got down to business and began discussing the new findings of the "Green Cheese Group," which they claimed had been passed to the Cult of the Dead Cow (thanks to some facilitation by Chasin) and would now be circulated around the hacker underground as a new textfile.[26] In the latest plot twist, the anonymous group had recovered evidence of "a cover-up instigated by the three-letter agencies and NASA, perpetrated upon the public with the unwitting aid of the media in the early 1970s, beginning with the death of three astronauts." Kubecka elaborated: "I don't know how many of you remember the Apollo fire, the Apollo project where three astronauts died; . . . according to the textfile, at least one of those guys got out, and is not dead, and figures somehow into this whole cover-up." As in any good conspiracy theory, spurious links between key government actors and agencies were established. Kubecka pointed out that the National Security Agency had already been implicated in the data dump Goggans and Chasin had leaked. Would the crowd be shocked to learn that the director who oversaw the agency during the period covered by the leaks had just been appointed secretary of defense—a position that would allow him to bury the story?[27] The pieces of the puzzle were coming together.

Where did the evidence of this cover-up come from? Kubecka had the full story:

> As far as we know, the same guys who were behind ALF were scanning some prefix in Virginia. Some prefix that seems to be unused. And every time they'd call a number they'd get a fast busy, they'd hang up and a person would call them back and ask them what they wanted with this prefix. And they persisted, they kept scanning it anyway. They came across some carriers and apparently they got to some machines and were able to get in, and able to log quite a bit of mail from around this period, from around the early 70s. This is in fact the stuff that's going across Quentin's screen that *Dateline* seems completely oblivious to again, and that's the most interesting part of the show.

Things were getting technical. Kubecka was describing a war-dialing effort, in which the hackers were calling all of the phone numbers within a given prefix (the first three digits of a phone number) in the Washington,

DC, area, looking for government computers they could connect to. The crowd at HoHoCon was no longer laughing. What Kubecka was talking about would have been familiar to everyone in the audience—this was standard practice for network reconnaissance in the early 1990s. Moreover, stories about mysterious interactions with telephone operators were frequently traded around the hacker scene, especially if they involved government phone systems, which were widely regarded as a dangerous legal boundary one should be wary of crossing.[28] Perhaps there was a grain of truth to this presentation after all.

Finally, it was time to release the new textfile, which the authors had titled "Better, Stronger, Faster" (fig. 2.4). To drive up interest through scarcity, Kubecka printed a limited number of hardcopies before heading to Austin. At the conclusion of the talk, these were tossed out to the audience, which by now was chomping at the bit, eager to see what the file contained. Boston-based hacker John Lester (aka Count Zero), who was to speak immediately after Kubecka and MacMillan, described the scene as a "feeding frenzy." Keeping with the Cult of the Dead Cow's aim

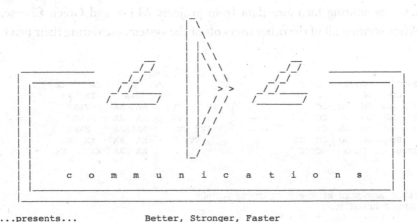

FIGURE 2.4. Cult of the Dead Cow Textfile #253: "Better, Stronger, Faster." Used with permission of cDc. All rights reserved. Bow to the Cow.

of "media saturation," HoHoCon was the first hacker conference that actively engaged with the press—a community that previously had only been able to observe hackers from the outside. A number of reporters were in attendance, and this talk in particular piqued their interest. They muscled their way into the fray of sleep-deprived kids to grab a copy. Despite the coverage NBC had already given to Quentin and the Legion of Doom, a few skeptical journalists finally began to ask the right question: "Is this for real?"

What exactly was in that textfile? Like the *Phrack* report, it adopts a blend of computer output and creative storytelling, but with far more emphasis on the latter. Teetering between the plausible and fantastic, the file takes a sudden turn toward the familiar, if the reader were acquainted with the cultural context. After alleging that a copy of the *Dateline* episode on hackers had turned up in the investigation of the death of Clinton Whitehouse aide Vincent Foster (an incident that was fertile ground for conspiracy theories), the file begins with a screen capture from a DARPA owned Digital Equipment Corporation VAX/VMS computer system (fig. 2.5). Following the terminal output, one can see that the Cult of the Dead Cow had gained access to a system discovered by the anonymous hackers hunting for more data from projects ALF-1 and Green Cheese. After booting all of the other users off of the system, escalating their privi-

```
DDDDD    OOOO   CCCC              VV        VV  AA     XX    XX
DD  DD  OO  OO  CC  CC            VV        VV  AAAA    XX  XX
DD    DD  OO  OO  CC                VV      VV  AA  AA    XXXX
DD    DD  OO  OO  CC        ----     VV    VV   AA  AA     XX
DD    DD  OO  OO  CC        ----     VV VV      AAAAAA    XXXX
DD  DD  OO  OO  CC  CC              VVV        AA  AA   XX  XX
DDDDD    OOOO   CCCC                 V         AA  AA  XX    XX
```

DEFENSE ADVANCED RESEARCH PROJECTS AGENCY
DOCUMENT REPOSITORY

W A R N I N G:

This computer system is operated by the United States Government and is protected under provisions of USC Title 23, Section 67. Unauthorized access is STRICTLY FORBIDDEN.

FIGURE 2.5. The network logs provided in "Better, Stronger, Faster" looked plausible enough to knowledgeable hackers. Used with permission of cDc. All rights reserved. Bow to the Cow.

leges, and adding themselves to the access list (username: Bovine; password: Cultee), the Cult of the Dead Cow members were ready to conduct their own investigation. What they found was a collection of CIA memos labeled "Violet and Sensitive"—material that was not meant for redistribution.

In Kubecka's talk, he made reference to the disastrous Apollo 1 fire, which killed the flight crew on the launchpad during a mission rehearsal, and the supposed escape of one of the astronauts. The memos reproduced in "Better, Stronger, Faster" continue to follow this thread. No stranger to aviation disasters, astronaut Virgil "Gus" Grissom is revealed to have suffered severe injuries in a near fatal crash of an experimental XF-17 aircraft in 1966, necessitating the use of an experimental treatment.[29] Secret, cybernetically enhanced prosthetics designed by DARPA called "Bionics" were implanted into Grissom, granting him superhuman physical abilities. During the Apollo fire, he was able to escape because of his Bionics, leaving his comrades to perish. On the lam, Grissom became a "loose-cannon," and the intelligence community grew concerned that he would go public with what he knew about secret governmental medical experimentation and broad plans to deceive American citizens, including an operation to fake the moon landing, dubbed project Capricorn.

Towards the middle of the file, a quotation appears that, like the similar one found in the *Phrack* report on HoHoCon 1992, simultaneously brings attention to the style of this form of writing and helps move the story along: "The most convincing lie is the one that's half true."[30] The CIA, it seems, aimed to "desensitize the American public to the potential existence of a Bionic-enabled man and secondarily, any allegations concerning Capricorn, the ludicrous portrayal of the first discrediting the second." Thus, the government would tip its hand by introducing Bionic technology to the public in a way that would immediately have it dismissed as implausible. This was to be accomplished through the production of a low-brow sci-fi show airing on broadcast television.

Does this sound familiar? The Cult of the Dead Cow was actually tipping its hand in the other direction. The story was being informed not by government secrets but instead by the television series *The Six Million Dollar Man* and *The Bionic Woman*, which had been popular in the 1970s. Today, Kubecka acknowledges the influence that *The Six Million Dollar Man* had on sculpting the prank: "It was a favorite show of mine and White Knight, we could quote from the plots of episodes verbatim." The show had all of the elements needed to fit a good hacker legend, but it was also campy, often poorly written, and suffered from obvious plot oversights. However, a little bit of humor is just what the hackers were looking for—it was a necessary ingredient for a successful textfile. As Kubecka has explained, "We picked out some of our favorite story lines from *The Six Million Dollar Man*, but also attempted to highlight how stupid many of the episodes were."

"Better, Stronger, Faster" can be viewed as a prototype for Internet conspiracy theories in general—a mosaic of loosely connected ideas arranged in such an intricate manner as to raise doubts about any possible critique. So what if it is obviously connected to a bad television show from the 1970s? Quentin's appearance on *Dateline* had happened, those were authentic VMS commands being typed out in the data dump, and many of the people, places, and events named were real. Conspiratorially minded readers would have also recognized that the plan to discredit a rogue Gus Grissom sounded suspiciously similar to the one the government actually did deploy in the Bennewitz affair. Things like this occasionally do happen. More crucially, the file bears a direct relationship with contemporary conspiracy theories like QAnon, where an obvious joke is set in a context that contains some factual elements, eventually becoming believable to some fraction of those exposed to it (Woolf 2018). However, it's important to note that in this case the content wasn't malicious—it was an exercise in mythmaking.

After covering surreal territory spanning from William Shatner to Sasquatch and back to extraterrestrial encounters, the textfile ends with the line "No Carrier." The computer had hung-up. For those who had made it all the way through this saga, there was probably one thing on their minds above all else: computer hackers could do it with flair. Those behind this caper had exploited the news media, virtual communities on BBSs and the Internet, and a couple of physical audiences to spin a highly entertaining yarn. Nobody had ever executed anything like this before. "Better, Stronger, Faster" would be remembered as one of the Cult of the Dead Cow's best textfiles. Technologists who experienced the hacker scene in that era are still talking about it because it is embedded within their shared culture. Mission accomplished.

Who was Quentin? To this day, nobody has divulged his identity. It could have been Goggans, whose role in the *Dateline* episode shifts in descriptions across textfiles and in interviews conducted with the people involved in this incident.[31] But the shadowy figure looked and sounded more like Kubecka, who maintains that he was drawn into things by the intense speculation around the episode he was reading on BBSs and another messaging technology called Internet Relay Chat, which was popular within the computer underground. Goggans suggested that other hackers may have played a role, including Lester, who also happened to be a member of the Cult of the Dead Cow. And it's plausible that the Quentin character was entirely somebody else's subculture prank, which the Legion of Doom and Cult of the Dead Cow co-opted. Nonetheless, everyone interviewed for this chapter talked about Quentin and the anonymous group researching projects ALF-1 and Green Cheese as if they were real. In some sense, to these hackers, the myth had become reality. And that's exactly the way they wanted it.

Who Put the News Media in Charge of the Truth?

Does the news media share some of the responsibility for what happened? In the present political crisis, the mainstream news media has portrayed itself as the arbiter of truth and the last bulwark against "alternative facts" spread by Donald Trump and his allies. Dramatic taglines like "Democracy Dies in Darkness" adorn the front pages of major news outlets, whose reporters now serve as soldiers engaged in the frontline battle against false narratives. In practice, the news media's effectiveness at not only defending objective truth but also packaging it up in unambiguous terms has been questionable in many circumstances. And this is nothing new. As many subjects who have been interviewed for a news story can testify, it is not uncommon to find oneself being questioned by a reporter who has already conceived the narrative they intend to use. Such narratives are crafted to be as compelling as possible, so that the resulting piece will be attractive to a large audience.[32] A common journalistic tactic is to lead subjects through a line of questioning that elicits the answers the reporter has in mind.

Goggans explained his experience with this during the filming of the *Dateline* episode. The original intent was to include an "Erik Bloodaxe" interview as a complement to the other two interviews with Legion of Doom members, but this material was cut prior to the episode airing. The reason was the reaction Goggans had to an aggressive line of questioning designed to sensationalize the Legion of Doom's activities—something that had been a recurring problem for the group since *Operation Sundevil*.[33] According to Goggans, "I pissed off Stone Phillips [then anchor of *Dateline*]. I tried to be frank with him, I didn't want to answer questions about all of the 'evil things I did' as a kid."[34] Phillips tried to reassure Goggans, but once the interview commenced, he began to press him to reveal fantastic crimes that he had committed personally. In response, Goggans would only deliver bland answers about the hacker scene in general.

Sensing that the story was not going where they wanted it, the *Dateline* production crew pulled the plug on the interview. Goggans continued, "Because I made him (Phillips) mad, he ended the interview by saying the crew needed to get some B-roll footage, and he left me to his guys." As Phillips departed the location of the interview, Goggans was ordered to walk back and forth on a street until the crew captured a scene that they liked. Exasperated by what he considered punitive action on the part of the production crew, Goggans called them out for their farcical behavior, and they stopped filming. To this day, Goggans asserts that "*Dateline NBC* only creates stories that they think their audience wants to watch."

This account is partially corroborated by Jim Thomas, a criminal-justice professor at Northern Illinois University and the editor of *Computer Underground Digest*, a weekly newsletter commenting on legal issues surrounding computing that he published in the 1990s. In an issue that appeared shortly after the *Dateline* episode aired, Thomas disclosed that he had been contacted by Susan Adams, the episode's producer, during preproduction. Like Goggans, Thomas was alarmed by the direction the questions from the *Dateline* crew were taking:

> She indicated that *Dateline* was going to do a story on hackers, and she wanted to know how many "hacker busts" had gone to court. She limited the term "hacker" to teenaged computer intruders, and did not seem interested in the more serious crimes of professional criminals who ply their trade with computers or with computer abusers who prey on their employers. Suspecting a pre-defined slant to the story, I attempted to make it clear that, despite increased visibility of attention to computer abuse, there have been relatively few indictments. (Thomas 1992)

Thomas was part of a larger group of activists attempting to push back against the rampant sensationalism surrounding hackers while still giving them credit for the new and innovative things they were doing with

technology. Others included famed computer-security researcher Doro-
thy Denning, prominent hacker defense attorney Jennifer Granick, the
science-fiction writer Bruce Sterling, and the staff of the Electronic Frontier Foundation, which had been founded partly in reaction to government
missteps during the investigation of the Legion of Doom. In their writing
from the nineties, these activists criticized journalists fishing for big scoops
on computer hacking, which inevitably led to misunderstandings about
what was technically possible, and subsequent government overreach in
cases against suspected hackers. Such conduct was not only disingenuous
but outright irresponsible, and it brought into question the integrity of the
free press. Thomas concluded his thoughts on the *Dateline* episode with
the following admonishment: "*Dateline* seemed uninterested in its responsibility to the public. It seemed more interested in presenting a sexy story."

The high-minded reader may scoff at any segment by *Dateline*, which
largely follows a true-crime format and has never broken a major story.
Reputationally suspect, the show has generated messy lawsuits against
NBC, including one concerning the production crew staging the explosion of a pickup truck in order to make false safety claims against General
Motors (Parrish and Nauss 1993) and another over the tragic death of a
man who committed suicide in front of *Dateline* cameras as they were filming a sting operation intended for the show's *To Catch a Predator* segment
(Stetler 2008). *Dateline* continued to pursue stories about computer hackers into the 2000s, using the same journalistic tactics they had deployed
in the early 1990s. But by then the hackers had grown tired of the show.
In 2007, an undercover NBC reporter prodding hackers to confess their
crimes at DEF CON, a yearly hacker conference held in Las Vegas, was exposed by conference organizers and heckled out of the venue (Zetter 2007).

Such missteps notwithstanding, the show's importance within the
news-media ecosystem cannot be overstated. *Dateline* is one of the lon-
gest running newsmagazines on television and is watched by an audience
of millions each week. Moreover, the show is a production of NBC News,
not the NBC Entertainment division. It belongs to one of the most storied outfits in journalism—a trusted source of information for viewers
across America. Violations of that trust undermine the basic principles of
journalism: truthfulness, accuracy, objectivity, impartiality, fairness, and
public accountability. The pattern of journalistic malpractice at *Dateline*
exposes a glaring weakness in the production of the news that we are now

confronting under more dire circumstances. Unsurprisingly, requests for comment on this story from NBCUniversal were left unanswered.

While some folks were taking a stand against the sensationalism exercised by *Dateline* and other news outlets, we know that a select group of hackers were exploiting it. The Internet Archive's Jason Scott has commented on why hackers in particular would be intrigued by the possibility of manipulating journalists. According to Scott, "there was a fascination in the 1980s and 1990s with appearing in movies and the news." This fascination anticipated the popularity of reality television and, ultimately, social media. In the era Scott is referring to, making a connection to those beyond one's immediate social circle was not easy for the average person. Hackers had discovered the utility of emerging information networks for this purpose, but mass communication technologies like newspapers, magazines, and television were still the best way to reach a large audience in the early nineties. If the objective was to weasel one's way onto television, it made sense to target journalists, as their desire to tell a story their way was the weak point in the system.

Once hackers figured out that they could exploit reporters who attempted to lead their subjects, faking news stories became part of their repertoire. The strategy was simple: the hacker gave the reporter exactly what they wanted in response to each question while also embedding their own cleverly crafted falsehoods into the answers. With its focus on media operations, the Cult of the Dead Cow excelled at fooling reporters. Ever interested in pushing the boundaries of creative communication, Kubecka had invented a story about the group's ability to move satellites in orbit, which he routinely fed to reporters eager for material about the hacker scene.

The story was inspired by a real incident in which John MacDougall, a disgruntled electrical engineer working at a satellite uplink station in Florida, seized control of a satellite television broadcast to protest the fee HBO was charging for its programming (Ewalt 2013). Calling himself "Captain Midnight," MacDougall was briefly able to send a protest message to millions of HBO subscribers before other engineers noticed. Reporting on this incident often confused moving a satellite dish, which MacDougall had done to send his message, with actually moving a satellite, which was not possible for him. This made the story attractive bait to rework and deceive reporters with—most didn't understand the associated technology.

However, good journalists saw through the ploy. According to Kubecka, "I tried this story with the *New York Times* guys, they didn't believe it."[35]

Humor played a significant role in many of these attempts to fake the news. In one of the more hilarious actions by the Cult of the Dead Cow, Luke Benfey (aka Deth Vegetable) and two associates did a serious interview with a Japanese news outlet. The producers deemed it too dry, so the reporter conducted the interview again, this time with Benfey and friends wearing outrageous costumes and simply making stuff up about their hacking capers, including recounting the satellite tale.[36] Sam Anthony (aka Tweety Fish) appeared on the PBS program *Net Cafe* (Net Cafe 1997) in the character of "Matt Force," the leading member of a parody hacking group called GO-FORCE![37] Not satisfied with merely adopting a comic-book name like the Legion of Doom, GO-FORCE! endeavored to bring actual superhero justice to the hacker scene. When asked by an interviewer why Matt Force had been elevated to the top leadership of this group, Anthony responded, "I have the best hair." With multiple disinformation campaigns running at any given time, the Cult of the Dead Cow was concerned that it might end up fooling itself. Anthony later explained, "Internally, we needed to keep track of what was real and what wasn't."[38]

Where does this leave us today? Not much has changed with respect to the incentives of reporters. Arguably, the situation is even worse, given the contraction of the news industry and the fierce competition for content engagement on the Internet and the ad revenue it brings. The same conditions that were exploited by hackers in the nineties are now being exploited by other actors for more serious purposes. Reporters looking for sensational political scoops are particularly vulnerable to this form of attack. Directly parlaying hacking into politics, the Guccifer 2.0 persona (presumed to be part of a Russian intelligence operation) worked with WikiLeaks to release hacked documents related to the 2016 election, along with pieces of disinformation, in an effort to smear the Clinton campaign. This action led to one of the most durable news stories of our era, with Trump administration officials continuing to defend the veracity of the Guccifer 2.0 leaks (Bump 2020). Modern politicians have recognized that reporters expect them to make ludicrous statements, and they are more likely to indulge them than ever before. In this context, it's easy to understand how adherents to QAnon end up in Congress.

That's not to say that we shouldn't trust the news. But it can't be the sole arbiter of truth. Hannah Arendt considered this dilemma in the shadow of the twentieth century's totalitarian regimes, which held a monopoly on mass media (Arendt 1967). According to Arendt, when a consensus view forms around an incontrovertible subject, the truth emerges. For instance, there is broad consensus that the sun rises in the east and sets in the west. This is reliably observed by the entire population of the earth every single day, rendering any argument against it, even by the most authoritarian government, completely absurd. Similarly, there is broad scientific consensus that the earth has not been visited by extraterrestrial spacecraft—there isn't a single shred of evidence to support such a claim. In Arendt's words, "Conceptually, we may call the truth what we cannot change; metaphorically, it is the ground on which we stand and the sky that stretches above us." If there are diverging viewpoints on the truthfulness of an incontrovertible subject, one should ask: Why is that happening? The motivations for bending the truth, as we have seen, are not always malicious, nor are they always clearcut.

Deny Everything

As any ethnographer will admit, there is a certain burden one must bear when interviewing subjects about a past event. The farther removed they are from the circumstances they are recounting, the hazier their memories will be. It is not uncommon to find different people giving differing accounts about the same event, not in order to deceive, but simply because their perception of the event has changed over time. And the possibility remains that a subject could be lying. But Sean Lawson, a professor of mass communication at the University of Utah who has been studying the social aspects of computer hacking, sees this as an interesting avenue of inquiry: "If they lie to you, they are revealing important things just as well."[39]

At the conclusion of his interview for this book, Goggans warned that "anyone providing information about Quentin and the *Dateline* episode might deny it in the future." Indeed, everything reported here about this incident could be false. Those responsible might deny everything after this book goes to press. The digital artifacts they have left behind might be reinterpreted by future observers. And the interpretation presented here might be yet another cultural mutation that will help this story evolve. When one is playing in the realm of mythmaking, that's the way it should be.

3

Photoshop Fantasies

THE POSSIBILITY OF AN ALTERED PHOTO revising history in a convincing way highlights a salient threat of imaging technology. After all, seeing is believing. Or is it? The examples history has preserved make it clear that the observer is more often than not meant to understand that something has changed. Surprisingly, the objectives of photographic manipulation have remained largely the same since the camera first appeared in the nineteenth century. The old battle-worn techniques have simply evolved to keep pace with technological developments. In this chapter we will learn about the history of photographic manipulation, from the invention of the camera to the present day. Importantly, we will consider the reception of photo editing and its relationship to the notion of reality, which is of more significance to our concerns than the base technologies themselves. Once again, mythmaking finds a new medium to embed itself in.

On the Practice of Changing Reality

One of the most provocative political artifacts from the twentieth century is a photo of Chinese leaders observing a moment of silence in Tiananmen Square on September 18, 1976, a week after the death of Mao Zedong (fig. 3.1). The drama of that moment in China's history is undeniable, but what is more intriguing is the photo itself, which exists in two versions (Brugioni 1999). The original depicts a lineup of the most senior leadership in close rank in the foreground, with thousands of others filling the square behind them. In November 1976, a second version was published in the state-sanctioned monthly *China Pictorial*, with two conspicuous gaps visible in the previously tight lineup. This was the version that would serve as the official photographic record of the event for not only China but the entire world.

Who was missing? Immediately following Mao's death, an internal power struggle displaced four staunch Maoists from their leadership posts: Jiang Qing, Mao's widow; Wang Hongwen, deputy party chairman; Zhang Chunqiao, vice premier; and Yao Wenyuan, politburo propagandist. Not satisfied with merely holding this group accountable for excesses committed during the Cultural Revolution, Chinese reformers saw fit to erase the so-called Gang of Four from the entire historical timeline. The naive interpretation of the November 1976 version of the photo is that the observer is meant to believe that this is how the senior leadership arranged itself for the photographer. However, given the disciplined military formation of everyone else present, something appears off in the scene. Even without direct knowledge of the event, an informed observer would suspect tampering, especially given the conspicuous absence of four key government players who had recently been arrested, including Mao's own wife. This brings to light a crucial but frequently ignored purpose of photo manipulation: the observer is meant to notice that the scene has been altered, which itself conveys an important message.

In China, there is a complex relationship between historical facts and competing realities. The global revolutions of the twentieth century that were ushered in by movements tied to distinctly new ideologies sought to bring about fundamental changes to the everyday reality of the people who inhabited the vanquished territories. Due in large part to continuity in its authoritarian government from 1949 to the present day, China remains the lone country where this is still unfolding. Mao's early revolutionary writing made the case for the practice of changing reality in order to achieve one's desires, be they personal, academic, or political:

> If you want to know the taste of a pear, you must change the pear by eating it yourself. If you want to know the structure and properties of the atom, you must make physical and chemical experiments to change the state of the atom. If you want to know the theory and methods of revolution, you must take part in revolution. (Mao 1996)

In other words, the capacity to change the state of the world gives everyone some mechanism for changing reality itself. Within a social con-

FIGURE 3.1. Following Mao's funeral, a political faction known as the Gang of Four was erased by darkroom technicians. The conspicuous gaps, left unfilled, convey a very direct message to the viewer.

text, one can bring about a mass change in reality through the use of the media, which, even in a developing country like China, was a focal point in the average citizen's life in the twentieth century. If a prominent individual finds themselves declared persona non grata, they can be removed from the historical record as transmitted to the public via the media, a space in which they had existed before. Not only does this revise the past, but it also redirects the arrow of time, as the behavior of those in the present and the future is modulated in response to any warning they accept from the revision. Such maneuvers are particularly effective in states with an authoritarian government that can, at will, exert control over all aspects of the media. This process has proceeded uninterrupted in China since the conclusion of its civil war, with the reception of such revisionism essential to the constitution of pan-Chinese identity (Da 2020). In this climate, one *expects* to modulate belief in response to perceived shifts in reality, and this, in turn, accelerates changes to the world. It also leaves a trail of competing realities.

But the complex relationship between the past that truly existed and the alternate realities that compete with it cannot be interpreted in a straightforwardly negative way. The achievements of China in the twenty-first century have allowed the country to buck the stagnation that sank the Soviet Union and put the handful of remaining communist countries in economic and social stasis. This is the paradox of information manipulation. A better future can be built in a society where endless possibilities exist in the minds of the people who live there. If an achievable change to the physical world can be conceived, it can be executed in some capacity, thus bringing a new reality into being in a physical space. China's capacity to rapidly build new cities and connect them with high-speed rail lines and information networks represents a modern revision to a historical reality associated with dynastic turnover, which has traditionally shifted populations and built lasting monuments to secure a legacy (Economist 2017). The Belt and Road initiative reflects another revisionist reality, one intended to resurrect the Silk Road as an alternate globalist infrastructure directed by Beijing (Maçães 2020). To make things like this work, the leadership and public must enter into a partnership, willing or forced, that embraces the reality being conjured.

Today, modern China exists as a fantasia, where fictions can be tuned into reality via an order from the politburo or the press of a smartphone screen. Xi Jinping has articulated this ethos as the "Chinese Dream," which he has describes as "the great rejuvenation of the Chinese nation," emphasizing the elements of strength, civility, harmony, and beauty (Allison 2017). This rejuvenation is all-encompassing, spanning everything from infrastructure to culture. In support of the latter, priority has been placed on the domestic development of sophisticated communication, entertainment, and AI technologies for mass public consumption, which reinforces the individual elements of the Chinese Dream.

Of particular significance to our discussion is the Chinese technology industry's fascination with software to digitally alter photographs. This takes the form of ferociously popular augmented-reality and virtual-reality apps that support the on-demand manipulation of imagery. Bytedance, the maker of TikTok (known in China as Douyin), specializes in the creation of computer-vision algorithms that can alter the human face to make it more attractive, or grotesque, or accessorized with virtual objects. Meitu, another app maker, aims "to let everyone become beautiful easily" through the application of digital cosmetics and image filters that convert blemished skin to eerily flawless flesh.[1] This is merely the contemporary instantiation of the media environment the Chinese market has always known, and the one it continues to need in order to realize the Chinese Dream.

These apps, of course, can be also found on the American market, which has an insatiable appetite for any technology that heightens engagement with the myth cycles that previously circulated through older, noninteractive forms of media (Maçães 2020). New Chinese technologies are routinely packaged, exported, and aggressively marketed to American consumers, creating what has become a divisive political issue for American leadership (McCabe 2021). China's success in this endeavor should hardly be surprising, as the Chinese Dream is merely a reworking of the American Dream, sharing the same hypercapitalist vision but forcing it into a communitarian rather than individualist, mode. The American Internet resembles the Chinese Internet in many ways,[2] as a site where elites have a predilection for promoting alternate realities through altered imagery and the same augmented-reality and virtual-reality apps are used by ordinary people yearning to become characters in stories of their own telling. The two cultures are now intertwined in cyberspace, in spite of the divisive rhetoric on both sides. This is a remarkable turn of events, and one that was inconceivable during the Cold War, when Western intelligence services were studying the photo of Tiananmen Square.

In the preface to the English edition of French journalist Alain Jaubert's landmark book on photographic deception *Making People Disappear* (Jaubert 1989), which chronicles the history of visual disinformation in the twentieth century, the national security scholar Roy Godson writes, "Jaubert suggests that, with the exception of wartime, it is unlikely that democratic governments would engage in systematic falsification even if they wanted to." This thinking betrays a startling failure of imagination in anticipating how the Internet would change politics and government—especially in democratic countries, where the expectation exists that guarantees of free expression and speech will always allow the public to push back against falsehoods propagating from the top down.

American political operatives in the first decade of the new millennium realized the potential of posting edited digital images to the Internet to steer public opinion. Early visual political disinformation portrayed plausible but easily debunked scenes—for instance, the famous photo montage of John Kerry and Jane Fonda appearing to share a stage at an antiwar rally in the 1970s, which was meant to tarnish Kerry's image during the 2004 presidential race by tying him to a polarizing figure. The photographer who took the original picture of Kerry, Ken Light, was able to produce an authentic negative to discredit the montage. He has since warned of how "professional-looking these distortions of truth have become in the age of Photoshop" (Light 2004).

But campaigns of this nature were rarely, if ever, effective, owing to the shadowy origins of the content and the authoritative responses that could be mustered against it—the exact responses Godson and Jaubert expected in democracies. What was not initially appreciated by creators and observers of visual disinformation was that a fake image could be more effective in a democracy if it were obviously fake. This would defuse any attempt to debunk the content, which would look hopelessly didactic. Thus today we find manipulations that are more reminiscent of the Tiananmen Square photo than the Kerry-Fonda montage.

A strategy to bombard the American public with clearly fake visual disinformation was taken up by the Trump campaign in 2016 and would continue through Trump's presidential administration, which believed itself to be in a permanent posture of electoral campaigning. This was an aggressive move from the topmost level of government—and effective, because it tapped into existing alternate realities associated with subcultures on the Internet. Prominent examples of systematic falsification emanating from the White House include Trump retweeting a photo of Chuck Schumer and Nancy Pelosi in Islamic garb (Pengelly 2020), Trump's reelection campaign circulating a doctored image of Joe Biden alone in his basement during the COVID-19 pandemic (Lajka 2020), and Eric Trump tweeting a photo of the rappers Ice Cube and 50 Cent wearing Trump 2020 hats, which had been spliced into the image (Williams 2020).

"Photoshop fantasies" are now as much a fixture of American as of Chinese culture. Much more than a political tool, filtered selfies, memes, and other forms of manipulated visual media tap into something fundamental within these cultures. Instead of viewing edited photos with suspicion, people across the globe are embracing them as a means of creative expression. This may seem counterintuitive, but as we have seen, in antiquity elaborate alternate realities that could be experienced visually were created through the more cumbersome medium of pottery. Photography lowered the bar, technically, for their creation and gave the creator more range in terms of what could be accomplished, compared to older artistic forms. Digital photography lowered it even further; unskilled users of the Internet are now creators via the apps on their phones. The motive remains the same, but a modern visual medium conveys the endless possibilities of the imagination better and faster than any other.

Darkroom Manipulation Techniques

How exactly was a photographer able to alter the photo of Tiananmen Square in the 1970s, without access to Photoshop or another digital photo-editing tool? Given the contemporary discussion around photographic manipulation, it might seem a new problem, unique to the Internet in its execution and reach. But it isn't: from tabloid photojournalism to misleading advertising, photos that have been edited in some way have been a fixture of print media for nearly two centuries. The creative potential of photography was recognized immediately in the nineteenth century—that it might be employed as an artistic tool in the same manner as the paintbrush or chisel.

Photography was even better than painting or sculpting, however, since the camera preserved a moment in time that could be reconfigured at will by the photographer—either before or after the shutter opened. While staging a photo was straightforward enough, one could go beyond that by adding effects directly to the negative which were not easily achievable through physical changes to the world. According to British art historian Aaron Scharf, shortly after the introduction of the camera, "retouching had reached such proportions, it seems, that it became difficult to find photographs which had not been embellished by hand" (Scharf 1965). Much like today's digital fakes, the resulting images could look plausible or over-the-top, depending on the intent.

FIGURE 3.2. *Self Portrait as a Drowned Man.* Appearing in 1840, this is one of the earliest fake photographs.

And naturally, over-the-top fake photos were the first to appear. One of the earliest known instances was staged by Hippolyte Bayard, who is credited with contributing to the invention of photography, in 1840 (Lerner 2014). The photo, titled *Self Portrait as a Drowned Man* (fig. 3.2), depicts the trailblazing photographer as a corpse in a morgue and was intended as a protest image. Having developed a process to compete with the daguerreotype, Bayard felt slighted when his direct-positive technique, which involved exposing photosensitive silver chloride paper to light for an extended period of time, did not catch on. *Self Portrait* was a ploy to draw attention to his plight, which he blamed on the French political establishment. A version of the photo that circulated in Paris was accompanied by a melodramatic text:

> The corpse which you see here is that of M. Bayard, inventor of the process that you have just seen, or the marvellous results of which you are soon going to see. To my knowledge, this ingenious and indefatigable researcher has been working for about three years to perfect his invention. The Academy, the King, and all those who have seen his pictures, that he himself found imperfect, have admired them as you do at this moment. This has brought him much honour but has not yielded him a single farthing. The government, having given too much to M. Daguerre, said it could do nothing for M. Bayard and the unhappy man drowned himself. Oh! The fickleness of human affairs! Artists, scholars, journalists were occupied with him for a long time, but here he has been at the morgue for several days, and no-one has recognized or claimed him. Ladies and Gentlemen, you'd better pass along for fear of offending your sense of smell, for as you can observe, the face and hands of the gentleman are beginning to decay.

One imagines Bayard would be right at home on 4chan, the Internet image-board community, where the practice of pairing weird images with brief outrageous stories is prevalent.

Bayard's histrionics aside, he demonstrated that photography could be a truly original form of creative expression. However, some were unsettled by the distortions to reality that could be induced by tinkering with the scene that the camera captured. In 1856, the *Journal of the London Photographic Society* published a series of complaints against the by then common practice of doctoring images (Holzmann 1988). A specific demand of the authors of these complaints was that the society stop exhibiting any photos that had been altered. But what did it even mean to doctor a photo? Were all altered images to be treated equally and denounced?

The filmmaker Errol Morris raised these questions in his own investigation of photographic veracity over a decade ago in the *New York Times* (Morris 2007). If a person is removed from a photo, as in the Tiananmen Square photo, that would be a large change to what is depicted and should certainly be considered doctoring. But what if a small object in the background of the scene being captured is moved by the photographer? Does that mean the image has been doctored, even though the change is trivial? No hard boundary exists between doctoring and an innocuous change. In fact, in Morris's view, a division between large and small changes to reality might not exist at all:

> The idea that photographs hand us an objective piece of reality, that they by themselves provide us with the truth, is an idea that has been with us since the beginnings of photography. But photographs are neither true nor false in and of themselves. They are only true or false with respect to statements that we make about them or the questions that we might ask of them.

To Morris, the relationship to a reality, real or imagined, is established by the act of an observer interpreting or interrogating what they are viewing and is not inherent in the photographic object itself.[3] Thus, a picture is a social object that is subject to the needs and desires of the society that produced it.[4]

As Bayard had showed, staging a photo was easy. But there were certain constraints to this form of changing reality: post hoc changes to the scene were not possible. Customers sitting for portraits were not always enamored with the final product (even if their own appearance was the fault), which necessitated some improvement after a negative had been exposed. This triggered a move beyond staged photos to a technical innovation in a new medium: film. By the end of the nineteenth century, photographers had demonstrated great ingenuity in the development of techniques for photo doctoring that could be executed in the darkroom. In general, these fell into one of two different categories: the deletion or the insertion of details.[5] Let's take a close look at both.

Deletion of Details

The quality of the images produced by early cameras was rather high, even by modern standards, meaning fine details could be resolved (Humphrey 1858). Too much detail wasn't always desirable, however, especially by the vain. Small-scale retouching of faces to remove blemishes, blotches, freckles, and other minor imperfections visible on a negative was an accepted practice at studios. In the 1890 book *Photographic Mosaics* (Wilson 1890), Virgil Williams defended this form of retouching, while rejecting more elaborate changes to facial structure, arguing that improvements to image quality did not impinge on the true character of the subject. In his words, "Defects in the complexion, like yellow blots, make the negative extremely spotted, and, of course, they should be eliminated, but to take out the lines caused by the irregularities of the features takes away so much of the character, and if you take the character from a man what is there left?"

As today, in the early days of photography the desire to become better looking was fulfilled via a technical process. In film photography, the negative is an inverse of the developed photo. Retouching a photograph by modifying the negative was straightforward, assuming one had a steady hand and patience.[6] Once the negative was fixed, so that any further exposure to light would not alter it, a basic strategy could be followed: to turn a light area of a photo darker, that area of the negative was made lighter, and vice versa. Seated at a special retouching desk, the retoucher would scrape exposed film with a knife to darken an area, or apply ink or paint to lighten an area. To remove an unsightly blemish, a small amount of ink could be applied in the spot that would appear lighter like the rest of the skin on the negative (fig. 3.3a). Special purpose tools like etching knives were developed to assist in this process, and in the hands of a skilled retoucher they facilitated very precise changes to the texture and geometry of the captured scene.

Through experimentation, darkroom specialists discovered that the same process used to alter a subject's complexion could also be used to alter their ethnic appearance. This was particularly appealing in countries, such as Russia, with significant minority populations that did not conform in appearance to the majority population. For example, with an etching knife and fine-tipped paint brush, facial features could be resculpted and skin lightened to make a swarthy subject look more European. A promi-

nent early instance is a photo of the Potemkin mutineer Afanasi Matushenko that appeared in Soviet history books. Matushenko, a Ukrainian,
had pronounced Asiatic features, which were reduced in his official photo
to make him look more European, and thus more prototypically Russian
(fig. 3.3b). In this instance, the majority population had modulated reality
to make the revolutionary hero their own. As with other forms of retouching, apps now fill this role. The San Francisco–based startup Gradient
promotes their AI Face app as a way to "find out how you would look like
if you were born on a different continent," thus moving this capability
from propaganda to entertainment.[7] Both historically and contemporar-
ily, the final product typically has an unrealistic look—too smooth, too
perfect.

Removing fine details was relatively easy. But how did one remove an
entire person? The most straightforward method was to simply crop the
photo. This could be executed quickly by cutting either the negative or
the developed photo. Depending on the positioning of the people in the
scene, a crop could have a dramatic effect on its interpretation. For ex-

FIGURE 3.3. Examples of the deletion of details from a photo. Subjects could be made
(A) more attractive, (B) less ethnic, or (C) persona non grata.

ample, in 1944, Mao Zedong and Zhu De, a general in the Red Army, were photographed inspecting the Yan'an airfield (Jaubert 1989). In the original photo, Zhu appears in front of Mao. During the Cultural Revolution, this photo was cropped to remove Zhu, thus putting Mao at the head of the review party (fig. 3.3c). By selectively deleting inconveniently placed people in historic photos, Chinese censors could strengthen the cult of personality around Mao by making him appear omnipresent. A similar effect could be achieved through effacement, the process of selectively cutting a negative and then putting it back together while leaving part of the severed material out.

Individuals targeted for deletion were not always as conveniently placed as Zhu De was. If a person could not be cropped out of a photo, an artist would have to repaint large regions of the scene. The practice of selective removal of people was known as *blocking*. After painting over a person, the resulting void in the photo would have to be filled with detail that matched the surrounding background. As we observed in the Tiananmen Square photo, conspicuous gaps in group photos betrayed an attempt to revise the past that also served as a stark warning to the observer.

Occasionally, the vanished left something behind. While a stray piece of clothing or body part might look like the product of sloppy editing work, these were frequently not mistakes—good darkroom fabricators knew exactly what they were doing. Albania's leader throughout most of the Cold War, Enver Hoxha, routinely purged his perceived enemies, as well as the historical record. In one particularly chilling photo, two high school classmates of Enver were erased, yet their shoes remained visible (Jaubert 1989). No matter where one looked in Albanian history, the same message was reinforced: beware of the control Hoxha and his party maintain over reality.

Insertion of Details

Newly created voids in a photo could also be filled with *cutouts*, individuals or objects taken from other photos, leading to the creation of a *photomontage*. However, the result was often implausibly bad due to lighting, perspective, and photographic inconsistencies. The manipulator in this case was nearly always trying to merge material that was incompatible with respect to visual appearance. Much as with deepfakes today, a crude edit was often enough to serve the purpose of presenting an alternate reality, as opposed to fooling the observer. A representative example of a badly executed cutout is the official team photograph of the gold medal winning 1960 US Olympic Hockey Team, which heroically defeated the Czech and Soviet teams on its way to Olympic glory (Grinter 2022). Three players missed the photo session, and their heads were later inserted into the picture over three heads of their teammates (Fig 3.4A). The result was an obviously doctored image, with all three inserted heads badly mismatched with the original scene in size and lighting. One wonders how the players erased from this landmark moment in sports history felt about their excision.

Beyond the simple insertion of a few objects into a photo, more elaborate photomontages could be achieved by combining significant portions of different images, thus creating entirely new scenes. In this mode, darkroom specialists could arrange complicated mosaics with a collection of photographic cutouts, giving them as much creative license as a traditional artist working with more conventional media would have. Importantly, creators of photomontages realized that it didn't matter if the photomontages were intentionally absurd—the more unusual, the more receptive the audience would likely be. At the turn of the twentieth century, whimsical scenes began appearing on postcards as advertisements for local regions and products; these became popular items to collect and trade. This takes us deep into historical meme territory. As time passed, distinct photomontage genres emerged, such as people in outer space, chimeras with human heads, and people posing with impossibly giant objects (fig 3.4b). The content most representative of fakes of this era was lighthearted material like this, not the more serious political material being generated by governments.

An additional, and very clever, technical approach that could be used to combine objects or people that were not present at the same sitting was the *double exposure*. This involved exposing the film in a camera multiple times, which, if done correctly, would capture multiple images on the same negative (Kantilaftis 2014). Double exposure was especially useful for generating eerie photos with an otherworldly appearance. Leveraging this trick, photographers in the late nineteenth and early twentieth centuries promoted "old spirit photography" as a way to reconnect the living with their deceased loved ones (fig. 3.4c).[8] By first taking a conventional

A.

B.   C.

FIGURE 3.4. Examples of the addition of details to a photo. (A) Photo of the gold-medal winning 1960 US Olympic Hockey Team. (B) Postcard promoting the impossibly large objects one could allegedly find in Wisconsin. (C) Ghosts among the living, courtesy of a double exposure trick.

portrait shot and then exposing the same film to an old photo of the departed, they could render the second exposure a far less clear and ghostly presence. The Victorian predilection for the occult, including seances and alleged hauntings, helped propel the popularity of double exposure photography for decades.

Digital Darkroom Manipulation Techniques

By the 1980s, digital cameras were available from multiple manufacturers, and the creative potential of computer programs to alter photographs became irresistible to engineers playing with the new and still expensive technology. Having a more efficient form of photography at one's fingertips opened up exciting possibilities for the art form. Why not revisit the old darkroom manipulation techniques in a digital context, engineers asked, and maybe try some different things as well? The emerging computer-science subfield of computer graphics had shown how it was possible to create fully synthetic scenes, from the photorealistic to the fanciful. And such scenes were already appearing as special effects in television and movies. But computer graphics would not lead the charge to develop algorithms for manipulating digital photographs.

Instead, it was a subfield of electrical engineering called digital-image processing that would upend photography. This surprised computer scientists, who in the 1990s had assumed graphics would come to dominate all of the digital visual arts.[9] Image-processing algorithms are a form of signal processing, which was originally meant to improve the quality and transmissibility of image content. As time progressed, there was a realization that some of the mathematical transformations used for improving image quality mapped nicely onto the old darkroom techniques. For instance, a low-pass filter generally used to smooth out noise in an image could also be used to improve the complexion of a face (fig. 3.5a). Thus, image manipulation was added to the image-processing repertoire. The continuity in the use of photography, as film faded and digital imaging ascended, is noteworthy. Instead of fake digital images suddenly appearing as novel threats at a particular time, familiar photographic practices continued, uninterrupted.

Certain advantages over traditional darkroom manipulations were realized, however, when using a computer instead of a retouching desk. First, when editing digital files, every operation is reversible, which makes experimentation much easier. Second, everything that could be done in a darkroom was possible on a computer, and more. New manipulations that could only be performed digitally were discovered and added to image-editing software—for example, various warping operations that drastically changed the geometry of the objects in a scene. Third, photographic editing became accessible to people with no training in traditional photography. This rapidly democratized digital content creation, and brought millions of newcomers to the practice of altering reality. And finally, because the images were just collections of binary bits, they could be moved around computer systems with ease, to let others modify them at will. Over time, digital cameras became integrated with information sharing technologies like printers, optical media (CDs and DVDs), removable media (SD cards), and smartphones. This last advantage would prove to be the most consequential one, turning digital photography into a dynamic form of visual communication on the Internet.

What exactly did the digital darkroom consist of?[10] For deleting details, we have already mentioned that retouching mapped nicely to image-filtering operations, which could blur or sharpen an image, depending on how they were applied. The previously painstaking process of removing a person from a photo could be replaced by the use of image-cloning algorithms. Instead of having to copy the look of the background of a photo by hand, a background region could be selected using the computer's mouse and then copied over the person targeted for deletion. The algorithm would interpolate the pixels on the border of the copied region to blend them with the existing background as seamlessly as possible (fig. 3.6a). Compared to the darkroom process, the quality of the product was dramatically better—enough so that if done well, the edit could only be detected by sophisticated forensic analysis by experts.

When it came to inserting details, the image-cloning process also made it possible to copy people and objects within an image, which might look realistic or silly, depending on the context. More powerfully, image-splicing algorithms facilitated the creation of complicated photomontages with a few point-and-click operations. Image regions across different photos could be selected and copied into a host photo, this time with the algorithm attempting to blend all of them as seamlessly as possible with surrounding regions. The more diverse the alien image content, however, the less plausible the resulting image would look (fig. 3.5b). This tends to be true even with today's best algorithms for the same operation. The basic image-splicing approach inspired later, more specialized algorithms, including face swapping (fig. 3.6b), the precursor to AI-generated deepfakes, which was introduced in 2004 (Blanz et al. 2004). Other techniques were

A.

Blurring for Retouching

B.

Image Splicing

C.

Head Shrinking, Artistic Stylization, and Corporate Logoization

FIGURE 3.5. These photos were altered using the popi editor, an early software tool for image processing created at Bell Labs by Gerard J. Holzmann (Holzmann 1988).

developed for stitching different photographs together. This was useful for panoramas but could also connect entirely different scenes.

The image processing operation that was most consequential to the social-media era of the Internet was also the easiest to accomplish through technical means: text overlay. This involved simply changing some of the image pixels into characters of a desired font, size, and color. The subtle brilliance of this feature was that the caption associated with an image could be inserted into the image itself. This would make image repurposing even more appealing, paving the way for Internet memes.

More impressive were the new effects that could only be accomplished through the use of image processing on computers. In the 1988 manual

FIGURE 3.6. Early digital examples of (A) image cloning to delete subjects from a scene (Rocha et al. 2011) and (B) swapping faces between people (Blanz et al. 2004).

Beyond Photography: The Digital Darkroom (Holzmann 1988), authored by Bell Labs engineer Gerard J. Holzmann, a host of inventive image transformations were introduced to computer enthusiasts for the first time. These included warping methods to shrink a person's head, shearing operations to give a scene a more abstract style, and procedures that could transform a face into an object reminiscent of a corporate logo (fig. 3.5c). Because all of these transformations were implemented in computer code, it was possible for anyone with some skill in programming to modify them, creating new variants that were then added to the growing collection of image-processing algorithms developers were trading. For convenience, Holzmann also released a software tool for the Unix operating system's command-line environment called popi, which could be used for general-purpose image editing.

Popi was part of a wave of image editing tools that appeared in the 1980s. Some of these tools, like popi and another command-line tool developed by DuPont called ImageMagick,[11] were intended for computer experts with specialized training. Others, like PixelPaint and MacPaint, had interactive graphical user interfaces and were marketed to graphic designers. All of the available software tools contained the traditional darkroom manipulation techniques as well as emerging new techniques. Many of these algorithms remain in use within social-media platforms and mobile apps, processing the billions of selfies taken by smartphones every day. By the late 1980s, professional designers had started their migration to purely digital work, as the use of a computer increased productivity, dropped the cost of production, and made the output easy to share across the globe. But the tools were still rudimentary in both user experience and in facilitating the actualization of one's imagination onscreen. Behind the scenes in this era, two brothers from Michigan were programming an application that would profoundly change how the world would interact with visual media.

"To Photoshop" is now synonymous with "to edit" in discussions surrounding photography. Why did this particular piece of software triumph over all of the others to become the Internet's favorite tool for altering reality? The answer involves the unlikely combination of a technological inflection point, calculated marketing, and one extraordinary family. Like the development of the commercial camera in the 1830s, the development of Photoshop in the 1980s would be a moment of consequence for the world, even though its implications would not be felt until the present.

Photoshop had its beginning as a pet project of Thomas "Thom" Knoll, a graduate student in the Department of Electrical and Computer Engineering at the University of Michigan, and John Knoll, an engineer at Industrial Light & Magic, the famed special-effects studio founded by George Lucas. The Knoll brothers were the sons of Glenn Knoll, a longtime professor of nuclear engineering at Michigan and an expert in radiation detection and measurement. Imaging was both a professional and personal interest of the elder Knoll, who invented nuclear resonance imaging technologies by day and experimented with film photography in his basement darkroom at night (National Academies Press 2016). Also in the Knoll household was an Apple II Plus, which Glenn had purchased to develop signal-processing algorithms but which soon became a platform for the boys to learn programming. The Knoll family was close-knit, and Glenn taught his sons how to create things through their shared hobbies, which also included woodworking, constructing model airplanes, and solving complex mathematical puzzles. Later in life, the brothers would combine their passions for engineering and creativity by doing what they had been training to do for years: writing software to realize their dreams.

After an awe-inducing visit to Industrial Light & Magic at the height of the Star Wars craze in the 1970s, John enrolled in the University of Southern California's School of Cinema and became adept at building physical models for special effects.[12] All of those years in the family basement had paid off. Thom stayed in Ann Arbor for college and entered a doctoral program in computer vision there following graduation. In his spare time, he began tinkering with code to implement various image-processing algorithms that were missing from the graphic-design software that he had installed on his Apple Macintosh Plus (Story 2000). This was everything from basic gray-level adjustment for image pixels to sophisticated visual recognition capabilities that could locate predefined objects in photos. While on a visit back home, John grew intrigued by the things Thom was doing on a PC that had previously been the exclusive realm of movie studios (Masson 1999). For fun, they began to collaborate to expand the set of image-processing capabilities for their own photography work.

Conveniently, Thom's PhD advisor, the well-known image-processing researcher Edward Delp, happened to be distracted just as the project was getting off the ground. According to Delp, "I was transitioning from Michigan to Purdue at the time Photoshop was created. Thom was working on microscopy in my lab, but I knew that he and his brother were into photography. They were very secretive about their after-hours activities, I didn't know what they were up to." Unencumbered by interference from his advisor, Thom spent perhaps a little too much time on his side project. Fortunately for him, the outcome would far exceed anything one could hope to achieve from a dissertation on microscopy. He would eventually drop out of his doctoral program to focus on programming full-time.

What the Knoll brothers initially had was a pile of individual code snippets that could do different things but needed to be used independently of each other. Thom wrote an application, which he called "display," for the Apple Macintosh that made all of the available pieces accessible to the user. Key advances were support for color images and different file formats— things that were not common in image-editing software in the 1980s. With these new features, plus a host of truly transformational image-editing tools, Thom and John believed they had something that might be commercially viable. Knowing that "display" would not fly as a product name, the program went through a series of name changes, becoming ImagePro, PhotoShop (with a capital S), and finally Photoshop (Schewe 2000).

As John began to prepare to demo the new software in Silicon Valley, it became clear that Photoshop had to better distinguish itself from competing products like SuperMac's PixelPaint, which was already popular with graphic designers. This led him to develop a facility in the application for users to add their own features. By creating a "plug-in," a user with a new idea for an image-editing technique wouldn't need to start from scratch by writing file-handling routines, a user interface, and other basic code when implementing it. Photoshop provided the scaffolding for creatives to innovate more quickly. And some plug-ins that would appear after Photoshop hit the market, like Aldus Gallery Effects and Kai's Power Tools, became essential photo-editing tools in their own right. But the most ingenious aspect of Photoshop plug-ins was the ability for communities of photographers, designers, and artists to form around the product, first on websites, and later on social-media services like DeviantArt. Writing in *PEI* magazine, the photographer Jeff Schewe noted that "Some of the Adobe people thought John's features were gimmicky and didn't belong in a serious application. They viewed the product as a tool for retouching, not special effects, so John had to find a way to 'sneak' them into the program. Those plug-ins have become one of the most powerful aspects of Photoshop" (Schewe 2000).

A harbinger of things to come on the Internet was the demo that John put together for companies interested in acquiring the rights to sell Photoshop. Armed with a vibrant topless photo of his then-girlfriend (and later wife) Jennifer, which he had taken while vacationing in Bora Bora, John would highlight what the new full-color image editor could do (Comstock 2014). And what could be more compelling than multiplying beauty with the click of a mouse? By cloning Jennifer in front of a live audience, John would show off a sequence of Photoshop's key features: the lasso tool to isolate a region of interest within the photo, the magic wand tool to select the relevant pixels in the region based on tone and color, and the copy and paste operations to bring the clone into being.[13] He'd leave a copy of the software at each company he visited, bundled with the photo of Jennifer, which became something of a standard test image over time.[14] Adobe Systems, a company with a growing reputation for making creative software products, loved all of it.

From a contemporary perspective, the Photoshop demo was obviously pandering to the adolescent needs of the male-dominated tech industry. It was also a troubling omen of the harassment campaigns against women that began with hacked nude photos (Olson 2012) and eventually devolved into the much easier creation of fake nudes (Randall 2012). But the standard critique isn't the entire story. Something far more significant was unfolding in the way the Photoshop software was conceived of, implemented, and used. The demo was also a reflection of that. In essence, Photoshop was a way to efficiently channel fantasies into a virtual space that others could experience immediately. When combined with the Internet, it would shape vast amounts of user-generated content and in turn be shaped by the user's themselves through the plug-ins they made. Quoted in the *Guardian* in 2014, Jennifer emphasized that "the beauty of the internet is that people can take things, and do what they want with them, to project what they want or feel." There was no practical limit to what users of the Internet could now show each other on their screens.

Adobe purchased a license to distribute Photoshop from the Knoll brothers in September 1988. The company released the first commercial version in early 1990. The timing couldn't have been better—the decade would bring multimedia technologies and the Internet to a global market of consumers eager to create and share their own content. By hitching their wagon to a major corporation, the Knolls were able to propel the marketing and reach of Photoshop to the point where it became the de facto digital image-editing tool for computer users. Its influence was so powerful that by the end of the 1990s, "Photoshop" had entered common parlance as a verb used to describe the act of manipulating a digital photograph (Macworld Staff 2000).

Importantly, the cloning of Jennifer prefigured how Photoshop would be commonly used. Looking back, Thom's former academic advisor Delp noted, "We worry about fake political stuff spreading on social media now, but the fashion and advertising industries were using Photoshop to change photos from day one." As we have already seen, the ability to remake the subject of a photograph was possible as far back as the nineteenth century. But for glamour shots, the darkroom process could take many hours (Zhang 2014). This was not at all compatible with the pace of content generation happening on the Internet. Photoshop let these industries grow their output, which aggressively expanded into online marketing as the world's consumers migrated to the Internet. Moreover, with Photoshop, things could be done to the human body that were not possible before. Entirely new forms of preternatural beauty and phantasmagoric pornography were conceived of to seduce the Internet's global audience.

In other corners of the Internet, creative communities were perfecting the art of parody using Photoshop and the trove of visual data that had been uploaded to the Internet over time. An epicenter of this in the early 2000s was the humor website Something Awful, which hosted a popular online forum that was a precursor to sites like 4chan and Reddit (Beran 2019). Started by Richard Kyanka (aka Lowtax) in 1999, Something Awful promoted a brand of antiestablishment, antisocial humor that would come to dominate the Internet in later years. A prime example was the Photoshop Phriday feature (fig. 3.7), which the website used to showcase "the tremendous image manipulation talents of the Something Awful Forum Goons."[15] Here one could find pop culture blended with history (e.g., a photo of John F. Kennedy making a speech while Robocop looks on), familiar entertainers used to spread absurd new messages (e.g., the band Kraftwerk telling the public that Santa Claus does not exist), and ironic reactions to the sentimentalism that was widespread in the 1990s and early 2000s in America (e.g., an idyllic home from a Thomas Kinkade painting set ablaze).

While it's easy to recoil at the transgressive nature of much of what appeared on Something Awful, it is more useful to consider the material in

Artist: Lowtax (2001)   Artist: darthfunk (2002)   Artist: Groggie (2006)

FIGURE 3.7. Three examples of manipulated images created for the recurring Something Awful feature "Photoshop Phridays."

context. For the most part, the Photoshopped images were a cultural experiment making use of unambiguous parody, as opposed to surreptitious manipulation intended to fool the viewer. The Something Awful forum users (affectionately termed "Goons") were beginning to explore parallel realities that diverged from a world that they increasingly viewed as too complex to understand and ultimately too flawed to fix through conventional means. By retreating to the Internet, they could experience the alternative narratives that were being created with Photoshop and shared by a growing number of amateur graphic artists. Thus the image meme was born.

Historical treatments of memes often begin with a discussion of Richard Dawkins and his book *The Selfish Gene*, but that may no longer be the best frame of reference for this analysis.[16] Dawkins argued that a biological model of evolution can extend beyond living beings to explain cultural transmission. While evolution might be a helpful analogy in this context, it is, in some sense, disconnected from what is transpiring on the Internet. Evolution is confined to living organisms in the physical world and cannot bring into being an alternate reality—it can only exert pressure on the single reality in which those organisms exist. Cultural artifacts transcend the physical world and are confined by nothing except the limits of the imagination. The meme, therefore, is a transcendent object. No wonder it now commands the attention of the entire globe.

More pragmatically, there is also something different about image memes, as compared to other forms of memetic content. Their success is tied to the intimate coupling of human visual perception and sophisticated information networks that can instantaneously deliver content anywhere on the planet. We are primarily visual animals, and we rely on our eyes for the rapid intake of information from our surrounding environment—even when that environment is virtual. It is far more efficient for people to gather information from an image than from a passage of text, thus it is not surprising that visual communication is now replacing textual communication on the Internet. And the "feeds" which are the primary interfaces to social media have been developed to get this type of content in front of users as fast as possible. Photoshop's enduring success relies on this formula, which was refined in the early days of 4chan, Tumblr, and Reddit—all prime breeding grounds for memes. Later, Twitter, Facebook, Instagram, Snapchat, and TikTok brought the meme to a nontechnical audience and solidified its position as an integral form of communica-

FIGURE 3.8. (A) The most effective disinformation is also the most ridiculous. Contrary to expectations, it was obviously manipulated images, not near-perfect fakes, that had an outsized role in disinformation campaigns in the 2020 presidential election in the United States. (B) Photoshop Fantasies at their best: the silliness that has been present since the dawn of photography.

tion. To this day, Thom Knoll's name still appears on the splash screen of Photoshop: credit to the original creator, the unwitting master of memes.

Are Manipulated Photos Truly a Cause for Concern?

On the Internet today, Photoshop versions of reality are as prominent as those resembling or approximating real life. Given what we have discussed about photography, this makes a lot of sense. There has always been a strong appetite for the fictions altered photos provide, and the more creative the better. A key innovation of the meme is the coupling of photographic manipulation with jokes, which used to be a primarily oral form of entertainment but are now exchanged visually. The most effective disinformation makes use of this formula as well: it matches what people want to see (fig. 3.8a). Take a look at any social-media platform—it will be awash in such content. While it is easy to automatically detect that a meme has been edited in some way, because it is highly likely that one of the doctoring techniques we have described has been employed (Farid

2016), it is not so easy to automatically determine whether or not it contains a malicious message. No reliable algorithmic mechanism for this currently exists. Adobe's Content Authenticity Initiative (Rosenthol et al. 2020) and DARPA's research programs related to forensics (Turek 2022a, 2022b) aim to develop new technologies that can flag all edited content that is potentially harmful, but it remains unclear if technology is a viable solution here.

Recent headlines have reinforced the mission of Adobe, DARPA, and others by declaring photo editing to be a driver of an "information apocalypse" that "threatens to rewrite history" (Knowable Magazine 2020; Edwards 2020). Yet it's overly alarmist to decry every manipulated image as bad simply because it somehow distorts the truth. Every digital photo is manipulated in some way these days. Computational photography pipelines have been integrated into modern digital cameras, meaning software, not an optical process, produces the snapshot that the photographer sees on their screen (Chayka 2022). And more often than not, those photos find their way to social-media apps, which provide a host of filters that can be applied to dramatically alter the content of the photo on-the-fly. In this regime, flagging manipulated content becomes a game of crying wolf—nobody will be listening when it matters. Manipulation detection is irrelevant in the world of Photoshop fantasies, where the observer is a willing participant in the fiction presented by an image (fig. 3.8b).

Perhaps, then, we shouldn't concentrate too much on technological band-aids. It's harder to change history than one might think. When the Gang of Four disappeared from the photo of Tiananmen Square, it was an easily noticed change to the scene—and that was the intended effect. As we have seen, the desire to manipulate photos is as old as photography itself. What has been routinely ignored in this discussion, however, is that this desire comes from an even deeper one: to escape from one reality and enter into others—others from the imagination. We know from photography that accuracy is not the question, instead it is how we absorb the content into our decision-making and culture-generation practices. Political threat is not equivalent to making a selfie look sillier. So perhaps the best path forward is through education in social norms, to steer content creators away from malicious activity. We continue to blame technology for long-standing social problems instead of confronting the unethical behavior that nourishes them. Don't starve creativity; starve bad intent.

4

Cheat Codes for Life

AS WE LEARNED in chapter 2, computer hacking involved a fair bit of misdirection to achieve its goals. Much of the misdirection was effected through textfiles, the primary digital medium hackers were using to communicate to each other and the public. It is worth pausing to consider the later history of this highly nuanced form of writing. At the turn of the millennium, the stakes were raised, as the technical content on security vulnerabilities that appeared in the textfiles became increasingly sophisticated. Embedded within the textfiles of this period is the story of the computer-security industry's genesis, including evidence of sharp divisions that fractured the hacking scene. Curiously, one frequently finds as much myth as fact in this material, which is unexpected given the rigorous nature of computer hacking in this period. With information asymmetry in the mix, new security vulnerabilities from technical disinformation appeared, which unnerved avenues of society reliant on the integrity of information networks.

Going Places Ordinary People Cannot

Early computer users were consumed with the idea of being able to go places that ordinary people could not. There was something tantalizing about the vast complexity of computer technology. Peering into the digital nooks and crannies, sometimes one could find oneself making a discovery that unlocked a door to a realm of the impossible (Murillo 2020). The most familiar example of this effect from the classic era of computing is the video game cheat code (Kirk 2020).

Cheat codes allowed the player of a game to do things that were not achievable in normal gameplay. In most cases, this simply meant gaining an unfair advantage to beat the game more easily, but any number of miraculous things could happen after entering one. For instance, if the secret code for games made by the publisher Konami[1] was in a player's bag of tricks, they could get thirty extra lives in *Contra* or nearly all of the power-ups offered in *Gradius*. Cheat codes existed for a variety of reasons. They were often intentionally programmed into a game by developers to use for debugging or for players to make use of for fun. It was also possible for cheat codes to be unintentionally introduced into the source code of games as bugs, which were then serendipitously located and exploited by players.

"Cheat codes were the currency of cool," according to Dan Amrich, an editor of *GamePro* magazine in the 1990s (Craddock 2016). Regardless of whether a code was deliberately introduced into a game by the developers, it was always treated as underground knowledge by the players. Rumors of new codes were whispered across high school cafeteria tables, eventually landing in a BBS post or Internet website after school. If one was in the know, one could gain quite a bit of respect within a technically savvy peer group by sharing the secret of a new code.

The popularity of some games was even propelled by the intensity of the conversation around the ways to cheat them. The more extreme the effect of a cheat code, the more players could be whipped into a frenzy (and ultimately a buying spree). The infamous cheat code that unlocked a series of grisly "fatality" actions in the Sega Genesis version of *Mortal Kombat* led to a full-blown moral panic in the early nineties (Crossley 2014). Suburban mothers were appalled that their children were deliberately changing the play of the game to witness various characters being murdered in spectacularly violent fashion. Yet as the controversy grew, so too did demand for both the game and the fatality cheat code. *Mortal Kombat*, of course, did not lead to any meaningful societal harm, and it is now considered a cultural touchstone for the millennial generation. For our purposes, the cheat code is a terrific illustration of a social phenomenon even more prevalent today: the increasing desire for subversive information that enables the impossible through computer technology while simultaneously contributing to a broader culture. And it is by no means the only example from the early days of personal computing.

Some of the gamers trading cheat codes were exchanging other pieces of underground information as well—a great deal of which was far more alarming to outsiders than any video-game violence. Nearly everything that is considered subversive on the Internet today could be found on computer networks as early as the 1980s, but in a much different format: the textfile. As we learned in chapter 2, textfiles were digital texts, often authored anonymously, which covered a broad range of topics: from UFO lore to instructions on how to break into computers. By sticking to just text, writers of these files got around the bandwidth and storage constraints of early computers, thus maximizing the potential of sharing. And the way these files were written and disseminated lent them an air of the mystical, as if they were arcane writings meant to be discovered only by a chosen few. Internet historian Jason Scott has described the textfiles as "the cheat codes for life," because they let the reader go places others cannot by manipulating reality. Remarkably, this material was massively influential in kickstarting the careers of many well-known technologists.

Scott's own history is relevant to the story here. Beginning in the mid-1980s, he was the system operator (SYSOP) of a hacker BBS based in New York called "The Works." By his own telling,[2] Scott was just a teenager when the board debuted in 1986, and his father was not pleased by the inordinate amount of time he was dedicating to it. By the time Scott left for college in Massachusetts, his family had expressly barred him from all distractions while he was enrolled in school—no part-time jobs and absolutely no BBSs. Thus, The Works was disconnected in 1988. It reappeared shortly after as a Boston-area board, this time under the control of a SYSOP going by the handle "Dave Ferret."[3] Scott very visibly continued his affiliation with The Works, organizing meet-ups of users around Boston and recruiting volunteers to help run the board.

In his self-described role of "master of lore" of the hacker scene, Scott obsessively collected textfiles that he considered gateways to places where ordinary people could not tread. This meant that several genres of subversive material were available for browsing on The Works. In its heyday of the early nineties, the board advertised itself as having 10 megabytes of storage space for over nine hundred textfiles—a veritable trove of underground information. It became a popular gathering spot for Boston-area hackers, many of whom were initially drawn to the scene via the discovery of the textfiles and were looking to connect with other local hackers to trade information with. Joe Grand (aka Kingpin), a hacker and influential figure in the maker movement, described wading into the board's content to *Decipher* in 2018: "The Works had all those text files, and it was sort of hacker related, but it wasn't evil hacker related. So I think The Works is the spot" (Fisher 2018).

The Works brought together one particular group of hackers that would fundamentally change the way that companies and governments would think about securing computer systems and networks. Incorporating themselves as a think tank called Lopht Heavy Industries, they contributed to the development of the "hacker space" concept for collaborative technology projects by moving their base of operations off of the BBS and into a physical space in Boston's South End neighborhood (later, suburban Watertown). As a tight-knit group working in concert, the members of the Lopht were able to release a number of high-profile security advisories for various operating systems and networking technologies, as well as a now infamous password cracker ("LophtCrack") for Microsoft Windows. Crucially, in this period the Lopht's output remained rooted in the textfile format, with the release of all of its information made in a mode that was instantly familiar to other hackers.

The Lopht's files attracted the attention of the federal government, which was monitoring developments in computer security outside of the establishment (and not always making the distinction between fact and fiction, as we saw in chapter 2). In what was a highly consequential moment in the history of the computer security, the members of the Lopht were invited to provide testimony to Congress, during which an astonishing disclosure was made that they had the ability to "take down the Internet" in a mere thirty minutes (CSPAN 1998).[4] Politicians and reporters took this claim seriously, as here was a group of expert hackers that had been engaged precisely because they had technical knowledge far beyond that of the establishment. But there was intense speculation within the computer underground about whether it was actually possible to shut down the entire Internet. Hacking culture blended fact with fiction in bombastic ways, after all. Had the Lopht merely invoked a cheat code of their own making to hack Congress?

Following the Congressional testimony, members of the Lopht were approached by other hackers who had attempted to determine if there really was a way to shut down the Internet. A handful of brand-new attacks emerged out of this genuine curiosity, but not the one the Lopht actually had in hand.[5] In the end, the hackers revealed that the attack they had described to Congress targeted a bug in the border gateway protocol, used by critical infrastructure at network providers to move packets of information around the Internet (Fisher 2018). Yet though there had been a real attack, the Lopht had indeed hacked Congress: vendors were informed of the bug before the testimony happened, and fixes were already in place by the time senators learned it was possible to bring the entire Internet down. This incident was shaped by what the members of the Lopht had been exposed to on BBSs like The Works: the convergence of sensational storytelling with real technical information.

Watching the Lopht's testimony today, one can see that this motley crew of technologists was on the verge of big things. Shortly after their appearance in Washington, the hacker think tank was acquired by the security firm @Stake (Fonseca 2000). Lopht members Chris Wysopal and Christien Rioux (aka Dildog) would go on to become founders of Veracode, a software-auditing firm that was later acquired by CA Technologies for $614 million (Owens 2017). Peiter Zatko (aka Mudge) has had an influential career in government and industry, with stints at DARPA and Google (Hesseldahl 2015). Lopht affiliate and denizen of The Works Katie Moussouris became famous in the security industry for popularizing "bug bounties," sums of money paid out if security vulnerabilities were disclosed to vendors before becoming public (McGraw 2015). All are now senior leaders of the computer-security industry.

In another instance of a programmer making good use of the cheat codes for life, famed software engineer and Stack Overflow cofounder Jeff Atwood got his start as a teenager who learned how to manipulate the telephone network via textfiles.[6] Writing in his popular blog *Coding Horror*, Atwood described his early experiences with BBSs: "I was always fascinated with the tales from the infamous hacker zine 2600. I'd occasionally discover scanned issues in BBS ASCII archives . . . and spend hours puzzling over the techniques and information it contained" (Atwood 2008).[7] That information eventually landed him in trouble with the law. After he wrote a program that let users make use of calling-card numbers they did not own (mainly so that he could make free long-distance calls to BBSs), Atwood received a visit from the police and a computer trespass charge (Atwood 2012). Yet he harbors no regrets over the incident, which only pushed him deeper into computing and the myriad directions it could take an enthusiast: "I must confess I've grown to love my own bad judgment. It's led me to the most fascinating places." Atwood was certainly not alone in this regard.

The textfiles written by computer hackers would get progressively more technical from the late 1990s through the early 2000s, but they never stopped blending factual information with creative storytelling. Nor did they stop encouraging sensational behavior in the real world. In fact, the stakes were dramatically raised as the Internet became an indispensable resource for the entire globe and security threats began to manifest themselves within it and against it. By looking at the activities of computer hackers in this later period, we can develop a clearer picture of common deception techniques used in technical contexts today.

Technical Files on Phone Phreaking and Computer Hacking

One specific genre of textfile, with an origin uniquely tied to computer networks, left a lasting impression on the technology industry: that was the *technical file*, which provided instructions on how to break into pieces of technology that possessed access controls—truly allowing one to go where others could not, through forbidden (and, in some cases, downright illegal) knowledge. The targeted technology was primarily the telephone system and networked computers, but various other devices were fair game as well. The reason this information became so enticing is that it attracted the attention of powerful forces within the government and large corporations. From the government's perspective, if the information in the technical files were real, that would undermine the security of critical infrastructure, including the Internet itself. But the files could also be valuable training material for intelligence officers, science and technology officials, and others within the government looking for new capabilities for both launching attacks against adversaries, and defending against new threats.[8] Elements in private industry felt similarly, except that a new dimension was added: the commercialization of offensive and defensive capabilities that were, in many cases, byproducts of the textfiles.[9]

Textfiles on phone phreaking, the art of breaking into the telephone system, came first (Lapsley 2014). Some of the earliest textfiles appearing on BBSs consisted of material that was lifted from print publications like the yippie newsletter *YIPL/TAP* and *2600: The Hacker Quarterly*. In the 1980s, computer-hacking zines emerged as original textfile content, and they were frequently associated with notable hacking groups (e.g., *The Legion of Doom/Hackers Technical Journal*). There was also a slew of independently authored files.[10] Stylistically, many of the technical files resembled creative writing, with fictionalized narration interspersed with real instructions on how to break into or disrupt some computer system. This was rather atypical for technical writing in any context, and it made vetting challenging, as real information could be mistakenly dismissed because the surrounding text was ridiculous. For instance, the editorial found in *Phrack* issue 48 opens with some humorous mockery of government security procedures:

> ~ WARNING! This is a TOP SECRET-MAGIC EYES ONLY document containing compartmenalized information essential to the national security of the United States. EYES ONLY ACCESS to the material herein is strictly limited to personnel possessing MAGIC-12 CLEARANCE LEVEL. Examination or use by unauthorized personnel is strictly forbidden and is punishable by federal law. ~
>
> Yes, it's the annual issue of Phrack you've all been waiting for, hopefully you have kept your security clearances current. (Phrack Editorial Staff 1996)

Any reader affiliated with the federal government who was turned off by this would have missed a trove of new and accurate technical information, including proof-of-concept code for the notorious SYN flood denial of service attack (Schiffman 1996) that wreaked havoc on the Internet for years. Further compounding judgment on the veracity of the technical files was the fact that they were rarely, if ever, published with the real name of the author attached.

A portion of the technical files were completely fake, however. And given the serious implications of the claimed use of many of the attack techniques and strategies, the genesis of any fake file is of particular interest. The motivations for the creation of bogus files varied. As time progressed, more people were drawn to the phreaking and hacking scenes. This led to changing social dynamics within these communities, which, given the nature of their activities, were fairly insular and wary of outsiders. Pranks had always been common in both scenes (to a certain degree thanks to their shared yippie lineage[11]), and they were meant in part to sort newcomers who were savvy and could recognize a joke from those who were easily fooled (or in hacker parlance, "lame") and not worthy of membership. Given the rather advanced nature of the technical content and the relative sophistication, in some cases, of the writing, there was a tremendous amount of information asymmetry present, even for technology experts. Thus it was no trivial feat to figure out what was real and what wasn't. Beyond their utility for vetting, the most memorable pranks became cultural touchstones for those who came out of these scenes.

An early prank by phone phreaks was the story of the "Blotto box." Scott explained the appearance of this apocryphal device on underground BBSs as the result of an uptick in interest in instructions on how to manipulate the telephone system through mostly illegal means:

> A good example of something spreading digitally that was false happened to be related to phone phreaking boxes. In the late 70s or early 80s, the black box came into existence. A black box messed with the voltage of a phone to keep it ringing, but enabled free calling. Combine interest in that particular new box, along with the blue and red boxes, as well as the cheese box, and you get a run on boxes on boards. One circulating is fake: the Blotto box.

Phone-phreaking boxes were home-brew electronic devices that served different purposes toward the end of cheating the phone company. The blue and red boxes allowed a phreak to place free phone calls, while the cheese box enabled a form of call forwarding, whereby the origin of the phone placing a call could be obscured. These boxes were real and widely used by phreaks in the 1970s and 1980s. By the early 1990s, after phone companies moved to digital infrastructure, boxes had largely ceased to work, but they remained cultural fixtures of the computer underground.[12] Plans for these boxes were distributed as textfiles that required a degree of familiarity with electronics to understand. Younger phreaks just entering the scene didn't always possess this and could be fooled by outrageous claims if the surrounding text was peppered with jargon or complicated-looking schematics. This was not an unfitting outcome, as the boxes that did work appeared magical to first-time users. The Blotto box is a representative example of a subculture prank targeting newcomers.

Several different versions of the Blotto box textfile exist, each providing similar directions for the construction of a device that allegedly could disable all of the phones within an area code.[13] The concept supposedly came from the box's namesake, King Blotto, a founding member of the Legion of Doom, though various versions of the textfile attribute the plans for a "working" implementation to different phreaks.[14] The long-version of the file makes it clear to the reader that it contains some very forbidden knowledge:

> The Blotto Box is every phreak dream . . . you could hold AT&T down on it's knee's with this device. Because, quite simply, it can turn off the phone \fe allowed out of an area code, and no calls will be allowed in. No calls can be made inside it for that matter. As long as the switching system stays the same, this box will not stop at a mere area code. It will stop at nothing. The electrical impulses that emit from this box will open every line. Every line will ring and ring and ring . . . the voltage will never be cut off until the box/generator is stopped. This is no 200 volt job, here. We are talking GENERATOR. Every phone line will continue to ring, and people close to the box may be electrocuted if they pick up the phone.

Proofreading, it seems, was not the phreak's strong suit. Nonetheless, over time the Blotto box became legendary, and former phreaks and hackers still speak of it with bemused reverence.[15] Part of its success as a myth can be attributed to the blending of familiar technology and apocalyptic elements. Given the promised destructive capacity of the box, the reader was most certainly in possession of information that was only to be deployed as an absolute last resort. But the box wasn't a weapon in the conventional sense; it was portrayed as a technical innovation that exploited an alleged flaw in the design of the telephone network. The skeptical reader likely questioned this: the only way to verify the design would be to test it. And if it had worked for the original author of the textfile, surely the results would have been reported in the news. Given that the instructions called for a "Honda portable generator or a main power outlet like in a stadium or some such place," it is highly unlikely that anyone ever attempted to deploy a Blotto box. The file was written in such a way that left the door open to an impossible outcome.

As time progressed, underground textfile writing evolved, including the fictional elements that were so essential to its popularity. Through the 1980s, there were groups creating distinctive spellings and terms for various technical materials associated with the hacking and phreaking scenes, and these became standard conventions in textfiles.[16] Turf wars, jealousies, and even some legitimate social criticism on the boards spawned textfile groups whose sole purpose was to poke fun at the more successful individuals and groups within these scenes, often by comically exaggerating the unique stylistic elements found in their textfiles. Metal Communications and its affiliate the Neon Knights, active between 1983 and 1986, were pioneers in this regard.[17] A tremendous amount of posturing can be observed in their textfiles, which tended to blend elements from hacker culture, heavy metal music, Satanism, drug culture, and other material young BBS users would have considered transgressive. The earnest activist holdovers from the 1970s and their acolytes within the hacker scene were enticing targets for a group like Metal Communications, which was mainly out to gain laughs through preposterous stories set in the underground world of technology. In this regard, its influence on the Cult of the Dead Cow, which emerged in the same period, is unmistakable. Remarkably, the success that group achieved spawned its own countermovement in the form of the Hogs of Entropy—a massively prolific textfile group that authored over one thousand pieces in the 1990s, many parodying the people, activities and files associated with the Cult of the Dead Cow.[18]

Comedy aside, by the mid-1990s the quality of the content found in the technical files had drastically improved—enough so that it attracted the attention of computer scientists working on operating systems, networking, and other fields that had only recently started to take security seriously. This coincided with the members of the underground technology scenes growing up. Phreaks drifted into computer hacking and acquired experience with nonproprietary systems that were not as opaque as the telephone switches operated by the Bell System. Hackers were going to college, getting real jobs, and leveraging the conventional knowledge they had gained along the way to get better at breaking into computers. But the posturing and lunatic storytelling of the textfile scene rolled along unabated. Just as the Blotto box had been used to vet novice phreaks, very sophisticated-looking fake technical files became a mechanism for vetting supposedly elite hackers whose reputations sometimes exceeded their capabilities. However, at the dawn of the Internet-era, with numerous corporate and government services moving online, these fake textfiles were considered a more serious security threat than any fake phone-phreaking box had been in the 1980s.

It is important to recognize that nothing even resembling a viable computer-security industry existed in the 1990s. There was some academic interest in computer security, but professors didn't produce the same type of practical security material as the hacking scene. They were focused on more theoretical aspects of security, primarily related to cryptography (this is still largely true). All of the security advisories that appeared in this period came from the hacking scene and were published in textfile form. Many contained a proof-of-concept source code called an *exploit*, which could be used to attack a computer system. Prominent exploits from the 1990s were often buffer overflows, which gave an attacker unauthorized access to a computer system and frequently targeted critical Internet infra structure with broad attack surfaces, like the Unix email server sendmail (Zatko 1996).[19]

In this setting, why would a fake exploit be dangerous? If the exploit code didn't work as advertised, wouldn't that become widely known? Not always, it turned out, depending on the level of sophistication of the bogus code. In some cases, fake exploits secretly did something to the would-be attacker's own computer system (e.g., added a backdoor that could be used later by the author of the exploit) while making it appear that the intended attack had simply failed. In other cases, the code merely needed to look plausible enough to fool people into thinking that a vulnerability existed, when it really didn't. The response would waste valuable time and resources, as software developers looked into the potential flaw. From a national-security perspective, both scenarios were threatening. Moreover, it wasn't terribly difficult to release a fake exploit to a large audience.

The Bugtraq mailing list, now considered a landmark initiative for vulnerability disclosure (Cimpanu 2021), was the primary resource for releasing advisories and exploits in the 1990s. The list was started by Scott Chasin (aka Doc Holiday, introduced as a major player in the hacking scene's manipulation of *Dateline NBC* in chapter 2) in 1993. Remarkably, it was not moderated in its early years. During Bugtraq's heyday, from the mid-1990s to early-2000s, Elias Levy (aka Aleph One) took over the responsibility of running the list and brought effective oversight of the messages that were approved for distribution.[20] Yet even in a moderated environment, vetting new exploits was challenging, as the technical complexity of computer hacking had grown dramatically, shrinking the pool of people who could actually understand the most complicated attacks.[21]

A look at some of the numbers for fake vulnerability disclosures is instructive. The Open Source Vulnerability Database (OSVDB) was a grassroots project that assessed and cataloged security vulnerabilities in a rigorous manner, without corporate interference (Rosencrance 2004). Active between 2002 and 2016, OSVDB became an authoritative resource for security researchers tracking and studying attacks. The project was an outgrowth of the hacking scene and saw the participation of several notable hackers over the years, including H. D. Moore, Jeff Forristal (aka Rain Forest Puppy), Jake Kouns (aka Zel), and Brian Martin (aka Jericho). The database sorted different types of vulnerabilities into categories that described how trustworthy they were, indicated by standardized flags.[22] There was a "Myth/Fake" flag, which indicated that a vulnerability was based on a lie, deception, or some other malicious motivation. There was also a "Not-a-Vulnerability" flag. This was different from Myth/Fake designation, which was intended to signal an intent to deceive. Not-a-Vulnerability indicated that a company or researcher didn't fully under-stand what a vulnerability was or meant, and subsequently misunderstood what the code they were studying was doing in practice. Vulnerabilities flagged Not-a-Vulnerability could still become misinformation, however, if the wrong message was conveyed to system administrators and others charged with securing networks.

In total, the OSVDB project cataloged 244,649 vulnerabilities, span-ning 66,598 products from 29,647 researchers. The vast majority were legitimate, but the numbers for the Myth/Fake and Not-a-Vulnerability categories were not insignificant: 567 for the former and 2,925 for the latter. But it was some time before fake vulnerabilities became widespread. There were very few vulnerabilities flagged Myth/Fake before 2004, when there were 24. According to Brian Martin, the reason for this was the gate-keeping procedures the community had put in place at the most-watched forums where vulnerabilities were disclosed: "The people who released fake exploits had no real visibility when dumping files to FTP servers or IRC channels that anybody could access. There wasn't a lot to gain by releasing code that way."[23] Martin has explained that concerns over trust were behind this: "You wouldn't see people run code like that compared to code that appeared on Bugtraq or another well known list, where new disclosures were reviewed." But even with expert vetting, fake exploits still got through.

The first Myth/Fake flagged vulnerability (fig. 4.1), an alleged bug in a Slackware Linux system administration utility that could grant a hacker

slackware-3.5 /bin/su buffer overflow

From: s8013006 () KMITL AC TH (Chatchai Watchakit)
Date: Tue, 18 Aug 1998 17:42:02 +0700

```
This message is in MIME format.  The first part should be readable text,
while the remaining parts are likely unreadable without MIME-aware tools.
Send mail to mime () docserver cac washington edu for more info.

---559023410-851401618-903436922=:3045
Content Type: TEXT/PLAIN; charset=US-ASCII


 From exploit4.c of Phrack 49 (P49-14) can exploit /bin/su of slackware-3.5
kernel 2.0.34


---------------------

endeavor:~$ gcc -o exploit4 exploit4.c
endeavor:~$ ./exploit4
Using address: 0xbfffb20
bash$ /bin/su $RET
bash#

---------------------

Chatchai W.
```

FIGURE 4.1. The first Myth/Fake flagged vulnerability cataloged by OSVDB. This advisory was posted to the Bugtraq mailing list and appeared real to the computer-security community, until somebody tried to replicate the results. The true purpose of the code that was attached to the advisory remains unclear to this day.

superuser access to a system, appeared in 1998 in a security advisory sent to the Bugtraq mailing list.[24] It included proof-of-concept exploit code that was fake. The circumstances surrounding this false report remain murky to this day. On its surface, the advisory looks plausible enough. It notes that the /bin/su program found on Slackware Linux version 3.5 systems is vulnerable to a buffer overflow attack, and that the included exploit is based on Bugtraq moderator Levy's own exploit code from *Phrack* issue 49. The message is signed "Chatchai W.," and the associated email address is from a user at the King Mongkut's Institute of Technology Ladkrabang in Thailand.[25] The advisory earned the Myth/Fake flag after a number of reports appeared that the vulnerability could not be confirmed on numerous platforms. Commenting on these reports in his own message to Bugtraq, Levy believed that this false disclosure "was either pilot error or there is something particular to his setup."[26] No follow-up message was provided by the original author, thus we cannot judge intent in this case. But since nobody analyzed the reference code, it very well might have been a malicious attempt to dupe users, with the exploit attempting to achieve something other than the stated objective. The mysteries associated with fake exploits like this one remain mostly unsolved. Martin hopes to one day investigate these cases in his archived copy of OSVDB: "Myth/Fake is fucking fascinating to me. There is probably a ton of good stuff in there to study and make sense of."

Fundamentally, the motivation for releasing fake material within the hacking scene boiled down to one thing: reputation. On the one hand, neophyte hackers had a tendency to release fake but rather technical look-ing material in an attempt to gain some quick credibility and impress those who knew even less than they. Scott had this to say about such behavior: "Search textfiles.com [Scott's publicly available archive of textfiles] for terms like 'loser,' 'leech,' 'lamer,' etc. You will find people talking about this phenomenon. Textfiles with titles like 'shitlist,' 'BBS losers' and so forth contained lists of people who were getting called out for spread-ing bogus stuff." On the other hand, there were elite hackers making use of fake material to discredit others in the scene who they believed were violating the unwritten code of computer hacking. A particular example highlights how problematic the fake material had become by the late 1990s and why its presence was so frustrating to the nascent computer-security industry.

The Blackhat Hacker Information War of the 1990s and 2000s

As the underground hacking scene started to professionalize and recon-figure into what we now know as the computer-security industry, a war of sorts started between different factions. The growth of the Internet, its commercialization, and an increasing number of attacks against high-profile networks spawned sudden demand for products and knowledge related to computer security. There was really only one source for security expertise: the hacking scene. Major hacking groups like the Lopht, the Cult of the Dead Cow, woowoo, and root all had members that sought to go legitimate and market their skills, research, and software to who-ever would pay. But whatever their motivations, the initiatives of these so-called whitehat hackers led to good outcomes for society. They would help improve the security of the Internet and get software vendors, who had largely ignored security problems in their products, to reform by working with them from the inside instead of attacking them from the outside.[27]

Not everyone in the hacking scene believed that the whitehats were acting nobly. Blackhat hackers who were still illegally breaking into computers felt that they had a duty to protect the underground subculture they had worked so hard to create. The philosophy of computer hacking had unfettered covert exploration at its core (Blankenship 1986). By humiliating perceived traitors who were marketing their elite technical skills in industry, blackhat hackers tried to intimidate the hacking scene at large. In their view, the best cheat codes to life weren't meant to be shared with the public. These you kept for yourself or maybe shared with your most trusted friends. And ironically, what the whitehats were selling wasn't always as good as they made it out to be. There has always been some element of fakery in the business of computer security—as is very much in line with the culture of hacking, while also opportunely compatible with contemporary marketing practices. With enough time and resources, any system could be compromised, regardless of the countermeasures in place.[28] Blackhats routinely exposed holes in sales pitches arguing otherwise by hacking into the accounts of prominent whitehat hackers and dumping stolen files and logs of the attacks on IRC as proof.[29]

What whitehat and blackhat hackers have to say now about this period is illuminating. Martin, a former blackhat turned whitehat, agreed with the analysis that blackhats were attempting to protect a subculture they feared would become extinct once its secrets were exposed. Even after leaving the world of illicit hacking, he still felt sympathy for the actions of the blackhats: "They were calling out security firms and researchers who had weak security practice." But he also acknowledged that the campaign had limits and ultimately "was a losing proposition across the fucking board." Martin believed that the argument against "selling out" didn't make sense, since nearly everyone in the scene was making money from their computer skills, whether or not their work involved security. To him, the entire blackhat reaction was a "very old-school proposition, but you have to move on. You can call what you're doing whatever you want, but at the end of the day, you're still a programmer, like many other people outside of the scene."

A representative from Gobbles Security, a prominent blackhat group of the period, emphasized that there was a lot of social insecurity on both

sides of the divide: "Blackhats were indeed upset with the change in culture in the computer underground. But what happens when you stir the
hornet's nest?"[30] Whitehats would routinely threaten blackhats with legal
action and physical violence when they encountered them in person.[31]
Nothing ever happened to this particular hacker though, who felt that
these counterattacks only advanced the campaign: "The people who tried
to discredit us gave us a bigger platform." As the audience interested in
computer security increased, so did the drama. When releasing evidence
of successful attacks against whitehat hackers, the Gobbles representative
emphasized that the strategy was to "always drop a little, and say that
more is coming. The most vulnerable thing is the human ego. You don't
need a technical hack if you are an authority that 80 percent of people
believe."

Stephen Watt (aka the UNIX Terrorist), was another blackhat associate of Gobbles Security in the late 1990s and early 2000s.[32] He too was
concerned by the money flowing into computer security and the changing
motivations of hackers within the scene.[33] A prime example he cited was
the hacking group woowoo, which started to lose members to the Silicon
Valley start-up world, and would eventually spawn several big exits, including Napster, WhatsApp, and Duo Security (Menn 2014). "We repudi-
ated these people," Watt said, in reference to the blackhat community's
views on woowoo and their ilk. Elaborating further, Watt landed on a
key facet of the animosity between the two factions: "Whitehats were
more attuned to 'what other people want'; the blackhats were a reaction to
this." In other words, the blackhats believed that they held the moral high
ground and did not pander to interests outside of the hacking scene. They
were not willing to cede that ground for any price.

Cris Thomas (aka Space Rogue), a member of the Lopht, acknowledged the motivations of the blackhats but didn't think that whitehats
entering the corporate world were a problem. He described the Lopht's
own reason for walking away from the scene: "This is 1999, VC [venture
capital] money is growing on trees. Our friends are getting rich left and
right. We couldn't do great big things with the money we were getting
selling junk at the flea market."[34] Moreover, he characterized the blackhat
turn on whitehats in the late 1990s and early 2000s as "jealousy and sour
grapes," noting that "back in 98/99, there weren't many security companies." Thus the first hackers to join companies or form their own made

headlines and a lot of money. There was quite a bit of bad blood over the Lopht's acquisition by @Stake as well. Shortly after the Lopht had vacated its rented space in Watertown, somebody broke into the building and spray-painted "Sell Out" on one of the walls. Feelings ran deep in the scene.

A primary weapon in the arsenal of the blackhat was, of course, the textfile. Much of the war between the whitehats and blackhats transpired in the pages of their respective zines. Underground hacker zines were usually produced through collaboration, which hackers who were most active in illegal activities tended to avoid, so as to minimize legal exposure. There was inherent risk in forming any sort of blackhat alliance, and maintaining trust between people was hard. Watt reflected on the dilemma of what would be needed to win the war against the whitehats: "The end of my era of the blackhats was like the end of the Renaissance. Attacks of this nature would require more than what any individual could do. It was a difficult time, most of the people hacking things were individuals. People really hacking things did not associate with the notable groups in the scene, who by the late 1990s were all whitehats." Some blackhats ultimately decided to absorb the risk and band together, becoming a more effective force, as well as a prototype for the shadowy activity that would appear later on the Internet, including targeted malicious hacking and coordinating trolling.[35]

Blackhat zines were largely inaccessible to outsiders, and even those deeply embedded in the hacker scene had trouble understanding everything that appeared in them. Zines with inscrutable names stylized with numbers replacing vowels ("leet speak") appeared on the Internet in the mid to late nineties and were linked to the blackhat groups that coordinated their activities on IRC. Two of the biggest blackhat zines of the era were *bog* (fig. 4.2) and *el8*, but hono, b4b0, Brotherhood of Warez, and the *ThE HaXoR bRoThErS NeWzLetTeR* also found audiences.[36] The content they ran largely consisted of humorous IRC conversations (some real, some fake), parodies of vulnerability disclosures, and logs alleged to be evidence of hacks against prominent whitehats. Given the highly unconventional nature of the writing, the emerging computer-security establishment didn't always know what to make of the blackhat zines. Hacker slang, raunchy ASCII art, command-line histories, and snippets of source code in various programming languages were littered throughout in seemingly random fashion.

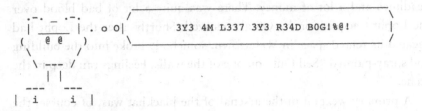

```
      .-.  .-.       /‾‾‾‾‾‾‾‾‾‾‾‾‾‾‾‾‾‾‾‾‾‾‾‾‾‾‾‾‾‾‾‾‾‾‾\
     |___  |. o o|        3Y3 4M L337 3Y3 R34D B0G!%@!      |
     (   @ @   )    _____/
      \    /
       \ --- /
        | |
       ---   ---
      | . i   i . |
```

```
b0g!#@!b0g!#@!b0g!#@!b0g!#@!b0g!#@!b0g!#@!b0g!#@!b0g!#@!b0g!#@!b0g!#@!

        TH4 4PR1L 1SSU3  1SSU3 IV ! 1N Y00R F4C3! PH33RN4T10N!

b0g            b0g!#              !b0     b0 #@!        b0g!#        #@!
b0g           !b0g!#@             !b0     b0 #@      @!b0g!#@        #@!
b0g         @!b0g!#@!             !b0    !b0 #@       #@!   #@!      #@!
b0g  @!      @!b  !#@!            !b0  #@!b0g!#@!b  1#@  0   @!b     #@!
b0g #@!b    #@!b    #@!  !#@!b0g! !b0 1#@!b0g!#@!b  1#  b0g!#@!b     #@!
b0g!#@!b0  #@!b    #@!  g!#@!b0g! !b0 1#@!b0g!#@!b g!# !b0g!#@ b0    #@!
b0g!#@!b0g #@!b   #@! 0g!#  b0g!  !b0    !b 1#     g! @!b  1#@ b0    #@!
b0g  !b0g #@!b   #@! 0g!#  b0g!   !b0   @!b 1#     g! @!b  1#@ b0    #@!
b0g  !b0g #@!b   #@! 0g!   b0g!   !b0   @!b 1#     g! @!b  1#@ b0    #@!
b0g  !b0g #@!b   #@! 0g!   b0g!   !b0 1#@!b0g!#@!  g! @!b  1#@ b0    #@!
b0g  !b0g #@!b   #@! 0g!#  !b0g!  !b  1#@!b0g!#@!  g! @!b  1#@ b0    #@
b0g!#@!b  #@!b0g!#@!  g!#@!b0g!   !b0 @!  g!       1#  !b0g!#@!b      #@!
b0g!#@!b  @!b0g!#@   g!#@!b0g!   !b0 #@! 0g!      1#@  b0 !#@!b       #@!
 0g!#@!      !b0g!#     !#@ b0g!  !b0 #@   0g      #@!           #@!
                         b0g!           @!   g!     g!# !b0g!#@!b0
                      g!#@!b0g                     !b0g!#@!
                      g!#@!b0                        b0g!#@
                      g!#@!b

b0g!#@!b0g!#@!b0g!#@!b0g!#@!b0g!#@!b0g!#@!b0g!#@!b0g!#@!b0g!#@!b0g!#@!
```

FIGURE 4.2. The header of the blackhat ezine *bog*, issue #4. Stylistically, *bog* followed the template of most blackhat zines, with excessive use of ASCII artwork and "leet speak" (swapping numbers for letters and using hacker-specific abbreviations for various words associated with the scene). Translated, the word bubble in the cartoon reads, "I am elite I read *bog*."

Watt recalled the historical progression of this form of writing: "There was a zine called *Citadel 666* that appeared in 1994 or so. It's older compared to the others, but you could see the style coming together—a style that carries through to later zines. It had more of a street vibe to it." That street vibe was key to the enduring influence of the blackhats. It was, in a sense, rebellious, and it attracted others to the cause. The representative from Gobbles Security noted that the style of the era never really went away: "Every couple of years a new zine comes out that has an old vibe. *ZFo* is an example of that." First appearing in 2009, *ZFo* (short for Zero for Owned) was associated with the antisec movement, a more aggressive offshoot of the blackhat movement of the late 1990s and early 2000s that did not believe in any form of public vulnerability disclosure and called for attacks against what was by then a more mature computer-security industry (Goodin 2008).[37] When it came to deception, however, the best examples of blackhat zine activity are the fake issues of *Phrack* (figs. 4.3, 4.4) published by a group calling itself the Phrack High Council (or pHC).

The fake issues of *Phrack*[38] were meant to resemble the real underground zine, in order to sow confusion with articles including malicious exploits that did not work as advertised—that is, were fake. Watt acknowledged his role in pHC, and he wrote most of the articles included in the five issues that were released (*pHC Phrack* issues 59–63) between 2002 and 2005. Watt described the thinking behind the fake issues, which was very much in sync with the broader antisec movement: "Nobody I knew wanted to have *Phrack* exist at all, we just wanted zines of hack logs and chat logs. We did not want to teach others about what we were doing, and we were against the release of all code that was useful to the underground." Beginning with Mike Schiffman's tenure as editor, *Phrack* had pivoted away from running articles about hacker culture and actual hacks in favor of more technical material about the security of the back-end infrastructure of the Internet. The anonymous *Phrack* staff that took

```
STOP POSTING, STOP HELPING THE SECURITY INDUSTRY, OR GET OWNED. THIS IS WAR.

                              ==#Phrack Inc.==

                   Volume 0x0b, Issue 0x3b, Phile #0x01 of 0x12

[-]=============================================================================[-]
#phrack #phrack #phrack #phrack #phrack #phrack #phrack #phrack #phrack #phrack
[-]=============================================================================[-]

*WHAT PHRACK IS ALL ABOUT*
*WHAT PHRACK IS ALL ABOUT*
*WHAT PHRACK IS ALL ABOUT*
"Phrack magazine, for hackers by hackers :D:D:D" - What a joke
Phrack magazine is nothing more than a bunch of whitehats posting
information they spend countless hours researching. Some of this
information is straight up NO-DISTRO-SUPER-PRIVATE, for example,
the ptrace insertion and strong arm shellcode articles. There is
a serious problem with this ezine though. Most of the people who post
articles to this ezine DON'T EVEN KNOW THEY ARE WHITEHATS. Researching
security related material or hacker techniques does not make one a hacker.
```

FIGURE 4.3. The rather combative introduction to *pHC Phrack*, issue #59 released in 2002 (Phrack High Council 2002), which was a fake issue of the popular hacker zine *Phrack*.

over after Schiffman stepped down continued to run the same type of articles. Watt alleged gatekeeping by the editors and, along with several associates, decided to take action against them: "We did this mainly to annoy the Phrack Staff. The zine was too Unix and vulnerability development centric. Overall, there was a sense that the zine had strayed from the good old days, and had become too narrow. We got a hold of a real copy of *Phrack* that hadn't been released yet. We burned it, but then decided to do something more creative."

Each fake issue of *Phrack* incorporated elements from the other blackhat zines, including plenty of hack logs and chat logs—everything Watt and his pals wanted in the real *Phrack*. But the source code each issue contained is of particular historical interest. Article 10 in *pHC Phrack* issue 62 (Phrack High Council 2003b) claims to be a collection of Linux kernel modules (LKMs) that add backdoor functionality to a compromised Linux system. However, the code for each provided module is obviously poking fun at prominent whitehat hackers including RLoxley, the maintainer of the #hackphreak channel on IRC; Niels Provos, a graduate student at the University of Michigan and OpenBSD developer; Eric Corley (aka Emmanuel Goldstein), the publisher of *2600* magazine; and woowoo members Andrew Reiter (aka awr) and Jonathan Bowie (aka Jobe). In the code for the module mocking Bowie, the infamous Unix command "rm -rf /", which deletes all of the files present on a system, is clearly visible.

Watt commented on the source code found in *pHC Phrack* issue 62, article 13 (Phrack High Council 2003c), which was meant to disrupt the open-source intrusion detection system (IDS) Snort and which had no other use besides causing mischief: "I wrote this fake code. It sends a barrage of data that makes an IDS go crazy. It was proof-of-concept antiwhitehat code." An IDS is meant to detect attacks by hackers that are in progress, allowing system administrators to take countermeasures, or, in the worst case, respond to an actual compromise. Snort, in particular, was a key piece of open-source security infrastructure that was widely used in the early 2000s. Watt's code was meant to trigger so many false alarms from the IDS that its operator would simply stop paying attention to it. This code wasn't really fake per se, but it was intended to spread panic, and an element of deception was present in its mechanism of operation. Watt had designed the program to mimic real attacks and trigger false alarms from the IDS. It didn't allow its user to break into any computers,

```
                          ==Phrack Inc.==

              Volume 0x0b, Issue 0x3e, Phile #0x0b of 0x0f

|=-----------------------=[ New Hacking Manifesto ]=----------------------=|
|=------------------------------------------------------------------------=|
|=------------------------=[ cr4zy c0nsuel0 ]=---------------------------=|
```

It happened again today. Another one sold out, sacrificing their dreams
to the corporate security machine.

Damn whitehats, noone believes in a cause anymore.

Another bug was released today to the security mailing lists.

Damn Whitehats, they know not what they do.

Another potential computer genius was relegated to an existence of nothing
more than than a 9-5 cubicle-dwelling promotional tool.

Damn whitehats, putting money before discovery.

FIGURE 4.4. The introduction to article 11 in *pHC Phrack*, issue #62 (Phrack High
Council 2003a), which is a parody of the textfile "The Conscience of a Hacker" by the
Mentor, which appeared in *Phrack*, issue #7 (Blankenship 1986).

but it did fool an IDS into thinking this was happening. In the writing that
surrounded the source code, Watt criticized the effectiveness of IDS technology in general, along with the quality of code that Snort maintainer
Martin Roesch had written. These were very real and valid points being
raised in a textfile that introduced each section of material with an over-
the-top quotation from boxer Mike Tyson.

   The fake pHC issues of *Phrack* remain important artifacts of the early
days of the computer-security industry, but another instance of fakery
is remembered by former whitehat hackers as being yet more frustrating, even though it spawned moments of hilarity that surpassed the best
issues of the blackhat zines. In late 2001, hacker group Gobbles Security
exposed a buffer overflow bug in the Unix operating system's gzip program on the Vulnerability Development (vuln-dev) mailing list (fig. 4.5).[39]
The accompanying advisory was written in broken English and appeared
to be intentionally hyperbolic in its claims ("The members of GOBBLES
practice the full disclosure of information but not the full disclosure of
exploits because we do not want to arm the many scriptkids of the world
with munitions to destroy the internet which we at GOBBLES love so

```
GOBBLES was sitting in his lab all alone one day wondering about
different ways to break into computer networks when he started thinking
about new ways to hack ftp servers.  Then GOBBLES thought "HEY I KNOW
SOME FTP SERVERS RUN DIFFERENT PROGRAMS FROM THEY OWN DAEMON AND MAYBE
THERE IS WAYS TO GAIN A SHELL ACCESS FROM EXPLOITING A BUFFEROVERFLOW
IN ONE OF THESE!" So the GOBBLES set out to download many sources for
popular FTP servers to look for the names of other programs that they
used and then he found that much of them use /bin/gzip that users on
the ftp server might use to compress files then send them back smaller.
So the GOBBLES decided it was a good idea to take a look at the
/bin/gzip on the lab computers to decide whether or not it was first
exploitable then to see if he could exploit a FTP daemon with the same
bug.

The first thing GOBBLES do is run gzip -option AAAAAAAAAA style things.
```

FIGURE 4.5. A snippet from the first Gobbles Security advisory for the Unix operating system's gzip program, posted to the Bugtraq mailing list. The bug described was real, but it was not the security threat portrayed in the advisory. This example exhibits the characteristic style of the supposed author of the Gobbles advisories: a fake persona that did not have a good command of English and who referred to themselves in the third person.

dearly.").[40] The bug was real, but it posed no real security threat. In spite of this, security researchers took the advisory seriously, and thus began a years-long blackhat campaign that whitehats couldn't ignore, nor could they always believe.

Former hacker Adam O'Donnell (aka Javaman) recalled the Gobbles advisories as being "bullshit upon bullshit."[41] Schiffman was clued into what was happening behind the scenes and had a lot of respect for one of real hackers behind the zany persona that the advisories were supposedly authored by: "The main guy behind Gobbles was a hacker who was really good at parody. Like V from *V for Vendetta*, he had a Guy Fawkes–like personality." Commenting on the Gobbles security advisories, the representative from the group, who Schiffman was referring to, had this to say: "People couldn't tell what was real and what wasn't with Gobbles. Nobody wanted to jump in and say something about it and be wrong. People did not want to risk their reputations." In essence, members of Gobbles were doing the impossible with their own cheat codes, and it fooled a lot of people.

When this started, the Gobbles representative was twenty years old, working professionally as a network engineer, and very bored. When he conceived of the Gobbles persona, the goal was to prey on the good nature of people who were trying to improve the security of the Internet. He explained his thinking at the time, which was shaped by the transactional fraud that plagued the textfiles: "A friend and I were making fun of the thousands of hacker sites that just repeated information without checking the content. Everyone would race to get content on their site. Many people were simply re-writing Aleph One's article on stack overflows." This lack of self-awareness made much of the computer-security world a target for parody. The Gobbles persona itself came from a related hacking incident: "At the time we defaced the website of a popular security portal," he recalled; "We found a ridiculous image of a Turkey on the site. It was funny, so we built a ridiculous persona on this find." Information asymmetry complicated the situation, however, as the stakes were high with respect to new vulnerability disclosure, and the material Gobbles blabbered about was highly technical. The representative noted that "Of course it was a joke from the beginning. But you still had 50% of people who actually believed us and another 50% who despised us."

Even the most outrageous claims made by Gobbles found believers. In early 2003, Gobbles Security released an advisory on the Bugtraq mailing list for mpg123, an open-source audio player for mp3 files.[42] Attached to the exploit was a backstory for its development, which made the astounding claim that Gobbles was working for the Recording Industry Association of America (RIAA), which at that time was actively cracking down on music piracy on the Internet via legal and technical means:

> Several months ago, GOBBLES Security was recruited by the RIAA (riaa .org) to invent, create, and finally deploy the future of antipiracy tools. We focused on creating virii/worm hybrids to infect and spread over p2p nets. Until we became RIAA contracters, the best they could do was to passively monitor traffic. Our contributions to the RIAA have given them the power to actively control the majority of hosts using these networks.

The Gobbles representative related the real backstory for this advisory: "I heard that somebody was listening to an Eminem mp3 that crashed the player. I found the bug, wrote a real exploit for it, and released it with a story that Gobbles was now working for the RIAA." The RIAA's actions against copyright infringement at the time had created a frenzy in the tech world, and journalists were always looking for big scoops that could paint the RIAA in a negative light. Many believed that industry associations were overstepping their authority in attempting to crack down on file sharing networks (the "p2p net" referenced by Gobbles), which weren't exclusively used for piracy. TechTV, a now-defunct television channel covering technology news, contacted Gobbles and expressed interest in conducting an interview about the RIAA situation. The Gobbles representative was excited about the prospect of exploiting the mainstream media, but the interview fell through: "I tried to jump on that for a free vacation, but they figured out it was fake."[43]

The leaking of secrets, which would become massively influential in the next decade of computer-security history with the activities of WikiLeaks and Edward Snowden, was also in the Gobbles repertoire.[44] Given the steady stream of lies emanating from Gobbles, leaked snippets of proprietary information that appeared in security advisories authored by the group were heavily scrutinized. For example, in April of 2002, Gobbles released an advisory through Bugtraq for a remote format string vulnerability in the Sun Solaris remote procedure call service that was commonly found on Internet servers.[45] A portion of the source code from the Solaris operating system, which was closed-source and the intellectual property of now defunct Sun Microsystems, was leaked in the advisory. The Gobbles representative expressed frustration over the blowback this particular advisory received from the computer-security industry, knowing that prominent whitehat hackers David and Mark Litchfield had been developing uncontroversial exploits using the same proprietary source code from Sun. Holding Gobbles to a double standard may not have been fair, but it was precipitated by the fear the group struck into the heart of network administrators everywhere. In June 2002, Gobbles Security claimed to have had in its possession for two years an Apache web server exploit for a hole that had just been discovered.[46] The representative from the group acknowledged that it was written a few days after the bug was disclosed and then released. The danger of claims like this was that they made administrators believe that they had been vulnerable (and potentially compromised) within a time window that was simply impossible.

Other reactions to the unusual advisories Gobbles released made it clear that some folks had no idea what was going on. Good-natured people offered to help rewrite the advisories for Gobbles, obviously not appreciating their intentionally goofy style. The Gobbles representative recalled one particularly amusing episode in which a prominent university tried to recruit the Gobbles persona that wrote the advisories, who appeared to be a top technical talent in need of some polishing: "We had a professor from MIT contact us asking if Gobbles wanted to join his program." Those who weren't fooled were simply annoyed. Whitehat hackers who were active on the mailing lists Gobbles regularly posted to were especially upset. They were trying to conduct themselves in a professional manner because computer security had become a more serious corporate endeavor. But this didn't quite jibe with what had traditionally been happening on the Internet. Gobbles was a reflection of the original spirit of the hacking scene, defending its traditions and values, as silly as they might have been.

Retrospectively, the Gobbles advisories are reminiscent of a much later and much more famous hacker persona: Guccifer 2.0. Guccifer 2.0 intervened in the 2016 US presidential election and was assumed to be part of a Russian disinformation campaign (Pollantz and Collinson 2018). One wonders if Russian intelligence services had been monitoring computer-security mailing lists fifteen years before the election. Reflecting on what is happening now with respect to disinformation on the Internet, the Gobbles representative expressed concern over the very same strategies he helped pioneer: "My father, a lifelong Democrat, and member of the public teacher's union in Michigan, now believes in fake news. Years ago, my mother was an Obama birther conspiracy believer. When the birther allegations were dispelled, it only galvanized her belief in it. This is how conspiracy theories work."

While it is somewhat ironic that fake information has come back to haunt the Gobbles representative later in life, the objective of his disinformation campaign was drastically different from that of the current political disinformation campaigns. Far from crackpot racist conspiracy theories, the grievances projecting from Gobbles were in fact legitimate and served to keep overly ambitious whitehats in check while futilely attempting to prevent the loss of an entire subculture that traced its roots back to imaginative BBS textfiles in the 1980s. All good things must come to an end, and the fate of the textfiles was already sealed by the first decade of the twenty-first century.

Twilight of the Textfiles

Textfiles worked as cheat codes for life because they were, in essence, digital windows into the imagination. The offbeat revelations one discovered when looking through one of those windows could appear plausible thanks to an intricate blending of fact and fiction—especially when difficult to understand technical material was weaved into the narrative. How far could one push the cyberpunk fantasy in this creative medium? At the twilight of the textfile era, a copy of a blackhat zine simply titled *GoD.txt* (fig. 4.6) silently appeared.[47] Enormous by the standards of the genre, it weighed in at 2.4 megabytes and was chock full of logs chronicling what appeared to be successful attacks against high-profile corporate and government targets; leaked emails; violent and offensive ASCII art boasting

FIGURE 4.6. The title ASCII artwork for *GoD*, issue #0 (presumably released in 2012), the only issue of this blackhat zine ever released. Here "GoD" is depicted as an executioner, exerting dominance over the Internet itself. This theme recurs throughout the zine, which portrays the blackhat hacker as able to enter and subsequently control any computer on the Internet.

about the skills of the zine's creators; and some really clever storytelling that connected all of the pieces. But a question remains to this day: Was any of it real?

Comparing it to other blackhat zines, Watt had this to say about *GoD. txt*: "*GoD* was a single release that was more elite by a mile. It was this super crazy zine that came out but got zero attention. There was more in there to send people to prison than anything that came before it." Watt was not joking about the elite nature of the contents of this zine. It contained plausible-looking evidence that somebody had penetrated deeply into the corporate networks of Cisco, Apple, Google, and other major corporations. This wasn't material harvested by targeting low-level employees who were careless about the security of their workstations. One of the published trophies was a password file from a server at Google that included entries for the company's cofounders, Larry Page and Sergey Brin (fig. 4.7). Equally astounding were logs of hacks undertaken against the National Energy Research Scientific Computing Center, run by the US Department of Energy out of Lawrence Berkeley National Laboratory, and the aircraft manufacturer and defense contractor Boeing. Naturally, a who's who of renowned whitehat hackers also appear as victims, including Thomas Ptacek (aka tqbf), cofounder of Matasano Security, Peter Shipley, an influential security software author, and Dug Song, a security engineer turned tech entrepreneur. Perhaps the most embarrassed victim was security professional Lance Spitzner, who, ironically, was leading an effort to lure hackers with computers that appeared to be vulnerable in order to study their ways (Spitzner 2003).

```
rjoseph:$1$E14tdJ4r$BkIKbYSLmCLzcfaDB7b1t/:4370:5000:Robert Joseph:/home/rjoseph:/bin/bash
dalb:$1$FGZCZPGg$r.5.LdbX1oWVWTxVHBOno0:4073:5001:Diana Alberghini:/home/dalb:/bin/bash
brendan:$1$8PpU4XU/$TAKLh83amzJNJr5ExSPvL/:4616:499:Brendan Schlenker-Goodrich:/home/brendan:/bin/bash
katiev:$1$2BKk2EAE$K6cqLQmzuJoTwQxxitptM/:4717:499:Katie Vijungco:/home/katiev:/bin/bash
sergey:XcaBm2sDpLDNc:503:5000:Sergey Brin:/home/sergey:/bin/tcsh
marc:$1$jaZRHzJm$lo1TtP5EiVkHuYc0L5Y911:3722:5000:Marc Felton:/home/marc:/bin/bash
dora:$1$9hoXDz8c$bezwul5K5P0o6x0nIjQbH/:3820:5000:Dora Hsu:/home/dora:/bin/bash
joohee:$1$Hd7FKFHb$lSxVsq.x4gBr/9/ouBpza0:4785:5001:Joohee Lee:/home/joohee:/bin/bash
reid:$1$yum446zb$WeF2gE3.hGO2KBEM7qxGV.:4275:5000:Brian Reid:/home/reid:/bin/tcsh
```

FIGURE 4.7. Were the hackers who wrote *GoD.txt* truly all powerful as claimed? The zine reproduced a password file, apparently from a server at Google, that contained the encrypted passwords for Google cofounders Larry Page and Sergey Brin. Even though the passwords were encrypted, it might have been possible to recover them using a cracking attack. This type of password file is always hidden from normal users of a server; only a system administrator should have access. Password files were big trophies for blackhat hackers, since they signified the complete compromise of a system. Is this one real? We may never know.

There are some very fishy aspects to the *GoD* zine, however. The technically savvy reader familiar with the Unix operating system might notice that no timestamps appear in any of the data related to these remarkable hacks. This makes dating the textfile particularly difficult and brings into question the provenance of the material. The textfile itself says it was released in January 2012, yet some of the logs are certainly much older. For instance, a section labeled "GoD GLOBaL HOLiDAY" appears to contain evidence that an account owned by Linus Torvalds, the creator of the Linux operating system, had been compromised. While no dates appear in the running program and file system listings provided, Torvalds' login information shows that he was forwarding his mail to torvalds@transmeta .com when the hack occurred. Transmeta was a semiconductor company that Torvalds worked for between 1997 and 2003 and that went out of business in 2009. Digging deeper into the file, we find evidence from operating systems that would have been very old in 2012 (e.g., Solaris 9, which was released in 2002) peppering the text. It makes only passing mention of the major hacking groups of the era: WikiLeaks, Anonymous, and Lulz-Sec. Those groups made use of social media to brag to a global audience about successful hacks (Coleman 2014), not the obscure textfile format, which had faded away by the second decade of the twenty first century.

It's almost as if somebody collected their hacking trophies from 2002 and spent a decade writing a zine around them—old jokes, rivalries, and all. What's most fascinating about this textfile is the lack of publicity surrounding it. Not a single mention of it exists anywhere on the Internet. The only place the file currently resides is in an exploit database maintained by Offensive Security Services LLC, a company best known for creating the Kali Linux Distribution, which is popular with penetration testers at security consultancies. Former hackers and those curious about the unruly beginnings of the computer-security industry learn about it through word of mouth, and reading it for the first time invokes strong nostalgia for the BBS days, when textfiles regularly took you to places others could not go. Watt provided some perspective on the closing chapter of the original hacking scene: "Whitehat hackers in general fell victim to their own success. When everybody got owned [hacked] and it became more of a rite of passage than an acutely shameful personal calamity, it all just became far less rewarding and amusing." The war pitting blackhats against whitehats? It's the stuff of legend now.

5

Speculative Sleuths

THE PROVENANCE OF ADVANCED ALGORITHMS FOR the modification of digital images is rarely considered by observers outside of computer science. This is surprising, given the intense scrutiny such technology is now under. Through the history of Photoshop presented in chapter 3, we have learned that the basic digital-editing operations emerged from the creative arts. But the algorithms that came later were sometimes adversarial, incorporating functionality that intentionally obscured evidence of tampering and exploited digital photography in ways no commercial software company would ever have endorsed. In a curious twist, these algorithms were by and large the invention of the very community charged with preserving the integrity of digital media. The work of these *media forensics* specialists frequently relied on mythmaking in order to raise alarm about potential problems with broader trends of image manipulation we have already discussed. Properly contextualized, the forensic analysis of images can be helpful for rooting out harmful information—though typically not in the sensationalized circumstances we hear the most about.

The Dilemma of the Self-Fulfilling Prophecy

Self-fulfilling prophecies abound in science and technology, but we often neglect to recognize them. The prediction that an expert, our modern-day prophet, makes may be too irresistible to scrutinize, because of the desires or fears attached to it. Thus the expert actively works to bring a predicted outcome into being, because they believe it must happen, even though there is always the option of questioning the premises that underlie the prediction. Rhetorically, the self-fulfilling prophecy is compelling because it combines the description of something that is indeed possible with the dictum of an inevitable outcome. When making a case for an inevitable outcome, the expert uses statements like, "It is inescapable that we will see this happen in the near future"; "I cannot imagine a world where this does not happen"; or, most insidiously, in fields dominated by quantitative metrics, "All of the data point to this happening." In some cases, the data may very well be diagnostic, but in others, especially those that unfold in a social context, there is no firm inevitability—people have the freedom to pursue alternatives to any predicted outcome.

That self-fulfilling prophecies manifest so frequently in science and technology is bewildering. The scientific method calls for rigorous questioning and skepticism, not proclamations of the inevitable. And yet we find entire intellectual communities attempting to fulfill their own prophecies. For instance, think about how many times Silicon Valley has predicted, with a tenor of inevitability, that a new technology would disrupt an entire industry, regardless of whether the technology was a needed advance. The Internet itself came out of this manner of thinking, but also unlicensed taxis, endless premium-content streaming services, and a host of other questionable inevitabilities. The philosopher John Searle's distinction between *brute* and *institutional* facts is useful here (Searle 1995). A brute fact is one that exists external to any humanly created institution. For example, the existence of our planet Earth does not depend on any human institution. An institutional fact is one that is solely the construct of human endeavor. For example, the existence of the state of Indiana relies on a human institution (the Constitution of the United States) for its legitimacy and the state does not exist external to that institution. Brute facts give scientists, engineers, and others who study what is possible in the world a path to successfully execute a self-fulfilling prophecy, because they exist in a verifiable reality.

The biologist Ruth Hubbard points out that scientific theories in particular tend to be self-fulfilling prophecies because they force experience into the fixed framework they provide (Hubbard 2003). Since science must seek consensus to weed out mistakes, falsehoods, and other inaccuracies, theories that stand the test of time are necessarily the product of collective action. Thus there is a long-standing tradition of social groups forming

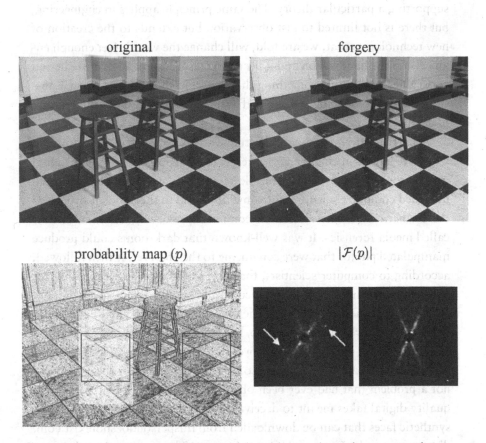

original   forgery

probability map (p) $|\mathcal{F}(p)|$

FIGURE 5.1. An early example of a type of digital forgery that makes some people very uncomfortable: the removal of an arbitrary object from a scene. Media forensics researchers knew such changes would be impossible to detect with the naked eye. In response, they developed countermeasures that let the computer see beyond the pixels of a digital image to detect the region that was manipulated (Popescu 2004).

around ideas supported by their own experiences. In practice, ideas that are both plausible and *en vogue* filter to the top of the scientific discourse. Of course, this can come at the expense of other, potentially superior, possibilities—especially those in conflict with the notions of any group supporting a particular theory. The same principle applies in engineering, but there is not limited to just observation but extends to the creation of new technologies that, we are told, will change the world. Get enough engineers on the bandwagon and it becomes feasible to make that prediction come true, by building something that is within the realm of known possibilities and convincing the public that its existence validates the promise of change.

A particularly intriguing case study in this regard has us picking up where we left off in chapter 3 with respect to the possibility of fake digital images so perfect as to be plausible revisions of history. This idea had intrigued computer scientists for some time, and in the 1990s it prompted the formation of a new research community working on what is now called media forensics. It was well-known that darkrooms could produce manipulated photos that were convincing to the observer. It then followed, according to computer scientists, that this would also be a capability for digital imagery and that it would become more of a problem, given the very low cost of the new medium and the ease with which it could be manipulated using software like Photoshop. For twenty years, the media-forensics community kept raising the alarm over this possibility (Farid 2003; Sencar and Memon 2009; Rocha et al. 2011; Farid 2016), even though it was not a problem that had ever been observed in practice. Eventually, high-quality digital fakes meant to deceive the observer, like the photorealistic synthetic faces that can be downloaded from thispersondoesnotexist.com, did appear on the Internet (Shen et al. 2021). The experts viewed the arrival of this content as a vindication of their dire warnings and assumed political turmoil (Wilbur 2020) and a breakdown of the judiciary (Reynolds 2020) would follow if action were not taken.

Media forensics would come to dominate the conversation on solutions to the problems associated with manipulated images and videos being shared on social media after the 2016 US election. Maintaining a bold ontological posture, computer scientists alleged that they could discern objective truth through algorithmic analysis, lending them the ability to inform the public of what on the Internet is real and what is not (Farid

2018; Delp et al. 2020; Verdoliva 2020). This claim was compelling, and it generated significant attention from tech companies, governments, and nongovernmental organizations. But very little has been written about the history of this subfield of computer science, whose members lent as much to the narratives around the problems as to those around the solutions. Moreover, a critical look at media forensics has been completely missing. For this we need not turn to complicated theoretical frameworks—the best criticism emerges from the voices of those researchers within this fascinating and eccentric community.

Media Forensics and Its Relationship to the Media Ecosystem

Media forensics can be split into two core parts that operate independently or in concert:. (1) The computer-vision part, which uses both physics-based models from computational photography and machine-learning-based models that are popular for visual recognition. The use of techniques from computer vision was initially suggested by University of California, Berkeley computer scientist Hany Farid, who invented algorithms to detect localized resampling, lighting inconsistencies, and color filter array irregularities, among other forgery clues.[1] (2) The signal-processing part, which draws on the lower-level techniques of image processing that had traditionally been used for data compression and image quality enhancement. This was largely pioneered by State University of New York at Binghamton electrical engineer Jessica Fridrich, who introduced the idea of sensor fingerprinting for identifying image-acquisition devices and figured out both how to determine the age of an edited image from accumulating defects and how to detect the "copy-move" (or cloned region) forgery operation. Both parts attempt to determine whether an image has been tampered with or is completely synthetic (Farid 2009). A positive determination, according to this style of forensic analysis, suggests that the image cannot be trusted.

The biggest challenge the discipline faced in its first couple decades was that it was trying to solve a problem that didn't exist. Research into digital photo manipulation from the debut of Photoshop in 1990 until the second decade of the twenty-first century reveals a distinct lack of recorded cases of malicious intent. Interviews with figures associated with media forensics turned up many anecdotes about early cases that proved unverifiable. In some instances, the claim was made that the official record behind an anecdote was protected by a veil of secrecy (e.g., "sealed court documents," "classified information"), while in others it was apparent that a faulty memory was involved (e.g., mistaking an old darkroom manipulation for a digital one). This is rather frustrating for the historian, as it leaves open the possibility that rumored evidence of early digital fakes is indeed just rumors. Accordingly, fiction had a hand in shaping the discourse from the very beginning.

The notion of a weaponized visual manipulation that could not be detected by the naked eye was strongly influenced by the popular culture of the 1990s. Shortly before media forensics was established as a discipline, author Michael Crichton imagined a world in which perfect fake images would upend courtroom evidence procedures in his crime thriller *Rising Sun*. As the character of Professor Sanderson, an imaging specialist, explains in the novel: "The case law isn't entirely clear. But it's coming. All photographs are suspect these days. Because now, with digital systems, they can be changed perfectly. Perfectly" (Crichton 1992). Real-life imaging specialist and scientist at the Woods Hole Oceanographic Institute Kimberly Amaral made extensive reference to *Rising Sun* in her 1999 essay "The Digital Imaging Revolution: Legal Implications and Possible Solutions" (Amaral 1999). She argued that altered digital images and video (what we now know as a deepfake) would indeed invalidate photographic evidence without technological interventions to label suspect content—all in a way that neatly fit *Rising Sun*'s plot. The unanticipated consequences of real technology was, of course, a theme of Crichton's novel. Yet the thriller genre often neglects the complexities of the environment in which a technology exists and the unanticipated reactions of society to it. Nonetheless, computer scientists gravitated towards the genre's straightforward interpretation of how the truth could be undermined through photo editing software.

Nasir Memon, a professor at New York University's Tandon School of Engineering, was also there at the beginning: "I got into media forensics through network and cybersecurity in the late nineties or early 2000s."[2] Because of his background in cybersecurity, he has drawn parallels between image manipulation and specific incidents coming out of the hacker scene. For instance, referring to a widely propagating email virus from 1999, he noted that "the Melissa virus was for fun, it wasn't supposed to be malicious. The early days of computer security were not as dark as today. The same is true with image manipulation then and now."[3] This is an important connection, given what we have learned about the creative motivations of computer hackers in chapters 2 and 4. Yet by invoking computer security, Memon still framed the issue in adversarial terms: "Remember that security is hard. Bad guys figure out ways to circumvent your security. The situation is the same with forensics." He was also critical of academic work in computer security from the 1990s: "You publish a paper, but so what? It doesn't really mean anything in the long run because what you did probably has no practical value. Forensics is a lot different. If you return a result, it has a direct actionable outcome. You are at least doing something that has an impact on the bad guys." The goal of producing an actionable outcome against bad behavior is admirable, but who exactly were the "bad guys"?

Memon recalled that "in the beginning, we stayed away from the Internet, because our techniques didn't work well." Turning to the Internet for malicious photo edits might not have helped much anyway—digital photos didn't become prevalent until the smartphone appeared a couple of decades later. This put researchers in a bind: Where else could they turn for the data that they needed? An easy solution was to simply generate it themselves. For years, work in media forensics was purely speculative, with published papers exclusively containing experiments that were run on self-generated examples. Alin Popescu, a graduate student advised by Hany Farid at Dartmouth, defended a landmark thesis on statistical tools for detecting signs of image tampering in 2004 (Popescu 2004). It made only passing reference to two real (and very recent) cases of digital splicing that had involved professional photographers. When it came to demonstrating how his new tools performed, Popescu used Photoshop to create what he believed to be plausible simulations of potentially dangerous manipulations, like the removal of an arbitrary object in a scene (fig. 5.1). Intentionally or not, media forensics was releasing the blueprints for manipulating content along with associated defenses. This is a common dilemma in any security-related field, but one that was rarely given adequate consideration within media forensics.

It took some time before anything even resembling a "perfect fake" would appear. Photoshop was still primarily used for professional photography and graphic design at the turn of the millennium. Media-forensics researchers would occasionally identify websites that were of interest be-cause they featured manipulated imagery created by the public, but the examples tended to be lighthearted. Fakeaphoto.com, Something Awful's Photoshop Phriday feature, and the PhotoshopBattles subreddit became important forums for this activity. The turning point would be the ap-pearance of the deepfake in 2017 (Cole 2018), which was viewed by the media-forensics community as vindication of their longstanding warn-ings. Commenting in 2020, Memon noted, "It is only within the last three years that people have gotten interested in this. If there was disinformation going around on the Internet before then, nobody in this country cared." Only after the public started seeing prominent figures in fake videos did the issue garner significant attention.[4] Memon also emphasized the sudden commercial interest in countermeasures to deepfakes, as the traditional computer-security industry had no viable products to offer and media-forensics startups had struggled to succeed in the marketplace: "I've had calls from VCs asking about solutions."[5]

It's not difficult to understand why venture capitalists are now very interested in media integrity. An onslaught of media coverage on deep-fakes, public outcry, and increased government funding translated into an upsurge in academic research.[6] That research is now providing a pool of algorithms for integration into software platforms tackling everything from image tampering in scientific papers (Xiang and Acuna 2020) to detecting deepfakes (Verdoliva 2020). The numbers associated with the growth of media forensics are striking. In 2004, the year Popescu's dis-sertation appeared, a mere 14 academic papers related to media forensics were published.[7] In 2020, that number was 440.[8] In the early 2000s there was no publication dedicated to media forensics. Today there is a highly selective IEEE journal dedicated to this topic, along with multiple meet-ings where researchers come together with law enforcement, government officials and corporate leadership to share the latest breakthroughs.[9]

The messaging in all of these outlets has been consistent: the technolo-gists maintain that the preservation of the integrity of digital media is the only way in which the blitz of fake content on the Internet can be defeated. Importantly, this perspective is purely technical; it disregards the rich and complex nature of the culture that generates the media. Inevitably, it ended up at odds with the situation on the ground as the Internet grew in popularity in the early 2000s. As we have already learned, humanity was more comfortable with competing realities than many experts believed. And this was documented early on. Writing in *Wired* in 2001, the technology journalist Jenn Shreve described the mismatch between fears over the societal impact of hoax images and how such images were actually perceived (Shreve 2001). Her article happened to focus on an example that was widely discussed by media-forensics researchers: the 9/11 "tourist guy" photo (fig. 5.2).[10]

Shortly after the 9/11 attacks against the United States, a sensational photograph made the rounds on various email lists. It depicted a tourist at the top of one of the World Trade Center towers who appeared to be unaware of the airliner barreling at him from behind. The text of the accompanying email explained that the photo had been recovered from the tourist's camera, which "was found in the rubble" of the Trade Center. The photo was subject to intense scrutiny from experts and the public, until a twenty-five-year-old Hungarian man named Péter Guzli stepped forward as both the tourist and the perpetrator of the hoax. Given the grim nature of the photo, it was surprising to many that it also generated a

FIGURE 5.2. The 9/11 "tourist guy" photo, an early Internet meme. The plane was copied into the photo from an external source.

vibrant meme genre, in which the tourist was copied into images of other famous catastrophes both real (e.g., the Challenger explosion) and imagined (e.g., King Kong attacking New York City) (fig. 5.3). Shreve used this example to highlight the emerging struggle between technologists who believed that the Internet was meant to serve as a database of factual human knowledge and ordinary users who treated it as a creative space where any idea, true or false, could flourish.

Kevin Christopher, an affiliate of a fact-checking organization calling itself the Center for Scientific Investigation of Claims of the Paranormal,[11] who was quoted in Shreve's article, expressed frustration with the direction content on the Internet was headed: "Given the things that people have to worry about, to have these idiotic hoaxes adding to that, that's detrimental and I don't think it's right. I wish I knew who these people were. They definitely deserve to be reprimanded in some way." The article also quoted Avi Muchnick, the founder of the now defunct humor website *The Satyr*, on his interpretation of the 9/11 tourist guy: "That picture of the World Trade Center man: People love hoaxes like that and love being able to create the hoax themselves. That sort of thing really takes off when you have the power to create that and send it around to your friends." He had it right. In the newly emerging memesphere, creativity could trump any social concerns, even when the underlying material was rather dark in nature. This is a lesson the media-forensics community is just beginning to learn: the interpretation of the content is more important than any technical analysis of its composition.

Misguided motivation didn't necessarily limit the utility of software

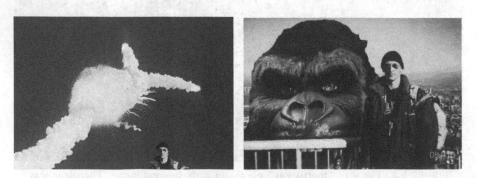

FIGURE 5.3. The 9/11 "tourist guy" spawns a meme genre.

tools to detect manipulations in specific cases. But it did limit the reach of those tools as a mechanism for preserving the integrity of visual information. Throughout the history of media forensics, the emergence of algorithms that are now applied broadly in defense of the Internet was sometimes incidental to the original objects of study and was always directed by simulated adversaries, to preserve the framing of the potentially dangerous scenarios to come. A look at two historical phases will shed light on how the field evolved under these conditions.

Early Inspiration from Digital Pirates

In the 1990s, television networks and movie studios quickly realized that piracy was becoming easier thanks to technological progress. High-quality digital videos of shows and movies were being uploaded to the Internet, where they could then be freely downloaded by anyone. To counter this problem, computer scientists were hired to develop sophisticated watermarking techniques that could verify the ownership of multimedia content. The idea followed from traditional watermarking on physical documents: embedded in a file was hidden data that facilitated automatic checks for illegally shared content by later recovering and verifying that data. During the development of digital watermarking, the individuals involved made several unexpected discoveries that would be the genesis of media forensics.

"The watermark is like a vaccine," Fridrich has underscored; it is "the first solution to many image forensics problems."[12] Reflecting on the beginnings of media forensics, Purdue University professor Edward Delp concurred: "This got started with watermarking, specifically with the SPIE conferences that published material on content authentication."[13] SPIE is an international society for optics and photonics that attracted the world's experts in electronic imaging in the mid-twentieth century and later those interested in digital image processing. SPIE conference papers on digital watermarks began appearing in the early nineties, and by the mid-nineties, the idea had gained traction in private industry. A consensus formed around the idea of the "forensic watermark," with industry representatives and technologists all agreeing that any intervention would need to surreptitiously tag content in a way that only the owner could control and later recover (hence the "forensic" aspect).

However, at the time the entertainment industries were deciding on a standardized approach to thwart piracy, turnkey watermarking solutions weren't readily available. An early commercial player was Digimarc Corporation, an Oregon-based technology company specializing in digital rights management. Entertainment was not initially a concern of Digimarc's founder, Geoffery Rhoads, an electronics engineer and amateur astronomer who had spent the early part of his career designing oscilloscopes.[14] Rhoads developed an interest in watermarking after realizing there was no easy way to prove that the pictures he had taken of planets in the solar system and posted online were actually his (Dyson 1995). A discovery that the image-processing procedures used to enhance the quality of astronomical images could be modified to add unique fingerprints to those same images led Rhoads to invent a rudimentary digital watermarking algorithm. In spite of his niche focus, he was able to attract external funding from investors who recognized the general applicability of watermark technology.

Customers pursuing dot-com businesses that relied on premium multimedia content soon followed. An early Digimarc client was Playboy Enterprises, which had identified the Internet's potential for marketing pornographic images and videos of women and was swift to develop digital offerings. Playboy also recognized the potential threat the Internet posed to their business if they didn't have a mechanism to limit the sharing of content that was their intellectual property. Digimarc's relationship with Playboy was showcased in a 1997 issue of *Wired* in which Rhoads declared that his technology could do even more than originally advertised: "We turn paranoia into brand management and a way to get your name out there" (Parks 1997).

In looking beyond intellectual property concerns, Rhoads was onto something. The nascent media-forensics community, which possessed state-of-the-art knowledge of watermarking, had been watching the developments at Digimarc with keen interest. But there were some technical challenges to be addressed before a good proof-of-concept could be considered a hardened product. Delp noted that the company's original algorithm was invented by people who had no background in computer security or signal processing: "They didn't really know what they were doing." Fridich concurred, and acknowledging Digimarc's commercial potential, offered her expertise as a consultant. But Digimarc not impressed with her work and declined. Shortly after *Wired* linked Digimarc to Playboy, Bruce Davis, a former video-game executive, was named CEO of the company. He remains in charge to this day.[15] Davis took steps to professionalize the business and bring in technologists with bona fide credentials in watermarking. Reengaging with Fridrich, Digimarc hired four of her graduate students, including one she considered her very best.

Important lessons about the nature of digital content came out of Digimarc's business activities and the academic research on watermarking that was happening in parallel. Min Wu, associate dean of engineering and professor of electrical and computer engineering at the University of Maryland, started working on media forensics as a PhD student at Princeton in the 1990s.[16] Wu began graduate school with a strong interest in multimedia retrieval, which involved linking related files together to make them easily searchable. Looking for new frontiers in multimedia research for her dissertation, she landed on a forensics-oriented question with broad relevance: Was it possible to determine if a copy of an image had been manipulated in some way? Finding big changes wasn't hard, but instances in which something very subtle had changed were far more challenging. The initial solution was, of course, the forensic watermark. By embedding a signal into an image to perform some other task (e.g., authentication), it was indeed possible to assess the integrity of an image. If it had been modified, but the watermark was still detectable, it would be possible to link it back to its original source and determine the scope of the changes.

It is here where media forensics starts to deviate from watermarking for copy protection. Wu singled out one algorithm for watermarking as being hugely influential to a generation of media-forensics researchers who took its concepts in new directions. It emerged out of the race for new copy-protection technologies in the late nineties. Digimarc eventually found competition in the watermarking arena, as research labs at major tech companies had been tasked to look into the matter as well. One was the famed IBM Thomas J. Watson Research Center, which had world-caliber expertise in multimedia systems and computer security. The algorithm Wu and others were so interested in was called "invisible watermarking," and it was developed by two IBM engineers, Minerva M. Yeung and Fred Mintzer (Yeung and Mintzer 1997). Invisible watermarking possessed two properties that would prove to be essential to modern media forensics. First, it was useful for manipulation detection, not just copy protection.

Second, it could look beyond the surface structure of an image to consider data invisible to the human eye.

With invisible watermarking as inspiration, Wu and colleagues figured out that it was possible to embed watermarking technology in the image-processing software of a digital camera pipeline, not just to prevent piracy but also to authenticate the images (Wu and Liu 1998). This made it possible both to determine if an image had been changed after it was released on the Internet and to trace it back to the camera that took it. The former capability addressed the concern that somebody might attempt to revise history with Photoshop, while the latter made criminal investigations involving photographic evidence easier, by linking suspects to the scene of a crime. Wu suggested this plan in 1998, but it never took off commercially, in spite of being technically feasible. Consumer electronics makers had very little incentive to add a watermarking capability to their products, because the industry's intellectual property concerns were at the corporate level of major content providers, and the two other security-related concerns were deemed insignificant. Media-forensics researchers saw this as a missed opportunity. Little mentioned was the manipulation technique Wu described in the same paper. In making the case for "ease of editing" of digital images, the paper showed that it was simple to change text overlays in a way that was plausibly authentic to the viewer (fig. 5.4).

FIGURE 5.4. Wu and Liu demonstrated that it was simple to edit text overlays on a digital image (*above*). But their method of watermarking could still authenticate the image by validating hidden data (*below*), making detection of the change trivial (Wu and Liu 1998).

Watermarks aren't the only solution to the image-integrity problem, but they can always be applied to solve it. Farid, who developed many of the early alternatives involving computer-vision techniques, acknowledged as much in his early papers. And watermarks remain relevant, even in face of new technologies like nonfungible tokens, which can only verify the provenance of an image if it hasn't been modified. Vindicated by the proliferation of visual disinformation spreading online, and recalling Wu's recommendation from the nineties, Memon has publicly advocated for watermarking all imagery (Ai4 2020). Farid has concurred, and he has speculated that media companies may already be doing this to prevent their content from being misused.[17] Legal considerations related to intellectual property influenced the initial period of media forensics, but a different and far more troubling legal context shaped the work of the next period.

Digital Victims Unit

Memon noted that in the period shortly before the 9/11 "tourist guy" photo appeared, and for quite some time afterward, "media forensics was more of a conventional law enforcement thing." Agreeing, Farid framed his early work in detecting manipulated media in this context: "When I first started, I was just thinking about courts of law. This is why we called it forensics." While the media-forensics community had expected to encounter a broad range of suspected forgeries in different contexts, time and time again they instead encountered illegal images of minors that required authentication. In fact, as far as anyone could tell, child pornography cases were the only instances in which law enforcement was handling digital images as evidence. Memon expressed puzzlement over this state of affairs, given the intense speculation around the use of image-editing tools by terrorists and other adversaries (Gaylord 2007). "To me, this was shocking," concurred Siwei Lyu, a professor of computer science and engineering at the University at Buffalo and a former student of Hany Farid. He described the dilemma investigators faced in these cases: "There were a lot of child porn cases and experts were needed to determine if those images were real or if they had been created using computer graphics."[18]

Investigating grievous crimes against children wasn't what the newly established discipline of media forensics was created for, but given the need of law enforcement for technical expertise, researchers stepped up to the challenge. Experts like Memon came to realize that the impact they could have in this realm might transcend everything that they were concerned about before: "If I saved one child, I would feel that I lived a meaningful life." The key challenge that the courts were facing was the 2002 US Supreme Court decision in *Ashcroft v. Free Speech Coalition*, which established that simulated child pornography was protected speech. Once computer graphics became sufficiently advanced, the way was open for a legal argument that the creation of realistic fake pornography "could happen." Using this argument, a confederation of pornographers, photographers, and artists calling itself the Free Speech Coalition managed to overturn the strict prohibitions on synthetic depictions of children in sexual situations established by the *Child Pornography Prevention Act of 1996*, giving themselves significantly more legal leeway for their own creative output. Writing for the majority, Justice Anthony Kennedy weighed the implications of banning certain types of fiction, and found a clear First Amendment violation in the Act's prohibition on speech "despite its serious literary, artistic, political, or scientific value" (Supreme Court of the United States 2002).

This opened the door to a new defense in child pornography cases: it was possible to claim that any recovered digital image or video evidence was fake and thus legal under *Ashcroft*. Success with this defense was assumed to be achievable because of the substantial burden of proof associated with authenticating digital images. Fortunately, the government was able to turn to the media-forensics community to recruit expert witnesses. In practice, making a compelling case in court that images were real was straightforward. In 2002 it was terrifically difficult and expensive to generate photorealistic scenes using computer graphics—this was a Hollywood-level skill. Prosecutors were wary of building a case around a single image, since it was possible to spend a lot of time and money to make one highly credible fake image. But this wouldn't be feasible for a large collection of images. If enough evidence could be collected, a credible expert witness could explain why the use of computer graphics in the creation of such a collection would be a technical impossibility, for all but the big digital animation studios like Pixar.

But this left cases involving just a few pieces of evidence vulnerable to the fakery defense. Further, any technical analysis performed on photographic evidence would have to adhere to two courtroom standards: the Frye standard for the admissibility of scientific evidence, based on what is generally accepted by a scientific discipline; and the Daubert standard for the admissibility of expert-witness testimony, which appeals to the scientific method to establish the credibility of what a witness presents to a court. It wouldn't be long before the Frye and Daubert standards were tested under *Ashcroft* in rather explicit terms.

In the mid-2000s, a Cleveland-area attorney named Dean Boland began serving as an expert witness for defendants in child pornography cases. Boland was concerned by the continued prosecution of suspects caught with child pornography following *Ashcroft*, which he believed left open the possibility of reasonable doubt in all of these cases. With photorealistic renderings generally assumed too expensive to consider, he ascertained that image-editing software like Photoshop could also be used to create a photorealistic scene. To make his argument to juries, Boland did just that. After downloading two stock photos of girls under the age of six from the Internet, he replaced a doughnut in one of the photos with a penis from a different photo, and copied the face of one of the girls into a pornographic scene featuring adults (United States Court of Appeals, Sixth Circuit 2011).

Boland's foray into expert witnessing did not go as planned. Armed with his two photos, which he believed were perfectly legal, he set off to provide testimony in a 2004 child pornography case in Oklahoma (United States District Court, N. D. Oklahoma 2006). Far from swaying the court with his argument, Boland found himself under suspicion as prosecutors raised the possibility that he had himself committed a federal crime because his actions violated the intent of *Ashcroft*. A federal judge weighed in, noting that Boland's photos were "prepared expressly at court order," but nonetheless admonished him to delete them from his computer. Boland declined to do so and used the photos in two other cases in Ohio.[19] This triggered a federal investigation, culminating in an FBI raid on his residence.

Importantly, Boland's edited photos were determined to be a case of image *morphing*, not image synthesis. This meant that Boland had blended elements of photos to turn innocent depictions of real children into pornography, which is far different from using computer graphics to create a scene that never, in any aspect, existed in the physical world.

It was a crucial distinction, as it led to a designation of content that violated federal law. In a dissenting opinion from an appeal of one of the cases Boland had testified in (Court of Appeals of Ohio, Eleventh District, Ashtabula County 2007), Ohio court of appeals judge Cynthia Westcott Rice recognized that

> Ashcroft did not address the issue as to whether morphed images of children, that is, the alteration of innocent pictures of actual children using digital technological means, is an appropriate ban. It appears from the record that Boland's activities in creating previous trial exhibits actually involves morphed images of children, activity still illegal under federal law with no exceptions.

Finally realizing that he faced serious legal consequences, Boland entered into a pretrial diversion agreement with federal prosecutors in 2007. The outcome was a relatively light punishment that included a public apology in the *Cleveland Bar Journal*, where he is quoted on record as stating "I do recognize that such images violate federal law" (United States Court of Appeals, Sixth Circuit 2011).

Boland's legal trouble did not stop there. Following the pretrial agreement, the two children who appeared in the photos, along with their guardians, sued him for "personal injury" stemming from violation of the federal code against child pornography (Heisig 2019). A judge ruled in favor of the children and ordered Boland to pay each $150,000 in damages. He declared bankruptcy in 2016, which would have prevented payments to the victims had his declaration not been overturned by a bankruptcy judge in 2019. In an initial ruling in 2017, US bankruptcy judge Jessica Price Smith found that Boland could discharge the judgment against him because he did not know the children at the time he morphed their likenesses into pornography, nor did he intend to do them any harm. However, a three-judge bankruptcy panel for the 6th US Circuit Court of Appeals ruled that Smith had been mistaken, in that any decision should have been made on the basis of violations against the interests of the children. Boland would have to pay up. This legal back and forth is another instance of a mismatch between the intent of a photographic manipulation and the reaction to it—a matter we explored in chapter 3. In this case, there were unintended consequences stemming from the creation of an alternate reality, which Boland learned about the hard way.

Boland's actions had major implications for the media-forensics community. With the idea of manipulated and fake child pornography now taken up by defense lawyers, investigators and expert witnesses needed tools to identify specific operations and artifacts that were the telltale markers of fakery. The earliest research paper on detecting manipulations in digital signals appeared in an *MIT AI Memo* authored by Farid in 1999, which suggests that natural signals and edited signals have different underlying statistics, which could be detected by looking for traces of the nonlinearities associated with editing operations (Farid 1999). This was a general idea, applicable to any signal. As part of an experimental evaluation of his approach, Farid described a method for splicing audio from one track into another, prefiguring the audio component of the deepfake algorithm. But it took several more years before the detection idea was fully developed to work on images and videos, in efforts that culminated in Popescu's dissertation. Farid continued to work on tools that would support investigations and his own expert witnessing, innovating by bringing ideas from computer vision and machine learning into media forensics.

At the same time, a different strategy was forming around the notion of device identification. In a sense, this was the holy grail of media forensics: to get back to the source of the content. If an image could be shown to have come from a suspect's camera, then it was real. The hard part was finding the clues in an image that could tie it back to a particular device. In principle, this was similar to Wu's idea of using forensic watermarks for image authentication. But for device identification it was some unique aspect of the camera hardware itself that would serve as the watermark. In the summer of 2004, Fridrich and her students Jan Lukáš and Miroslav Goljan were thinking about this problem. Inspired by earlier research that had used hot pixels (always on) and dead pixels (always off) on a sensor as a fingerprint for a particular device (because these artifacts would show up in its images), they wondered if there were other such fingerprints. Some sensors didn't have such obvious defects and thus could thwart identification attempts.

Holed up in the laboratory with a Canon PowerShot G2 camera and software that could analyze sensor noise, Lukáš and Goljan made the key observation that individual pixels on a sensor exhibited different levels of defect, not just hot or dead. And these defects were stable, meaning a reliable fingerprint could be created for any sensor. What they had stumbled upon was photo-response nonuniformity noise (PRNU), or the variable light sensitivity of pixels caused by the material nonhomogeneity of silicon wafers and imperfections induced during the manufacturing process. PRNU would become one of the most reliable signal-processing-based indicators in media forensics, with application to tying evidence to cameras and detecting postprocessing and manipulation (Lukáš et al. 2006).[20] Fridrich has noted that she was on vacation when this discovery was made—Lukáš and Goljan deserve most of the credit.

By 2010, the legal landscape had changed, and the expert witnesses with their sophisticated forensics software were no longer a frequent presence in child pornography cases. A major shift took place in how reality was discerned from photos used as evidence. Instead of depending on a technical determination of the veracity of an image based on difficult-to-understand artifacts of the digital image creation process, cases started to be built around a demonstration that the child in a photo is a real victim and the abuser a real suspect. Memon credited this strategy, which was far simpler for juries and judges to understand, to a Department of Homeland Security special agent named Jim Cole[21]:

> In child porn cases, a lot of effort is put into finding the people who make and spread the images, so they can be arrested. Jim Cole asked the right question: where is the child? That's the most important thing. Jim started doing forensics to look at objects in the scene, for example, this type of curtain is used by Holiday Inn.

In the present day, the media-forensics community has adapted to this new legal landscape by developing software tools that can assist investigators in identifying when and where a photo was taken. For example, Abby Stylianou, a professor of computer science at Saint Louis University, has designed an algorithm that can match photographic evidence depicting the room where a crime is presumed to have occurred to a large database of hotel room photos contributed by the public (Stylianou et al. 2017). Identifying a location by hand may be impossible, given the enormous number of possible locations to sift through. This is an important new capability for investigators working on child exploitation cases. The shift toward a presumption of truth here is significant, given the latent paranoia within the media-forensics community about perfect fakes. This perspective was also taken up by defense lawyers, who no longer argue that photographic evidence has been faked. A presumption of falsehood is a ludicrous proposition if the victim and abuser are real people who can be linked together in time and space—even if that space is virtual.

A Flood of Fakery

Institutional facts facilitate the creation of fake photos promoting false narratives, while brute facts facilitate the self-fulfilling prophecies about the creation of that very same content. How can this be? The seeming paradox stems from the constructed reality of the Internet, which needs institutional facts to support its content and brute facts to support its infrastructure. And because the setting is the Internet, where narratives and technologies rapidly come and go, their relationship is amorphous. As was pointed out earlier, the fake digital photo situation today doesn't exactly match what was foretold by media-forensics prophecy. Yes, the perfect fakes did arrive as predicted, but they do not appear to play any significant role in disrupting civil society. Manifestations of fakery that were not directly anticipated, yet still fit the general pattern of the prophecy, are taking precedence. These include obviously manipulated images like memes and crude-looking fakes that aren't believable but are still socially damaging. While the prophets of media forensics failed to provide clarity on the social aspects of media manipulation, they did develop useful countermeasures to real problems through their various investigations.

In recent conversations, researchers have provided honest reflections on this state of affairs. Memon was blunt in his acknowledgement that what was actually happening was disconnected from the discourse in the academic world: "Real shit has been happening on the Internet for over a decade. This has raised many new questions for the field." Lyu noted that the problems the media-forensics community had been using to justify its work didn't resonate as expected: "In general, the field languished for years, because we did not do a good job to promote its future importance. It took a flood of real fake content on social media to put the field into the spotlight." With manipulated images now endemic to social media, the low-level signal-processing techniques that detect edits have become less useful. Thus new capabilities will have to determine if the messages conveyed by manipulated images are of concern.

Cutting against the sentiments of the others, Farid doubled down on the implications of Boland's actions in the mid-2000s in the context of the Internet and near-perfect fakes. He contends that the legal arguments made in early child pornography cases involving digital evidence had a lasting impact on society because of the questions they raised around the burden of proof: "Just because you can do it, you have to now prove that this content being used as evidence in any circumstance is not fake." What started as a child pornography defense was adapted to other criminal contexts. For instance, Bashar Al-Assad has rejected photographic evidence of war crimes committed by the Syrian government during his country's civil war because of the possibility that each and every image could have been "Photoshopped" (Syrian Arab News Agency 2017). We now see this rhetorical dodge across the board. By pointing to a technological possibility, it is easy to dismiss anything, which fuels conspiracy theories on the Internet. Commenting on this, Farid stated, "This is what really scares me."

In the shadow of the COVID-19 pandemic, the most insidious manifestation of the near-perfect digital fake has been the falsified output of scientific experiments. According to the journal *Nature*, "up to one-fifth of published life-sciences papers contain at least one digitally altered image" (Else 2021). Most of these alterations are innocent changes to improve interpretability, but some are intentional modifications meant to change the result of an experiment (fig. 5.5). The popular blog *Retraction Watch* has cataloged scores of retracted papers on pandemic-related research, some flagged as problematic because of irregularities in figures.[22] Material of this nature could influence public-health policy if believed, leading

FIGURE 5.5. Cloned western blots (a technique to detect proteins in biology) from a scientific paper that was retracted from the *Journal of Biological Chemistry* (Niture et al. 2011).

to wasted time and resources in the best case and bad patient outcomes in the worst.[23] This is something the media-forensics community never anticipated and yet is stepping up to address with automated detection capabilities for journals and scientific-integrity offices at funding agencies (Xiang and Acuna 2020). By leaving prophecy behind, this quirky discipline is finally finding its footing.

6

Virtualized Horror

IN THIS CHAPTER WE VISIT another dark corner of the Internet where computer hackers played a central role in establishing strategies for fakery: shock-content sites. The chapter is based on interviews with hackers who were witness to the rise of extreme forms of entertainment in the 1990s and early 2000s, as well as newly collected source material from rotten.com, 4chan, and early business plans for social media. The primary goal here is to examine why shock content is so alluring and whether we should be alarmed by its prevalence on the Internet. Often ignored in the controversies around this phenomenon is the cultural significance of the darker side of humanity on display. What does shock content say about us? Much of it is situated in the realm of myth, like the other forms of transgressive material we have looked at.

The Retina of the Mind's Eye

One of the more perplexing aspects of media manipulation has been its significance for the creation of shocking yet entirely plausible scenes. It is frequently unclear why something has been faked when circumstances would have permitted it to actually occur. For instance, the Islamic State caused a stir in 2015 when it released a video depicting the barbarous beheading of a Japanese hostage (fig. 6.1). As it traveled across the Internet, leaving aghast viewers in its wake, analysts determined that the video exhibited several signs of tampering, bringing the veracity of the footage into question (Mendoza 2015). But this raised an obvious question: Why would the most murderous terror organization on the planet go through the trouble of faking something it could have easily accomplished with the quick swipe of a blade? Perhaps then the analysts were mistaken and the video wasn't fake at all. Counterevidence to this effect soon surfaced (West 2015). So who was right? In some sense, it didn't really matter to the casual viewer on the Internet—the ambiguity made the footage even more intriguing. It also harkened back to an infamously prescient cinematic moment.

In the 1983 film *Videodrome*, the actor James Woods portrays Max Renn, a television executive obsessed with bringing increasingly extreme content to a fledgling broadcast station in Toronto. Through graphic depictions of sex and violence, Renn believes that he can break through to a new audience. Describing a recently discovered and particularly grotesque show of shadowy origin titled *Videodrome*, he brags, "It's just torture and murder. No plot, no characters. Very, very realistic. *I think it's what's next.*" Importantly, the characters in the film are never certain of the provenance of the *Videodrome* footage. But fundamentally, it did not matter to the business of running the station—the more outrageous, the more viewers would tune in. If we credit this insight, the forms of extreme content— from possibly bogus execution videos produced by Islamist militants to pornographic deepfakes—that we are now subjected to on the Internet should not be surprising (Romano 2019).

Videodrome is a horror film, and an imaginative one at that. As Renn is drawn further into the *Videodrome* mystery, the camera captures how increasingly grotesque everything around him appears—especially the people he encounters. The film's writer and director, David Cronenberg, is well known for surreal depictions of violations of the human body that moved the horror genre into a space that blurs the boundary between the mind and the physical environment. In *Videodrome* this is evident in the blending of elements from Renn's real existence in Toronto with his perception of the horrors he observes on television. Through the character of Brian Oblivion (portrayed by Jack Creley), a reclusive professor of media theory who appears only via videotape, the film makes the point that telecommunication devices have become an extension of the nervous system's sensory modalities. In Oblivion's words,

> The television screen is the retina of the mind's eye. Therefore the television screen is part of the physical structure of the brain. Therefore what-

FIGURE 6.1. Why go through the trouble of executing somebody when you can simply fake it? A frame from an allegedly fabricated execution video released by the Islamic State. The reasons for the creation of this video remain uncertain, but its ability to generate press and viewership is not disputed.

ever appears on the television screen emerges as raw experience for those who watch it. Therefore television is reality, and reality is less than television.

Through dialogue and visuals, Cronenberg was able to channel the ideas of famed media theorist Marshall McLuhan, who served as the inspiration for the Oblivion character (Ripatrazone 2017). McLuhan is best remembered for his trademark phrase "the medium is the message" (McLuhan 1994), which anticipated the global spread of interactive information networks like the Internet. The medium, he argued, was the most important component of technological communication because of its visceral influence on the body itself (Chun 2014). As that technology becomes more sophisticated, so does its ability to arouse emotions and bodily reactions. McLuhan revised his phrase when titling *The Medium is the Massage* (McLuhan and Fiore 1967), a bombastic media manifesto that he coauthored with the graphic designer Quentin Fiore, using the pun in the title to emphasize that a medium was more than just a conduit for information:

> It takes hold of them. It rubs them off, it massages them and bumps them around, chiropractically, as it were, and the general roughing up that any new society gets from a medium, especially a new medium, is what is intended in that title. (McLuhan 1967)

By shocking both his characters and his audience through the specific medium of recorded video, Cronenberg demonstrates McLuhan's observation first-hand. The *Videodrome* footage in the film does not contribute to any meaningful narrative. It is literally just short clips of torture and murder, which the medium exploits to shake the viewer up. And it did not matter if it was real or not. From a practical standpoint, when shock content is fake (as it certainly is in the film), it is simply easier to produce. It is no small feat to torture another human being for hours on end, let alone kill them.

Videodrome left an unusual legacy within the technology world. The film bombed at the box office but gained cult status within the computing world.[1] Retrospectively, it appears a case in which some viewers, consciously or not, ignored Cronenberg's critique of where information networks were headed and instead attempted to replicate Renn's business plan (Podoshen 2020). Renn, of course, was right: horrific content is easily monetized. It glues users to the medium conveying it, eliciting the physical reaction described by McLuhan over and over again. A canonical example is the social-media platform Reddit, which in its infancy followed a growth-first strategy, largely taking a hands-off stance toward the content appearing in user-generated subreddits. Unsurprisingly, some of the most popular subreddits were boundless feeds of violent, misogynistic, and, in general, disgusting content (Lagorio-Chafkin 2018). Reddit as a medium was highly amenable to delivering such material, as the entire platform revolved around user-generated posts and comments, which could include imagery. Importantly, nobody from the company was vetting the content to any great extent. Regardless of its authenticity, if it attracted users to the platform, it satisfied the founders and their investors.

That social media is awash in disturbing material is news to nobody. But the discussion on what, if anything, to do about it has only superficially examined the nature of material meant to shock the observer and such material's relationship to the medium by which it is conveyed. On its surface, all shock content appears to be socially unacceptable. Yet that does not hold the public back from consuming it en masse. An important data point here is that *Videodrome* is a horror movie, and that particular fictional genre serves a specific cultural purpose through its provocations. Ethically, we should be alarmed by a depiction of actual violence that undermines the dignity of a person. But is that what we really see in all instances of shock content on the Internet? Once again, fake stuff has an outsize influence, and the boundaries between the real and virtual are amorphous.

The Original Website from Hell: Rotten.com

In 1996, a computer hacker going by the handle "Soylent" registered the domain name rotten.com. The appearance of the shock website that would inhabit this domain was a landmark moment in the history of the Internet (fig. 6.2) and a harbinger of the deluge of disturbing content to come on social media. The man behind the Soylent moniker was Tom Dell, an eccentric computer programmer who worked at Netscape developing some of the fundamental technology that would power the dot-com era. Dell cut his computing teeth in the BBS world as a member of the textfile crew Anarchy Incorporated and was known for authoring files lampooning the

today
daily
rotten
news
tshirts
press
words
porno
fmax
mugshots
nndb
boners

www.rotten.com

**When Hell is full,
the dead will walk the earth**

PURE EVIL SINCE 1996

Flush please

rotten dot com

An archive of disturbing illustration

The soft white underbelly of the net, eviscerated for all to see:
Rotten dot com collects images and information from many
sources to present the viewer with a truly unpleasant
experience.

FIGURE 6.2. Active between 1996 and 2012, rotten.com was one of the web's original
shock sites and a harbinger of what was to come on social media.

more earnest elements of the hacker scene. Like P. T. Barnum, Dell had a
predilection for curiosities and the acumen to effectively advertise them.
Bringing his web-development expertise and a willingness to antagonize
to his after- hours pursuit, Dell ended up making rotten.com his primary
project for more than a decade. Over the years, the site became a repository for an increasingly grotesque collection of photos depicting bizarre
sex acts, mangled corpses, and other material meant to horrify the viewer.
It was phenomenally popular.

An early win for the site was a surge of interest in a photo Dell posted
in 1997 of Princess Diana's battered body being extracted from the car
wreck that killed her.[2] But it turned out to be a hoax. In fact, like a carnival freak show of yore, much of what could be seen on rotten.com was not
what it appeared to be. Immediately after the alleged image of Diana was
posted, French authorities pointed out that the first responders in the scene
were not wearing the right uniforms, nor did their vehicles match any of
those used in France at the time (Harmon 1997). Yet even a solid debunk-
ing could not stem the tide of curious visitors. Shortly after the photo was

exposed as a fake, traffic on rotten.com climbed to a record seventy-five thousand visits per day[3] (an impressive number at the dawn of the World Wide Web). The mainstream media picked up the story, and Dell found his site featured in the *New York Times*, Reuters, and Agence France-Presse, among other outlets.

Dell frequently wrote with a playful ambiguity, leaving visitors guessing over the nature of rotten.com's content and his intentions. Addressing the fake photo of Diana, he had this to say: *"At no time did we actually claim the photo was genuine.* Of course, once we receive a genuine photo of the accident, it will get published." This was seemingly in conflict with the site's own policy on content, which stated that only real photos would be posted, including those that depicted dead bodies.[4] Noting the prevalence of fake photos of dead bodies on the Internet, Dell wrote, "We see a lot of fake pictures, and can spot them fairly easily. Real pictures of this nature aren't particularly rare; they are merely hidden from the public in most cases."[5] A visual medium that could manipulate the behavior of its users, the utter shock of viewing a mutilated corpse, a public left guessing—rotten.com looked an awful lot like the plot of *Videodrome.*

An important chapter of the rotten.com origin story is Dell's history in the hacking scene, where, as we have already learned, ingenuity and misdirection thrived. Hackers active in the 1980s and 1990s remember him as one of the most creative early textfile writers,[6] crafting edgier and more clever material than his contemporaries.[7] He was also an expert programmer. In the 1980s, Dell wrote an influential piece of BBS software called Waffle, which was easy for fledgling SYSOPs to get up and running and brought various Internet protocols used to exchange information to the DOS operating system for the first time.[8] Conveniently, Waffle became a vehicle for transmitting the textfiles put out by Anarchy Incorporated, which Dell had a hand in writing.[9] Given the wide variety of strange writing that could be found on BBSs, it's not difficult to make a connection between the shock content that would later appear on rotten.com and the often confrontational obscenity contained within the textfiles. A brief analysis of the Anarchy Incorporated files is instructive here.

Emerging in 1984, Anarchy Incorporated specialized in surreal writing, in rather tongue-in-cheek fashion, on kinky sex, grotesque violence, petty strategies for seeking revenge, and other transgressive topics. A significant aspect of these files was that they explored changing perceptions of reality in cyberspace. In one file, titled "Murder at 300 Baud," the various members of Anarchy Incorporated appeared as characters in their own profane murder mystery tale.[10] Through this story, the group explained its mission to leverage the new digital medium of computer networking to disseminate troubling material:

> "What exactly is the purpose of this group, Jude?" he asked. Jude shifted her weight.
> "They . . . write." she said.
> "Write?"
> "Yes . . . Electronic media. Mostly fictional work, but nothing more. They have this nasty habit of going out and causing distruction [sic] while getting research. Why, once in K-Mart, a member did horrible things to a cashier, the poor girl is still suffering from third degree—"

In another file, titled "Why Reality Isn't," the above theme was further developed by the group, now anticipating that computer networks would convey information directly to the mind's eye, making them irresistible to the user:

> What's real for you is -=-not-=- real for another person. For instance, most people don't have modems. Perhaps since you have a modem telecommunications has become a large portion of your life. This is bad. Real bad. A little telecom is good, but only so much.[11]

Dell's technical skills did not go unnoticed by companies in the dot-com era. Having earned credibility for his efforts developing Waffle, he found work at Apple and later Netscape (Schroeder 2014),[12] where it was rumored he made a considerable amount of money in the company's IPO.[13] Assuming those rumors were true, in the mid-nineties Dell would have been a programmer of means with sufficient flexibility to work on personal projects. In a 2001 story about rotten.com published by *Salon*, journalist Janelle Brown reported that the genesis of the site was the simple act of Dell (identified in the article only as Soylent) registering the domain "because he liked the name" (Brown 2001). His next move was to put up a barebones website with a few "joke pictures." But Dell's sense of humor, already on display in his Anarchy Incorporated stint, was not universally appreciated. Naturally, other hackers were aware of what he was up to, and the site immediately became something of a cultural touchstone within their scene. Mike Schiffman (aka route), then editor-in-chief of the hacker zine *Phrack*, expressed dismay at the mere mention of rotten .com years later: "I have images and videos from that site burned into my mind." In essence, rotten.com was a logical extension of the textfile scene, bringing bizarrely offensive material to the masses in a visual form that was faster to consume and delivered a harder body blow.

Dell had a stroke of good fortune when rotten.com was discovered by the radio shock jock Howard Stern, who encouraged his audience to visit the site. This, coupled with the posting of the Diana photo, sealed the site's status as a must-see destination on the early web. While underground textfiles never found mainstream acceptance, the photos of gore and exotic sex posted to rotten.com did. The key differentiators are not difficult to understand within the context of an older form of shock entertainment: the freak show. Exhibitions of curiosities had existed for centuries, but the American showman P. T. Barnum sensationalized the practice in the nineteenth century through his own museum in New York City. Stepping through the door's of the American Museum, one entered a parallel universe where Barnum controlled the narrative, which was intentionally crafted to attract customers. The historian Nadja Durbach writes:

> Barnum and many other successful showmen combined the genuine and the fake, drawing on a mixture of illusion, assumption and reality. According to the English showman Tom Norman, it was not the show itself that entertained but rather "the tale you told." (Durbach 2009)

The freak show worked as a medium because of the psychological priming induced by the tale that was told immediately before the patron viewed the exhibit. Even if the exhibit was obviously fake, it didn't matter, as long as it conformed to the narrative in an entertaining way.

What Dell shrewdly did was update the freak show for the new era of the web. Stylistically, the rotten.com website looked like it had been designed by a carny to lure hapless web surfers away from the Internet's family-friendly midway to its seedier side alleys (fig. 6.3). With cheesy horror cartoons and over-the-top text promising the viewer "a truly unpleasant experience," the site situated itself within the carnival tradition. Importantly, the website was littered with claims that everything that could be viewed on rotten.com was authentic, even though contradictory information, like the explanation about the fake photo of Diana, was also

 rotten
dot com

An archive of disturbing illustration

 www.rotten.com
PREPARES FOR IMMINENT RAPTURE
Make your Fin de Siecle
a Sin de Faecal
Sodomites Run Rampant

YOU DAMN DIRTY APES

The soft white underbelly of the net, eviscerated for all
to see: Rotten dot com collects images and information
from many sources to present the viewer with a truly
unpleasant experience.

Cadaver.org
An archive
of gruesome and disturbing
images from
the rotten.com collection

FIGURE 6.3. *Top*: Cheesy horror cartoons are a staple of freak show advertising. *Bottom*:
Rotten.com made use of this graphical style in its own branding on the Web. Top photograph © CP Hoffman. Licensed under CC BY-SA 2.0

present. The overall narrative set by Dell overrode any priggish critique of the content on his site, in the same manner that previous narratives had ensured the enduring popularity of Barnum's obviously fake exhibits like the "Feejee" mermaid (Meier 2018).

However, Dell didn't merely copy the freak show format to the Internet, he adapted it using the new medium in a way that had been predicted in Anarchy Incorporated's textfiles. McLuhan's vision of the future of information networks was realized in the sheer amount of shock content that Dell posted and the rapid way it was processed by observers. By the turn of the millennium, rotten.com had become a conglomerate of affiliated websites that spewed out horror at regular intervals. These sites included the *Daily Rotten*, which parodied mainstream news sites, Boners.com, which alternated between photos of embarrassing mistakes and phallic imagery, and the *Gaping Maw*, which published original satirical writing. The *Daily Rotten* was particularly innovative, in that it accepted user-submitted content and allowed registered users to comment on posted material. According to Luke Benfey (aka Deth Vegetable), a noted textfile author in his own right and member of the Cult of the Dead Cow, "people were getting angrier and angrier" because of these new participatory features, which channeled heated arguments over the site's controversies into the site itself. Eventually, rotten.com stopped being "fun," and Dell gradually backed off adding new content. The site disappeared from the web entirely in 2018.

There has been much debate over the years about what Dell was actually trying to accomplish with rotten.com. Some within the hacking scene believed that the site was intended to be a viable business, making money through merchandise and advertising sales. Benfey, who knows Dell personally, strongly disputed this: "Rotten.com was not a money making scheme. Sure, Rotten.com was meant to shock, but it was not meant to be popular. Though it did end up finding a large audience that Tom didn't anticipate." The *New York Times* reported that the site was the product of a "Mountain View, Calif.-based group of anti-censorship activists" (Harmon 1997) that was reacting to moves in the 1990s to regulate the Internet. In this context, the site made a lot of sense: as with the more transgressive textfiles, Dell was making forbidden information available as a form of protest. Supporting the assertion in the *Times* was a manifesto that Dell penned explaining the mission of rotten.com:

> Rotten dot-com serves as a beacon to demonstrate that censorship of the Internet is impractical, unethical and wrong.
>
> To censor this site, it is necessary to censor medical texts, history texts, evidence rooms, courtrooms, art museums, libraries, and other sources of information vital to functioning of free society.

Yet given Dell's earlier writing and the spontaneous genesis of the site, this explanation would seem only part of the story. While Dell was no doubt invested in anticensorship activism, he was experimenting with media in a way that resembled Max Renn's experimentation with torturing a willing audience. In this regard, the site's legacy is not in dispute. Benfey noted a curious link between rotten.com and a far more famous website renowned for spreading shock content: 4chan, which launched in 2003. Dell was friends with Christopher Poole (aka moot), a programmer who was adjacent to the hacker scene and the creator of 4chan. The 4chan site shared some of the *Daily Rotten*'s features, notably having users generate content and comment on postings. But it took things a step further in letting users post anonymously, thus making it more comfortable for ordinary people to wade into the murkier waters of the Internet. The growing legion of "anons" thrived on provocations that often extended well beyond the confines of 4chan, firmly establishing the site as a mass exporter of Internet culture (Knappenberger 2012). Shock content is now found on every social network, where users consume endless feeds of it every day.

Fabricated Horror Can Be Evil Too

While Dell and Poole likely didn't cash in on the *Videodrome* business plan, the tech industry eventually did.[14] The lasting influence of rotten .com can be observed everywhere—from scenes of prison torture on YouTube to reels of naked women being asphyxiated on Pornhub (Kristof 2020).[15] In 2020, YouTube's revenue was in excess of $19.8 billion (United States Securities and Exchange Commission 2020), while the scrappier Pornhub raked in $460 million (Nilsson 2020). Importantly, these platforms minimize cost and legal liability by largely refraining from original content production, leaving that to their users so they can focus on lucrative advertising and subscription businesses. And no company seems to be interested in verifying the authenticity of the videos users are uploading unless they become subject to a criminal investigation. In the midst of this deluge of horror and money, the person of conscience wonders: How is the new medium of user-generated video production, to paraphrase McLuhan, roughing up society?

To answer this question, we must reconsider the distinction between the medium and the message. In his landmark book *Understanding Media*, which endorsed the primacy of media in mass communications, McLuhan wrote that the "content of any medium is always another medium" (McLuhan 1994). Thus the underlying significance of the higher-level medium to society isn't undermined by any vulgarity present in the lower-level medium/message. The higher-level medium could be transmitting meaningful messages, but it doesn't necessarily need to in order to deliver the visceral effects McLuhan was so intrigued by. The purest manifestation of "the medium is the message" is content like the *Videodrome* footage—devoid of meaning but amplifying sensory stimulation through its sheer shock value. This is why vacuously vulgar content like Internet porn is so popular: it has the ability to deliver repeated blows through continual user uploads that are transmitted around the globe via social-media feeds.

In contemporary culture, the compulsive consumption of grossly indecent material is frequently depicted as self-destructive. Cronenberg makes this point by juxtaposing horror with eroticism: in his film, anyone who is so obsessed with sex and violence that they would view the *Videodrome* footage for pleasure develops a fatal brain tumor from the medium of delivery. *Videodrome* anticipated a significant social problem that has now arrived, contributing to the fraying mental state of millions of people.[16] The novelist Tao Lin makes this point in his book *Leave Society*, where the protagonist attempts to amplify the visceral experience of pornographic feeds through chemical stimulants:

> On modafinil that night, drinking 250 percent as much coffee as planned, he wrote for five hours and masturbated to online porn, which he hadn't looked at in five months, for four hours, alternating sessions. "You terrible fucking piece of shit," he thought throughout the night, sometimes grinning manically. (Lin 2021)

Lin is using online porn as evidence that people should "leave society"— that is, abandon the facets of modernity that lead to self-destruction, including the aspects of information networks that he views as irreversibly damaging to the user. Fundamentally, it is the recognition by the protagonist that his behavior is socially isolating that prompts his self-flagellatory exclamation. From the perspective of *Leave Society*, intimate social relations with family, friends, and romantic partners reduce McLuhan's vision of technology to just one possible way of living—not an inevitability. Yet today that vision tends to override the alternatives.

Surprising to even the most ardent promoters of *sex positivity*, a feminist movement that celebrates pleasure and rejects the repression of niche sexual practices, has been the growing popularity of degradingly violent pornography, particularly that which depicts the brutal torture of women (Goldberg 2021; Holden 2021; Emba 2022). This content has intrigued experts on gender relations, who do not possess a clear understanding of why it spread beyond subcultures that celebrate misogyny (Srinivasan 2021). Within the context of McLuhan's theory of communication mediums, a rather simple explanation can be offered: there is a universal inclination to maximize the physical impact of a medium on the body by seeking increasingly exhilarating content. In *Videodrome*, Debbie Harry's character Nicki Brand makes the explicit connection between the horror and eroticism of the *Videodrome* footage, which had initially escaped Renn:

> *Nicki Brand:* Got any porno?
> *Max Renn:* You serious?
> *Nicki Brand:* Yeah. It gets me in the mood. [*looks through cassettes*]
> *Nicki Brand:* What's this? "Videodrome"?
> *Max Renn:* Torture. Murder.
> *Nicki Brand:* Sounds great.
> *Max Renn:* Ain't exactly sex.
> *Nicki Brand:* Says who?

If the medium is decoupled from the message, unforeseen audiences for violent pornography suddenly make more sense. The journalist Daisy Schofield has interviewed women who have become compulsive consumers of extreme forms of pornography, documenting the accelerating behavior expected with a medium that manipulates the body's senses. In a piece that appeared in *Refinery29*, the feminist imprint of Vice Media, one interviewee confessed: "The realisation that my tastes were escalating into truly harmful content such as rape and abuse turned me off completely" (Schofield 2021). Like Lin, all of the women interviewed by Schofield recognized that online pornography was fostering antisocial attitudes within themselves and took corrective action to reestablish meaningful connections with real people. Investigations as to why a sex positive embrace of pornography might take such an inwardly dark turn tend to overemphasize the prescribed conflict between men and women and deemphasize the technological manipulation behind the scenes.

The technology, as we know, does not need real tortured bodies to deliver its intended effect. Writing in the *Atlantic*, journalist Elizabeth Bruenig has scrutinized the consequences of the collision between the fiction of pornographic shock content and the reality of the consumer of that pornography (Bruenig 2021). In interviews with high-school students, she learned that mimicry of extreme sex acts was now endemic in the adolescent population (frequently to the dismay of the person on the receiving end). All of the students were seemingly unaware that what they had observed on sites like Pornhub was generated to exploit a specific technological medium in order to monetize compulsive behavior. Only when students broke away from the repetitive cycle of excess porn consumption and could clearly reflect on what they had been watching did the problem become apparent:

> "You see some fucked-up stuff," Thalia said about scrolling through sites such as Pornhub. "People looking like they're in pain . . . people pretending to be raped." Those scenes had stayed with her, though she hadn't sought out porn in some time.

Morally, this form of shock content is problematic because it undermines the dignity of the actor in the message, as well as that of the observer, inducing a destructive detachment from a healthier reality.

A prevailing concern, from the feminist left to the religious right, is that violent pornography is a catalyst for premeditated attacks against women. Like everything involving some aspect of fiction on the Internet, the landscape of digital misogyny is complicated. Various online subcultures, like the Incels (Tranchese and Sugiura 2021), Men Going Their Own Way (Lamoureux 2015), and other organizations associated with the "manosphere," frequently invoke violent language and imagery in their posts about women. Previously, we saw something similar from authors of the textfiles, like Anarchy Incorporated, who, as it turned out, were not violent maniacs seeking to unleash mayhem in real life. This raises the question: How much of that misogynistic content is catharsis and how much might lead to real violent action?

Undoubtedly, misogyny is repugnant on its surface. Yet as of 2021, only a handful of violent attacks worldwide have occurred where misogyny coordinated on social media was an established motive (Beckett 2021). As with the average reader of the more controversial textfiles, the average consumer of violent pornography does not take to the streets to act out a ghoulish fantasy. The sensational nature of these attacks has obscured a more pressing problem that does occur at mass scale. Bruenig's observations suggest that pornographic shock content fosters a repressive culture of everyday violence against women through behavioral modulation affecting both men and women. In this sense, violent pornography is truly malicious in a way the textfiles and other forms of shock content never were.

Violence is a key amplifier for a communication medium and frequently stands alone when the message depicts some form of death—real or imagined. Brand's dialogue in *Videodrome* emphasizes that recorded violence, of itself, provides a form of intense sensory experience on par with sexual stimulation. Given the popularity of violent pornography, then, the mass consumption of footage of raw torture and murder on social media should not be surprising. Naturally, authentic material of this sort was originally difficult to procure, as those involved in unsavory acts typically want to avoid establishing any record of their crimes. However, in the popular imagination, real recordings of torture and murder proliferated—you just needed to know where to look to find them.

This urban legend got its start with the 1978 horror film *Faces of Death* (fig. 6.4), which was shot in documentary style and through a variety of individual segments depicts people dying in particularly unusual (e.g., man killed by alligator) or savage (e.g., execution by electric chair) ways. However, with the exception of some archival footage of corpses, the film was fake (Szabo 2021). Thanks to a clever video rental marketing campaign in the 1980s and an enduring cult following,[17] there remains to this day a persistent belief that the film is real and that more content of this sort must be available. Rotten.com exploited this belief when it released its own questionable depictions of death. Remarkably, criticism

FIGURE 6.4. The VHS cover for the film *Faces of Death*.

from fact-checkers pushing back against the claims surrounding the movie (and later snuff footage appearing on the Internet) set up a messy dilemma for investigators looking into actual crimes. A wave of real depictions of death did eventually flood social media, when activists began using cell phones to document war crimes and other abuses in the world's most violent conflict zones. However, to the perpetrators of those crimes, such as Syrian president Bashar al-Assad, video evidence is easily dismissible as merely another iteration of *Faces of Death*, which places a high burden of proof on investigators to demonstrate that it isn't fake (Syrian Arab News Agency 2017).

Also problematic is the fact that the reception of recorded violence is shaped by repeated exposure. Because people who binge on shock content have been conditioned to fictional depictions of death, they often assume that death in real life proceeds in a manner stylistically consistent with a horror movie. Evidence of this has surfaced in a handful of bona fide murders that were filmed and uploaded to the Internet by truly deranged perpetrators. Writing for *The Verge* on the 2012 murder of Jun Lin, a student at Concordia University in Montreal who was stabbed to death, dismembered, and then eaten by his killer Luka Magnotta, the journalist Lessley Anderson discovered that a video of the crime was being enjoyed by an audience that did not seem to process the grave circumstances they were witnessing (Anderson 2012). Instead of offering respect for the deceased and his family by working to get the video off of the Internet, "many wished there had been more 'gurgling' or otherwise eerie sound effects."

But Horror Isn't Necessarily Evil

Horrifying content can, however, take on more significance than it has as a mechanism of titillation—especially when the observer is paying attention to and learning from what they are seeing. *Videodrome* is a visually disturbing film that induces physical discomfort in the viewer. Yet it's also a culturally significant piece of art that has framed the analysis of shock content in this chapter. Similarly, 4chan is the scion of rotten .com, yet it too churns out culturally significant material that provides useful commentary on contemporary social concerns. The communication medium and its message aren't necessarily working against us, even if both conspire to rough the viewer up a bit. McLuhan himself was fundamentally upbeat about the potential of information networks operating in this capacity, with their "electric speed in bringing all social and political functions together in a sudden implosion," which, he argued, "has heightened human awareness of responsibility to an intense degree" (McLuhan 1994).

Thus we shouldn't automatically resort to moral panic, even when what we see on social media disturbs us. Each piece of shock content must be properly contextualized. Much of it, of course, can be dismissed as vulgar schlock. This is the content that exists as noise on the Internet. After the thrill has subsided, it induces in the compulsive observer that blank stare that is the physical manifestation of desolation. But some of it fits neatly into a myth cycle and conveys meaningful signals that we should pay close attention to. Instead of giving up agency while observing, we can think and synthesize when locking onto a particular signal of interest. The medium makes us feel its impact, which forces us to look and

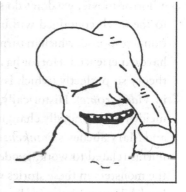

FIGURE 6.5. Comic commentary on male sexuality has been seen since time immemorial and hasn't changed very much over time. *Left*: Oltos, fragment of drinking cup, Attic red-figure, 525–500 BCE. *Right*: Brainlet meme; 2021. Left, Museum of Fine Arts, Boston, 08.31d. Photograph © 2022 Museum of Fine Arts, Boston.

understand. What happens here affirms McLuhan's vision and reflects the changing nature of how one's virtual existence now plays out.

Shocking imagery served an important social function long before it moved onto the Internet. For instance, ancient Greek pots decorated with an exaggerated eroticism are treasured artifacts, not profane rubbish. They provide a window onto an older myth cycle that folded sexuality into a larger explanatory narrative for the very nature of human existence. This frequently involved depictions of sexual violence, humiliation, and silliness, reflecting the diversity of experience one would likely encounter in life. This material is a far cry from pornography, yet shares a strong relationship to the racier memes that proliferate on the Internet today, which are sometimes misidentified as vulgar (fig. 6.5). Similarly, P. T. Barnum is celebrated as America's original celebrity entertainer, not reviled as a monster. His fictional characters and bogus curios were adopted into American culture, with some, like the Feejee mermaid, enduring as icons to this day. Barnum's fantasies were projections of the imagination, and precursors to how entertainment would evolve as information networks began to appear in the twentieth century. Pieces of rotten.com fit into both of these frames, and it can likewise be seen to have substantial cultural value, as compared to purely vacuous sites like Pornhub.

This brings us back to the very nature of horror as a genre of fiction. What function does it serve beyond mere entertainment? When we watch a horror movie, we don't do so out of malevolent desire. Instead, we look to the myth contained within the narrative to give us a heightened emotional response, which in turn helps us to remember and reflect on what we have experienced. Horror has endured as a genre because it fits McLuhan's theory so perfectly (which is likely why Cronenberg put the two together in *Videodrome*). Historically, its emergence in the nineteenth century coincided with a rapidly changing world. Stories like Bram Stoker's *Dracula* and Mary Shelley's *Frankenstein* reflect the disruptions of changing social norms related to work, gender roles, and technology. The black hearts of the monsters in these stories were nourished not by spilt blood but instead by the deep anxieties in the real culture they are imagined to inhabit.

The genre grew in popularity as media became more sophisticated in the twentieth century, in ways that mirrored serious philosophical discussions concerning technological progress and its consequences through two world wars, the Cold War, and beyond. Throughout his career, philosopher Noël Carroll has commented on the aesthetics of horror and how it situates itself in a world of constant upheaval driven by market capitalism, where everything from employment instability to physical violence fills the average person with dread daily. It is his conclusion that, as compared to the writings of contemporary philosophers on the subject, horror is a more organic and accessible critique of the forces that generate anxiety:

> As social expression, rather than as persuasive philosophy, postmodern rhetoric may reflect the recent experience of the collapse of the conceptual fixities, or more aptly, the presuppositions of Pax Americana. In this respect, the current ascendancy of the genre of horror may be the mass popular expression of the same anxiety concerning criteria that preoccupies the more esoteric forms of postmodernism. (Carroll 1987)

The overall aesthetic of rotten.com was situated within the traditional confines of horror, providing popular criticism of a form different from conventional philosophy but spurred by the same anxiety. If Dell's personal motivation for posting certain content was frequently juvenile (e.g., for Boners.com), the reception would still fit into the standard horror framework. And from the activist bent of rotten.com, we know that his overarching motivation was to draw attention to perceived misuses of power, knowing that corporations and governments were making moves to control information on the Internet—something that persists to this

FIGURE 6.6. An "Accelerationist" meme that spread across 4chan and other social media platforms. Accelerationism, as defined by various political groups on the Internet, refers to a process of enacting radical social change. Writing about this particular meme, academics at King's College London alleged, "Given the context in which it was deployed, we can assume that this meme is intended to glorify and promote violent accelerationism" (Crawford 2021). However, familiarity with that context (4chan) leads to a different possibility (Coleman 2012): perhaps this meme is simply meant to mock alarmists on the Internet with shocking imagery. The depiction of the fascist fighter is so over the top that it's possible this image was never meant as a serious threat.

day. Thus rotten.com reflected newfound anxieties around the control of a medium that was rapidly changing the world.

At present, there are more social critiques embedded in shock content than ever before. The memes of 4chan scroll by at a dizzying pace on its most popular boards, like /b/ and /pol/, subjecting visitors to a barrage of profane and exaggerated representations of real social concerns—with messages seemingly arguing for accelerating whatever problem is at hand (fig. 6.6). This form of transgression tends to be mistaken for literal extremism, especially by academics (Crawford et al. 2021) and the news media (Abad-Santos 2018), which misses the more important, underlying story. Similarly to how changing social norms helped the horror genre get off the ground in the nineteenth century, wrinkles in today's social fabric force certain types of discourse into virtualized horror.

Notably, there has been a rapid decline in real-life forums where social concerns can be aired in the exaggerated form that people are highly receptive to. For instance, consider the recent puritanical backlash against stand-up comedy. Contemporary social norms have made it completely unacceptable to discuss certain things in the open, especially if ideas are raised that push back against dominant media narratives (Jeffries 2019). Yet there is still a strong impulse to do so. Forbidden ideas of this sort are now channeled into disquieting social-media posts that are released under the veil of anonymity to jolt the masses into thinking critically. The question is whether this activity will truly heighten human awareness of responsibility or simply drag us all to hell.

7

Dreams of a Clairvoyant AI

THE TECHNOLOGICAL CAPACITY TO CREATE FAKE images has improved dramatically since the early days of Photoshop. To alleviate the laborious process of using traditional computer graphics or image processing, AI researchers have designed a new tool for the automatic production of photorealistic fakes: the generative adversarial network. This specialized form of machine learning is now a drop-in replacement for manual image editing and synthesis tasks. In operation, generative adversarial networks have appeared so impressive that computer scientists have made astonishing claims about their predictive capabilities, with implications for the temporal nature of reality that warrant scrutiny. What are the practical limits of this technology? Should we believe the stories an AI tells us about the future, or are they myths from a synthetic imagination? In this chapter we will seek to answer these questions and others around this fascinating new technology.

A Treacherous Unknown

A disquieting fact of life is the persistent unease one experiences when pondering what lies ahead. How should we plan for an uncertain future that may bring trouble our way? If risk can be mitigated, good. If an advantage can be gained, even better. But there are reasonable and perilous paths forward available to each of us. Which one we take can irrevocably alter our life for the better or worse. Historically, this dilemma has led desperate people in some form of trouble to make bad decisions, often magnifying the problem they were trying to fix. A good example comes to us from the Old Testament.

When confronted by an invading army of Philistines and no obvious strategy for countering their advance, Saul, ancient king of Israel, takes the drastic step of consulting with a sorceress to divine a viable course of action. Legitimate sources of information having failed him, Saul turns to an age-old source of dubious information: the occult. But having cast all of the fortune tellers out of Israel by commandment of the Lord, he has to go underground to locate his quarry, a clairvoyant witch in the village of Endor. Upon meeting her he requests that she conjure the spirit of the recently deceased prophet Samuel, whom Saul believes will provide him good advice on the impending battle. Predictably, this plan backfires in spectacular fashion. Saul's disobedience does not go unnoticed by God, who has directed Samuel's spirit to foretell inescapable doom as a punishment. A poor outcome, to be sure, but it's not hard to relate to Saul in this situation. At the present moment, we live amidst a great deal of uncertainty but crave stability. Thus the prevailing wisdom of our age is that we must grasp the past, present *and future* to bring focus to the amorphous circumstances we find ourselves in.

The story of the Witch of Endor is a warning against such a desire for power over time. And it exposes a stark disconnect between acting on that desire and the delivery of useful results. Reconciling one's yearning to make predictions about the future with the limits of human ability is difficult for someone struggling with a dilemma, often forcing a shift from rational planning to a pursuit of the impossible. Clairvoyance, of course, is not supported by observable evidence and frequently misleads its adherents, yet it has not gone away, in spite of thousands of years of admonitions. Remarkably, we continue to see Saul's story play out in our own age. But more recently, the manifestation of clairvoyance has taken a curious turn: the seer of yore has shape-shifted into a computer algorithm.

In 2019, a scientific paper was published through a prominent artificial intelligence conference that described an algorithm purportedly able to "bring the future closer in the viewer's mind" (Schmidt et al. 2019). A future, the authors tell us, in which climate change has taken hold to usher in catastrophe. Given a geographic location and a climate model as input, the algorithm generates an image of a potential future for that location—allowing the viewer to experience the consequences of climate

FIGURE 7.1. A vision of a swampy future foreseen by artificial intelligence, or just a synthesized fiction? (Schmidt et al. 2019). Licensed under CC-BY 4.0.

change both "rationally and viscerally." The markers of climate change are all around us, and its impact on the future could indeed be dramatic. And while it is not surprising that computer scientists would want to contribute to the fight against a warming planet, this particular method for doing so raises a few eyebrows. The algorithm is the product of famed Canadian computer scientist Yoshua Bengio and his laboratory at the University of Montreal, which is leading an area of research within AI called "deep learning" (Goodfellow et al. 2016). It has already spawned a follow-on publication (Cosne et al. 2020) and media coverage (Davis 2019; Yuan 2020). But is it really possible to see the future using artificial intelligence?

Learning from Data to Make Predictions

To answer the question at hand, we need to consider a few others about how the algorithm works and related matters in predictive modeling. First, is such a thing sound science? From a computer-science perspective, generally accepted practices from machine learning, a discipline within AI that promotes learning statistical models from data, are being used. Specifically, the algorithm makes use of an approach known as a "generative adversarial network" (Goodfellow 2014), which is able to synthesize photorealistic images or alter existing images in specific ways. To make a prediction about the impact of climate change on a particular location, the algorithm learns a mapping between an original image of that location and images of natural disasters, using a climate model as the go-between to determine whether or not to transform the original image into a flood, fire, or some other product of extreme weather. Computer graphics technologies have been able to perform similar operations for quite some time,[1] but the technological innovation here is that it no longer takes manual effort to generate the content. Through the use of AI, the process can be automated.

To make this work, the generative adversarial network needs to be trained with relevant data, in the form of thousands of images of locations under good and bad conditions. This is an example of the "big data" strategy in AI research, where an algorithm is shown as many examples as possible of what it is supposed to learn (Mayer-Schönberger and Cukier 2013). Big data powers many of the software applications we use every day, from ad placement on the Internet (Livingstone 2017) to photo filters on our phones (Gershgorn 2020). An important question is where the data for these applications comes from. The answer as of late has been public sources on the Internet. Vast photo collections are available on social-media platforms like Facebook and Instagram, which ingest hundreds of billions of images per year (Eveleth 2015). If these are representative of the world we are trying to make predictions in, a model can be trained for the task at hand—in this case, one for predicting the consequences of climate change based on what many different normal structures and flooded structures look like. The research group at the University of Montreal turned to photo-sharing websites to find examples of different types of homes and neighborhoods under both normal and flooded conditions. During training, the generative adversarial network learns how to transform one class (normal) to the other (flooded) in a gradual manner, allowing for the simulation of a range of disaster conditions. Following training, the model is able to make predictions about any location provided to it.

So far, so good, but are we missing something in the formulation of the problem? How exactly does learning from data allow us to make a prediction about the future? And are any of the predictions accurate? The algorithmic sleight of hand is in the assumptions that underpin the predictive model. First, the designers of the algorithm have assumed that it is possible to predict the future consequences of climate change, in visual form, using machine learning. To make those predictions, it is also assumed that we know the probability of an extreme weather event occurring and what its outcome will look like given past experience with similar events. But the future must look almost identical to the past for these assumptions to hold true. Given that burden, can we determine what is predictable, and what is not?

The problem is as one of short-term versus long-term predictions. For example, consider a form of forecasting that we are all familiar with: weather prediction. The weather cannot drastically change a few seconds into the future, which makes it easy to predict the conditions in that limited time frame. Even hours into the future, meteorologists can still rely on measurements from radars, barometers, hygrometers, and other instruments to make reasonable (if not always perfect) evidence-based judgments about the conditions in that longer time frame. But farther into the future—can we say anything about the weather at this time next year? The editors of the *Old Farmer's Almanac* may claim to,[2] but in reality, at this timescale one must abandon per point weather estimates and move to more general statements about climate. In spite of the known temporal limitations of weather predictions, the group at the University of Montreal claims that it can generate visions of the weather in the far future—a full five decades from now. Is it possible to make specific long term predictions in any capacity?

Nate Silver, who is perhaps the best-known figure in the world of predictive modeling, has commented extensively on the types of predictions that are reliable in his sports and politics site FiveThirtyEight.com and his book *The Signal and the Noise* (Silver 2012). According to Silver, casino games like poker are somewhat predictable because they happen in a limited time frame under closed conditions (i.e., the rules of the game don't change). Human behavior and elements of chance guarantee imperfect predictions, although not enough to dissuade savvy players from attempting to make them. Elections are also somewhat predictable, because they too happen in a limited time frame—albeit one that is much longer than a poker game—and operate under closed conditions (i.e., a winner-take-all system can't change to a proportional system on election day). Information to make predictions in elections comes from history and polling, and the impact of time can be mitigated through incremental polling. Again, human behavior and chance conspire to make this very difficult, but not so much as to keep millions of viewers away from FiveThirtyEight.com in an election season. In contrast to games and elections, earthquakes are not predictable, because they are driven by random processes that scientists do not fully understand (i.e., the rules of earthquakes are undefined). Further complicating their prediction is that severe earthquakes, the ones we are most concerned about, happen quite rarely over very long time spans. This leaves only a handful of data points for the construction of a model. Thus time and unknown conditions work against a predictive model.

Silver's success in game and election forecasting lent an enormous boost to the nascent field of data science a decade ago, inspiring an entire generation of predictive modelers to follow his methodology. When Silver and his disciples make forecasts, they account for a range of possibilities, all of which are assigned probabilities. The most rigorous way to do this also reflects the variance of the model's predictions, allowing one to view its uncertainty (i.e., error). This is why we see a prevalence of approaches based on Bayesian statistics—approaches that employ a sampling procedure that captures uncertainty by simulating different outcomes and incorporates prior knowledge to modulate probability scores. As a model looks farther into the future, its uncertainty necessarily increases, because there is less basis for a decision the further it is from the data it was created with. Without sufficient recent prior knowledge, many outcomes become plausible—there simply isn't enough information to make a good decision. This, of course, is also true of human-generated predictions.

Did the Montreal group characterize the uncertainty surrounding their predicted visions of the future? The short answer is no: we are only shown the final output of the model, an image. Could they have done so? The answer is complicated. Even though the model outputs images, it shares characteristics of the predictive models used for gambling, sports, and elections that make estimations of uncertainty possible. However, the execution is difficult. To test the idea, one could "predict" the present, by collecting old photos of a neighborhood under different weather conditions and corresponding historical climate data, creating a model based on that information, and then generating images of what the neighborhood should look like now. By taking the difference between real images of the present and the predicted images, the error can be calculated, thus quantifying the uncertainty of the model.

But because we're dealing with image synthesis, the error calculation is more complicated than it first appears. How far away is too far away for a predicted image to be right? Consider the space of all possible images. The resolution of the images created by the Montreal model is 300×300 pixels. Each image is color, meaning it has three channels, giving a total of $300 \times 300 \times 3$ pixel values. And each pixel value can be a number between 0 and 255. This means that there is a total number of $256^{(300 \times 300 \times 3)}$ possible images. This number far exceeds the number of atoms in the universe (around 10^{80}) and, practically speaking, defines a functionally infinite space. It is unclear how an assessment of the similarity between real and predicted images should proceed, given the vast unknown space of related images and no predefined thresholds. Human perceptual thresholds may be diagnostic for this purpose (Rajalingham et al. 2018), but no published evaluation of a generative adversarial model incorporates them. Paradoxically, the set of all 300×300 images contains all of the scenes that have ever occurred in the universe, and all of those that ever will, but the space is so large that you will never find the future you are looking for.

Even assuming that uncertainty can be estimated in some way for a set of possible outcomes, things can still go wrong. Prime examples can be found in the collection of highly touted models meant to predict the winner of the 2016 US presidential election. In an incident still fresh in the minds of Democratic voters, an array of models promoted by the news media, including those from FiveThirtyEight.com and "TheUpshot" at the *New York Times*, confirmed Democratic preferences right up until election night. This possibly relieved the anxiety of some voters in the short term, but it turned out to be flat wrong. These models weren't just suggesting that Hillary Clinton might win the election; they were making highly confident predictions that she would. FiveThirtyEight.com, the most conservative of the prominent models, had Clinton as a 72 percent favorite on the morning of the election (Silver 2016). "The Upshot" gave Clinton an 85 percent chance of winning (Katz 2016). In the most outrageous example, Sam Wang, a neuroscientist at Princeton, created a Bayesian predictor that gave Clinton a 99 percent (+/- 0.8) chance of winning (Wang 2016a). Wang, so confident in his ability to predict the future with mathematics, pledged to eat a bug on live television if Donald Trump won the election—an outcome he believed impossible. He did end up eating the bug (Wang 2016b).

Predictive Algorithms in Historical Context

Writing in *Harper's* magazine shortly before the 2016 election, the novelist Walter Kirn questioned the underlying logic of predictive modeling in circumstances with a social dimension (Kirn 2016). Contrarian recipients of algorithmic predictions can actively work against a future they don't want to experience, thus altering the course of time. This is, of course, not always a bad thing. In Kirn's words, "Flip people like coins enough times and they might flip back." In a remarkable case of foreshadowing, he pointed out that Silver's 99 percent certain prediction of a Clinton win over Bernie Sanders in the Michigan primary broke down when Sanders pulled off a narrow upset in the state. With respect to the social dimension, it was almost as if Sanders being an underdog turned the tide after enough contrarians rejected the inevitability of a Clinton win, as was emphasized over and over by polling in the state. This scenario would again play out in the general election. What Kirn describes, however, reinforces a consequentialist outlook on algorithmic predictions, with an underlying assumption that the predictions are correct at least some of the time. The entire debate was rehashed in the 2020 presidential election, this time with more sober assessments of the utility of election forecasts (Tufekci 2020).

Critical thinking around this topic is not new. In spite of the prevalence of soothsaying in their time, Classical writers were skeptical of the
formulaic behavior induced by the reception of predictions, as it stood in
opposition to freedom of choice. In *On Interpretation*, Aristotle proposed
an alternative way of reasoning about future contingencies by suggesting
that one wait until the realization of a contingency before commenting
on the nature of the possibilities (Aristotle 1938). Using the example of a
naval battle, he explained that foreknowledge of the outcome isn't necessary, but an accounting of the possibilities is:

> A sea-fight must either take place on the morrow or not. No necessity is
> there, however, that it should come to pass or should not. What is neces-
> sary is that it either should happen tomorrow or not.

This doesn't mean, however, that behavior isn't driven by the possibilities
of future events. We observe such responses to contingencies in nature all
of the time. For instance, when chased by a predator, a rodent will randomly vary its movement, anticipating possible interactions with its pur-
suer, but not committing to any of them (Moore et al. 2017). This suggests
that the anticipation of the future has a social dimension, regardless of
whether or not probabilities have been assigned to the possible outcomes.

So if predictions have a social dimension, how does one set the odds?
Kirn seemingly overturns his first consequentialist thesis by observing that
in gambling, odds-making bookies aren't actually concerned with predicting the future, they simply want to equalize the bets on outcomes. This is
accomplished by dispensing with the odds surrounding who wins or loses,
and setting a line on the points a team needs to win or lose by. In sports,
this is known as the "spread," and it is always manipulated by the bookie
to manage risk. It doesn't matter what the behavior of the gamblers is—
they could be acting randomly—the objective is to build suspense around
the game to maximize engagement (and thus bets placed on both teams).
The designer of a predictive model can do the same thing to elicit emotions
around potential outcomes—especially for polarizing events like elections
and climate change. Indeed, an underlying motivation of the Montreal
group when designing their model was "to channel the emotional response
into behavior change." But the bookie has the luxury of working with a
closed system—a sporting event will always proceed by following the rules
and resolve with a definitive outcome. Forecasters of unconstrained events

like weather generated by climate change don't have that luxury. Hence more concern for the believability of our AI looking glass into the future.

Novelty is a significant and underappreciated difficulty for predictive modeling. If something completely unexpected happens, how does the model react? Upon reflection, this complication should not be surprising. All of us are stymied at some point by bad luck that was impossible to foresee, from personal challenges, like the unexpected death of a loved one in an automobile accident, to global events, like the sudden appearance of the pandemic respiratory illness COVID-19. This is where things truly unravel for any person or algorithm attempting to make predictions. Without a proper accounting of all of the possibilities at some point in the future, even Aristotle's notion of contingencies is stymied. Former US secretary of defense Donald Rumsfeld famously described this situation at a news briefing in 2002 (Rumsfeld 2002). Referring to the 9/11 attack on the United States, Rumsfeld suggested that the things we don't know that we don't know are the most difficult to plan for. He dubbed these "unknown unknowns." In order to create a supremely effective predictive model for climate change, we would need something akin to Aristotle's complete accounting. How many unknown variables are at work influencing the climate at any given time? We will likely never know.

Compared to humans, AI algorithms are especially brittle, because they know only a relatively small number of things that have transpired in the past. This is a function of how they are trained: relevant data are collected from available sources, usually up to an amount that will fit in the memory of the hardware being used. Even in a big-data regime with millions of samples, this process necessarily undersamples the world. The computer will never see as many data points as a human experiencing the world around them. Moreover, today's algorithms do not learn in the same way people do. They fail to generalize beyond their immediate experience and have trouble learning new things in their environment (Marcus and Davis 2019). As is true of making predictions in general, there should be no expectation that a model can make predictions in settings that are far beyond its past experience as gained in training. As concerns the Montreal model, a lot can happen in fifty years that does not resemble anything experienced previously. The appearance of a brand-new technology that can mitigate or exacerbate climate change is possible. A once-occupied home may be abandoned and later demolished by government order. Even seemingly insignificant events decoupled from climate (e.g., the local township decides to clean its sewers in 2045) may head off a catastrophic flood. In a dynamic universe, the possibilities of what can happen over the span of decades is limitless.

Within the field of AI, one can find a boneyard of algorithms discarded because the predictive models they relied upon were grossly inaccurate. These bad predictors often have an ethical dimension with troubling social implications. For instance, a consortium of data and social-science teams found that AI algorithms could not predict six life outcomes for people when trained on 13,000 data points for over 4,000 families (Salganik et al. 2020). These algorithms made use of a select set of variables that accurately described the training data but failed to generalize as a description of new data, seen after training. Given that these models have been touted for criminal-justice and child-protection use, this finding brings the recent fascination policymakers have with predictive analytics into question. In a more extreme example of AI applied to the area of criminal justice, claims have been made that predictive models are effective at discerning future criminals from photos of faces (Hashemi and Hall 2020). All models for this purpose, however, have been shown to exploit irregularities in the datasets they were trained with in order to yield an illusory effect (Bowyer et al. 2020). In automatic job-candidate assessment, algorithms fail to account for diversity and disabilities when predicting the future success of applicants, because examples of these things are not always present in the data for this application (Burke 2019). This can lead to discriminatory hiring practices that leave perfectly qualified candidates out of the running. In all of these cases, false premises concerning what leads to successful predictions were formulated in order to achieve the desired outcome. It is not difficult for the designers of algorithms to be misled under such circumstances.

As we have seen, there are tremendous technical hurdles to generating visions of the future. Some are insurmountable. Plainly stated, the images generated by the Montreal group's models are fake. Nonetheless, these scientists and others may indeed believe that they can see the future by learning from past experience, because it works in some constrained cases, like predicting what a frame of video should look like a fraction of a second into the future.[3] But the past doesn't necessarily inform the future in a predictable way in all cases, and this line of reasoning becomes subject to the overgeneralization fallacy. The most troubling aspect of all of this is that ascientific work is being cast as science. The claims of the papers authored by the Montreal group could not be verified at the point of peer review; one must wait fifty years to see if the predictions made by the model are accurate. The conference that published this work simply took the authors' word.

Regardless, a believing public routinely buys into questionable prognostications when they are supposedly grounded in rationality and promoted by renown experts. A computer scientist of the stature of Yoshua Bengio, who leads the AI lab at Montreal, should be taken seriously when he comments on topics aligned with his expertise and experience. However, there has been great reluctance to challenge experts in technical disciplines on matters that fall outside their purview. It would be prudent to be critical when computer scientists veer off script and venture into metaphysical exploration through their algorithms. Without opposition, the computer scientist can assume the role of cyber-guru—a spiritual guide able to see beyond direct experience through mastery over arcane technologies. Having achieved so much success in other endeavors, how could the cyber-guru be wrong in making predictions about the future—especially ones that cannot be falsified?

It turns out that parlaying rationally grounded expertise into a scheme for forecasting is hardly a new phenomenon (Gardner 2010). Writing recently in *First Things*, the historian James Hankins has pointed to the example of Niccolò Machiavelli, a political genius whose own slavish devotion to scientism led him to make a string of bad predictions (Hankins 2020). Using a form of behavioral analysis based on observation, Machiavelli came to believe that humans followed a set of rules that dictated outcomes, determined by actions. Thus a leader with access to the rules could safely predict the effects of policies—*if* such rules existed. This reductionist approach, of course, suffers from the problems that have already been outlined in this discussion. In Hankin's words:

> Machiavelli was in general a poor prognosticator. On salient issues he predicted the exact opposite of what turned out to be the case. At the end of *The Prince*, he foretold that Italy was ripe to reclaim its liberty from foreign invaders; Italy remained under foreign dominance down to the nineteenth century.

Examples of people being fooled by charismatic experts making bad predictions abound. From Paul Ehrlich's population bomb that fizzled (Roane and Weiser 2019) to Elon Musk's frequent misses concerning when his cars will achieve full autonomy (Matousek 2019), audiences remain receptive to potential futures, both bad and good.

The question of why in the present moment people believe that any entity has the capacity to predict the future deserves a closer look. Civilization's move from ignorance to reason, so the conventional narrative goes, begins at the dawn of modernity with figures like Machiavelli. A turn toward reason means a rejection of interpersonal human interests that are not always based on reason or logic, especially those rooted in supernatural beliefs. Thus any trust in oracular pronouncements should have faded away as science uprooted religious practice, from the Enlightenment to the present. AI is the most extreme example of the modern adherence to rationality, in that it is wedded to the logic of the computer, and cannot stray from the mathematical rules embedded in its design.

Yet resistance to a complete immersion in a perfectly rational existence has surfaced, and indeed a blending of scientific and supernatural ideas can be observed in popular conceptions of capacities to predict the future. A 2018 report from the National Science Board noted a significant decline between 2014 and 2016 in the number of Americans who believed that astrology was unscientific (National Science Board 2018). Many respondents to the board's survey gauging the public's understanding of science and technology believed that supernatural phenomena such as astrology, lucky numbers, and extrasensory perception contained some scientific elements—seemingly combining ideas they were exposed to via education and mainstream media with traditional folk understandings of the operation of the universe.

This phenomenon is consistent with the recent uptick in public interest in the occult (Burton 2019; Bosker 2020). Social alienation leads many to seek a connection to things outside the realm of rational human experience, which in the twenty-first century is largely shaped by rationally grounded market forces. The impulse towards spirituality has traditionally been satisfied by organized religions, which established communities around a shared notion of transcendence through virtue. In contrast, late capitalism seeks to organize society as a collection of individual rational agents interacting only within the confines of the market. The consequence has been a profound reordering of society over the course of the past several centuries. In the West, market orthodoxy has led to the precipitous decline of Christianity (Pew Research Center 2019), which historically attempted to reconcile faith and reason and, in so doing, emphasize the social good of a spirituality that unites the faithful and warn of the consequences of belief in supernatural practices like clairvoyance that run contrary to the natural order of things.[4]

In the contemporary social order, the occult is a convenient alternative to both organized religion and strict adherence to the market, in that it reconciles forced individualism and spiritual need. And importantly for our discussion, information pertaining to the occult is now widespread on the Internet, where budding acolytes interface with esoteric beliefs and practices within the confines of their social-media feeds. Because this information is delivered via technology, it is understandable that nonexperts often associate it with other emerging technologies like AI, which also exist on the Internet. In this context, an AI that can see into the future will seem plausible to its intended audience. In essence, we have a return to primitive impulses in the midst of technological upheaval: individuals alienated by the uncertainty wrought by contemporary existence seek out clairvoyants, but only those appearing from out of the rational world in which they are immersed (Breen 2015).

A Practical Dilemma

The core problem with all of this is that it will inevitably lead to bad choices by both the designers and consumers of AI technologies attempting to predict the far future. Most obviously, the technology is exceptionally vulnerable to abuse by scammers exploiting society's anxiety over the future; it adds a new tool of deception to the boardwalk psychic's bag of tricks. The story of the Witch of Endor is diagnostic here, because it suggests that clairvoyance is a racket. In one interpretation, the witch is simply running a scam against the king of Israel. She has no capacity to predict the future and is perhaps looking to make some money or exert power over a king. Her fraud is betrayed when she cries out in horror at the apparition of Samuel: this wasn't supposed to happen. With Samuel's admonishments reflecting divine judgment, the scheme unravels. It is God, not the witch, who is in control of time and space (Beuken 1978). Like Carravagio's *Fortune Teller*, the Witch of Endor fits the stereotype of the fortune teller in art and literature: a low-level crook who seeks to deceive targets of opportunity. Not much has changed over time when it comes to the fortune-telling business.

Beyond the scam lies a more basic ethical dilemma: there is potential that the audience viewing the climate-change predictions will be primed to think that they solved a problem that was never a problem in the first place. Given the tremendous uncertainty surrounding localized events in the far future, an attempt to manipulate the behavior of individuals through fear will inevitably misdirect society's attention from where it needs to be. For example, if a concerned homeowner believes that their house will indeed be underwater in the future, they might focus on fortifying their property from catastrophic flooding, while ignoring the systematic changes that need to be made at global scale to mitigate climate change. After all, a person can only devote so much attention to any one problem, and thus the one most immediate becomes the primary focus. There is no guarantee that anything will actually happen to a particular homeowner's property, but there is a strong likelihood that somewhere on planet earth, bad things will happen to vulnerable buildings. The whole business is a distraction from the present reality of the fundamental problem. Indeed, the underlying motivation for the research from the University of Montreal was to better inform the public about the problem of climate change.[5] Why go about it in a disingenuous way? Presenting the public with unlikely potential futures is a bad course of action. And it remains unclear why information technology should play any role at all in this discussion. Climate change is a policy problem that cannot be addressed with AI.

So what can we do to relieve the anxiety that we feel about the future? The advice here is simple: one must learn from the past and react to the present. This will likely lead to a better future. When it comes to climate change, we already know the impact it is having on the planet right now and what we need to do to address it. A clairvoyant AI isn't needed to tell us anything more. The world will be much better served if fossil-fuel consumption is drastically reduced, investment in clean energy sources is greatly increased, transportation networks are reconfigured, and cities are rehabbed with modern infrastructure. This is the territory of world governments, not of computer scientists. Of course, even if public servants are acting in society's best interest, that will not be enough to head off all problems that might come down the pike. Coming to terms with this is essential to avoid fooling ourselves into being seduced by technologists selling the impossible. To reject a futile grasp at the future like the one that undid Saul, we must accept the unease of not knowing what comes next.

8

Creative Spaces

A GOOD HISTORY SHOULDN'T BE COMPILED just to satisfy intellectual curiosity. It should contribute to our understanding of the present and help us make better decisions and avoid repeating the mistakes of the past. When it comes to digital fakery, this is especially important, given the recent politicization of such content and worries about historical analogs to totalitarian media control. However, what has been revealed through the course of this book's investigations is that we don't have as much to fear about fake things on the Internet as we might initially have assumed. The future won't be completely awful—in fact, it looks pretty good. Many of the anticipated threats have not been realized, and those that have tend to fizzle. Instead of turning malicious, most people are finding new ways to communicate, collaborate, and create through their own storytelling. Entirely new subcultures have been forming on the Internet, some proving to have an overwhelmingly positive influence in the physical world. Thinking about the emerging technologies that will steer this process in new directions isn't terrifying—it's intriguing. Immersive virtual worlds, mesmerizing interactive memes, and a robust harmonization between real life and the Internet are just around the corner thanks to the collective imagination of the globe.

And it is the human imagination itself that is perhaps the most important part of this story. Notably, the capitalist project sought to deemphasize the role of the imagination in society by prioritizing rational thought and behaviors that supported the profitability of markets. Through the decades in America, a persistent strain of Puritanism has propped up a rigorous work ethic, at the expense of all else: there was simply no time to daydream. The gradual teardown of civic, cultural, and (ironically) religious institutions limited the outlets for thinking beyond one's immediate experience, and, in general, made life rather boring. A startling decline in the use of the word "imagination" can even be observed in writing from the early nineteenth through the late twentieth century, the point at which information networks began to appear.[1] Yet capitalism could not write the imagination out of existence—our inner lives are as active as ever.

What exactly is it about the imagination that makes it so indispensable? From a purely biological perspective, we can say that it supports survival by allowing us to account for contingencies in the environment and generate knowledge to solve problems in a manner that isn't exclusively dependent on observation. But the imagination also supports activities that escape Darwinian interpretation, allowing engagement with the arts, prompting our own individual creative acts, and producing figurative language on the spot (Liao and Gendler 2020). All of these things can be combined to address complex circumstances in an appealing manner. We see this explicitly in the construction of myths.

Claude Lévi-Strauss writes in *The Raw and the Cooked* that "if the human mind appears determined even in the realm of mythology, *a fortiori* it must also be determined in all its spheres of activity" (Lévi-Strauss 1969). In other words, there is a certain necessity in a person using their imagination to engage with a myth, as in all areas of human cognition. This is the way the mind works: we simplify complex situations and amplify imagined solutions. The most remarkable aspect of mythmaking is that the process is not specific to an individual but rather is a common experience shared by every person on the planet. Evidence for this comes from the discovery made by Lévi-Strauss that motifs can be found that are common to the myths of cultures that never came into contact (Downey 2009).

It is therefore no surprise that the key technologies that we have discussed in this book have been intentionally designed to make the Internet an extension of the collective imagination of humanity. Guided by the suppositions of market-driven rationalism, accounts of the history of computing tend to valorize the optimization of routine calculations for the military (e.g., Alan Turing's groundbreaking work on the digital computer at Bletchley Park during the Second World War) and corporations (e.g., the storied rise of IBM in the mid-twentieth century). Thus the undercur-

FIGURE 8.1. Vermeer's *Girl with a Pearl Earring* (*left*) restyled to resemble the look of the Netflix animated television series *Arcane*. This effect was achieved with the ArcaneGAN algorithm (Khaliq 2022), a variant of NVIDIA's StyleGAN (Karras 2019). Courtesy Ahsen Khaliq. Reprinted with permission.

rents propelling the Internet forward have been de-emphasized, leading to misunderstandings about the origin of certain technologies, along with how and why they are being used. To gain a better understanding, all we need to do is listen to the people who have brought us to this current technological moment.

How We Arrived at the Metaverse

In 1965, the computer graphics pioneer Ivan Sutherland drew a bold connection between the imagination and the opportunities newly invented multimedia systems afforded users: "A display connected to a digital computer gives us a chance to gain familiarity with concepts not realizable in the physical world. It is a looking glass into a mathematical wonderland" (Sutherland 1965). This echoes the contemporaneous thinking of media theorist Marshall McLuhan, who believed that "electric circuitry" could be "an extension of the central nervous system," thus allowing consumers of media to transcend the boundaries of the physical world (McLuhan and Fiore 1967). Through the formalism of computer code, Sutherland was able to instantiate entirely new visual realms, laying the foundation for today's augmented and virtualized realities.

But the real power of the imagination, stressed by Lévi-Strauss, is its collective dimension, mirrored in the seeming requirement that the interfaces designed by Sutherland and others be connected together. Thus we find that early Internet figures were enamored with the idea that the imagination could be set loose across a global network limited only by its silicon substrate. Writing in 1990, Internet activist John Perry Barlow was enthusiastic about this possibility:

> I know that I have become a traveller in a realm which will be ultimately bounded only by human imagination, a world without any of the usual limits of geography, growth, carrying capacity, density or ownership. In this magic theater, there's no gravity, no Second Law of Thermodynamics, indeed, no laws at all beyond those imposed by computer processing speed . . . and given the accelerating capacity of that constraint, this universe will probably expand faster than the one I'm used to. (Barlow 1990)

While it was easy for someone like Barlow to embrace an expansive vision after it became apparent that it was technologically possible for every person on earth to unleash their imagination on the Internet, the power of the underlying computers was for a time a substantial limitation. Slow networks, slow processors, and very limited file storage capacity all contributed to a clunky user experience in the first few decades of the Internet. Moreover, software engineering was also immature, forcing developers to spend a lot of time programming from scratch because of a dearth of software frameworks and user communities sharing languages and tools— both essential sources of reusable code. This changed in the first decade of the twenty-first century with the appearance of broadband, smartphones, and colossal back-end data centers. The software running on top of these hardware systems consisted of common platforms and mature protocols, meaning there was far less overhead involved in creating something new.

This system works well. Anyone with some basic programming skill can now create highly usable software and release it globally without expending much time and money. Blogging in 2007, venture capitalist Marc Andreessen observed that these technological innovations were finally enabling the imagination to run wild: "The world is a very malleable place. If you know what you want, and you go for it with maximum energy and drive and passion, the world will often reconfigure itself around you much more quickly and easily than you would think" (Andreessen 2007). Andreessen's world was one where software systems, running within the Internet, could alter circumstances in the physical world to conform to the programmer's vision. For instance, services that existed physically, like shopping, banking, and entertainment, were virtualized and enhanced in new and engaging ways. This has disrupted the economy in profound ways, by moving more of life online, which consumers have come to have a clear preference for. As Andreessen famously put it in an op-ed penned for the *Wall Street Journal*: "Software is eating the world" (Andreessen 2011).

Even so, minds within the technology world currently believe that this mode of restyling reality is still far too constrained. The act of programming continues to require some modicum of human effort and is limited to what the mind's eye can project when a person is behind the keyboard. Alternatives are emerging from the field of artificial intelligence, which is designing algorithms that can work tirelessly for free and, more importantly, surprise people with synthetically imagined outputs for many different applications. Jensen Huang, CEO of NVIDIA, believes in a future of computing in which the programmer is replaced by a more efficient and inventive AI. As he emphasized in an interview with *MIT Technology Review*, "Software is eating the world, but AI is going to eat software" (Simonite 2017).

NVIDIA makes graphical processing units (GPUs), powerful hardware components that can both render virtual environments in real-time for a device's display and accelerate the primitive operations necessary for AI algorithms to learn from information. The twenty-first century AI paradigm is frequently referred to as "programming with data," where large datasets collected from the Internet are used to provide examples to an algorithm of what it should learn to do. This could be the generation of program source code, but more commonly the task is to solve a problem in a way that cannot be described by a human programmer using a conventional programming language—for example, the creation of a program that can generate an infinite number of different looking worlds for a virtual environment. The creative arts can expect in the very near future an influx of AIs that will augment the work of animators, special effects shops, and graphic-design studios, thanks to this new paradigm.

More broadly, AI will be the foundation of what has been described as the "metaverse," a newly emerging immersive virtual space that Meta CEO Mark Zuckerberg has characterized as an "embodied internet" (Newton 2021).[2] Users of this successor to today's Internet will notice a gradual change in the interfaces necessary to experience the new information network, first in the shift to augmented-reality software running on a smartphone, then away from phone displays to peripherals that trick the body into thinking it is someplace else, and finally to brain-computer interfaces that deliver information directly to the central nervous system. Seemingly drawn from the pages of science fiction, the latter technology is being seriously pursued by Facebook Reality Labs and Elon Musk's company Neuralink. Zuckerberg feels so strongly about the metaverse concept that he has staked the future of his stable of technology companies, including Facebook, Instagram and WhatsApp, on it.

Critics point out that the metaverse is merely a rebranding of the existing technological trajectory we have been charting. Yet it should not be trivialized. It is the natural culmination of decades of thinking from multiple arenas on what the Internet should be. Portuguese political scientist

Bruno Maçães, whose thoughts on today's technological transformation we began this book with, projects that the metaverse will facilitate a rich and fulfilling parallel existence:

> I imagine it as a virtual world with some of the characteristics of a city. There will be stores where users can buy the products which will later be delivered to their physical homes (does Facebook want to beat Amazon in the metaverse?). There will be beaches and parks where we can meet our friends to chat and play, much like what Fortnite already offers today (but better). There will be concerts and art galleries. Is there a reason to travel to Venice in order to visit the Biennale instead of jumping into the metaverse and enjoying all the video art and installations with the latest fully immersive technology? Around these possibilities it is easy to imagine the development of a new digital economy where creators will be less dependent on mediators of all kinds (Maçães 2021a)

Crucially, none of this will be real in any conventional sense. The metaverse will be the most elaborate fiction ever imagined. In *History Has Begun* (Maçães 2020), Maçães argues that virtual reality was already a stratum of American society in the twenty-first century, and that technology and crisis were conspiring to give it global primacy. This is consistent with all of the evidence we have surfaced in this book, much of it going back decades. Maçães has termed the political philosophy behind these developments "virtualism," and he suggests that it will replace liberalism as the dominant world order. The COVID-19 pandemic highlighted in grievous terms how politically challenging it is to transform a real world under siege by a complex emergency. Thus, the logical response is to simply leave that world behind and build alternatives that do not suffer the same problems. Maçães describes this shift in revolutionary terms in his *Manifesto of Virtualism*: "Once the real world has been abolished, nothing is inescapable" (Maçães 2021b). Notably, he released *Manifesto* as a nonfungible token (Clark 2021), to be bought and sold in the new digital economy in the form of an object with no physical reality.

But we're not quite there yet in terms of the technology needed to make the metaverse work and the social contract needed to make it worth using. The optimism exuded by these thinkers should not lead us to simply ignore our current real problems. Something must be done to rein in the Internet's worst aspects, lest the metaverse end up a cyberpunk-esque hellscape. Politically operationalized conspiracy theories, memetic disinformation campaigns, and other antisocial manifestations are problems not exclusive to technology. Manipulation detection, content flagging, and increased regulation of the Internet do not get at the heart of the problem—the mistaken belief that accepted ethical practices and social norms do not apply online. A viable solution may well involve an entire reframing of the problem. Platforms shouldn't have to tell people what they're doing wrong, they should instead be showing them a better alternative. There are constructive ways to channel the unease induced by the pressures of contemporary life. Why target an outgroup to soothe your woes when you have the building blocks to create a globally inclusive alternative culture? In the remainder of this concluding chapter, a few words will be said about some absolutely amazing technologies and movements that give one hope, and a few recommendations are provided for how to negotiate the fine line between creativity and destruction in a rapidly changing technological landscape.

Technology for Myth Building

The satisfaction of producing something that is both one's own creation and truly new has been central to the activities of computer hackers, digital artists, media-forensics specialists, and AI researchers throughout the life of the Internet. Now it is enjoyed by nearly everyone on the planet. And this DIY attitude has driven the boom in technology development that supports the emerging metaverse. Never before have so many creative tools been at the disposal of anyone with an imaginative idea. What was once the exclusive realm of professional designers and computer programmers no longer requires extensive training and experience. All one needs to do is to pick up one's phone and make use of the available technology—with AI lending a helping hand.

AI's immediate triumphs will not be in highly touted technical applications like automated disease diagnosis, whose development has been slower than anticipated (Heaven 2021). Instead, it will be in creative endeavors where a silent insurgency is already underway. The relentless emphasis on logical reasoning, planning, and decision making in AI tends to shift the conversation away from other significant achievements: generative algorithms that have the ability to create new things, as opposed to simply analyzing existing things. Some of the apprehension in acknowledging such capability likely stems from a belief in the innate specialness of the human imagination and the perceived difficulty in replicating it. By initially prioritizing cognitive tasks, computer scientists avoided abstracting a little-understood phenomenon in favor of processes that appeared to be more amenable to formalization. Surprisingly, the introduction of the programming-with-data paradigm showed that it was easier to replicate components of the imagination than it was to build a system (like a self-driving car) that relies on a cognitive model.

Today's generative algorithms can do everything from creating songs and works of art to enhancing image and video content on the fly. Where did this ability to automatically generate new data come from? The history begins decades ago with a group of mathematicians at Brown University led by Ulf Grenander and David Mumford, who believed that the entire world could be decomposed into recognizable patterns, which could then be learned and synthesized to account for future variability. Calling this idea "pattern theory," the group went on to investigate a class of algorithms known as probabilistic generative models, which can learn patterns from data and then generate new instances of those patterns. Different aspects of the world can be considered in this regime. For instance, Grenander discovered that marching-band music was particularly well structured and thus especially amenable to being modeled and synthesized. As early as the 1970s, he was able to generate novel compositions using a computer (Mumford and Desolneux 2010). Compared to other tasks, like recognizing objects in photographs, the creative generative processes were more functional and did not need to be perfect in order to be useful.

Flash forward to the present: generative algorithms are better than ever. Coinciding with the widespread adoption of deep learning in the 2010s, artificial neural networks designed to generate data appeared as open-source tools in public repositories maintained by university and corporate researchers as well as hobbyists. Compared to the older pattern-theory work, which was constrained to simple signals like one-channel audio, these networks were able to process more complex signals like 3-D images. Success was thanks largely to the enormous amount of data used by the algorithms in training, which gives a sense of the variation in the world so as to plausibly bound the conditions in which new things can appear.

Denizens of the Internet are no longer asking when particular generative algorithms will become practical for general use. Instead, they want to know about the coolest stuff that is readily available and making waves across different platforms. In chapter 7 we learned about academics at the University of Montreal who promoted the use of generative algorithms for seeing into the future. That is not a representative use of the technology, nor a good indicator of where things are heading. Far more people are using it to interact in a socially constructive way. The community building pioneered by computer hackers in the early days of the Internet, as discussed in chapters 2 and 4, has evolved to move faster; integrate emerging technologies from different areas of computer science, like AI; and be generally accessible to everyone instead of limited to an elite cadre of specialists. So where on the Internet do we find the communities working with these new technologies?

Visual artists were early to appreciate the potential of generative algorithms for synthesis—a genuinely new medium of expression that opened up possibilities beyond the features of Photoshop described in chapter 3. This has led to a vibrant collaboration between artists and AI researchers—a natural extension of the existing collaboration between artists and computer-graphics researchers (the past few decades of computer graphics in movies have been impressive, to say the least). Early buzz was generated around AI-generated art at auction, with the first offering by Christie's in 2018 selling for the astronomical price of $432,500 (Christie's 2018). That particular piece (fig. 8.2) was produced by a Paris-based artist collective called Obvious using an adversarial generative network (incidentally, the exact same type of algorithm the research group at the University of Montreal was attempting to predict the future with), largely as an exercise to demonstrate the novelty of the medium.[3]

Gimmicky auctions aside, the interesting work is not in the realm of fine art but in community art. Also in 2018, computer-vision researchers started organizing workshops at their conferences to figure out ways in which the technical divide between creatives and engineers could be bridged.[4] The workshops involved representatives from large tech companies, startups, and university labs that were working on generative algorithms for creative applications like fashion, art, and design. One participant was Devi Parikh, a professor at Georgia Tech and a researcher at Meta Fundamental AI Research. Parikh noted on Twitter that she had been looking for a fun side project in the creative AI space when she happened upon the new trend of algorithmic art.[5] Having both good design

FIGURE 8.2. *Edmond de Belamy*, a portrait synthesized by a generative algorithm under the guidance of the Paris-based art collective Obvious. It sold for $432,500 at auction. The title is a play on words in tribute to the computer scientist Ian Goodfellow (*bel ami* in French means "good friend"), the inventor of the algorithm used to create the work (Goodfellow et al. 2014).

sense and the technical sophistication to innovate, she began to moonlight as a self-described "generative artist," initially releasing her work on social media (fig. 8.3).

Parikh had joined an emerging algorithmic art movement that was impressive enough to warrant new outlets for exposure and for establishing the provenance of works. Algorithmic art eventually migrated to the block-

FIGURE 8.3. AI-generated artwork guided by the imagination of the "generative artist" and computer scientist Devi Parikh. Courtesy Devi N. Parikh. Reprinted with permission.

chain ecosystem for generative information. Platforms like Art Blocks and Brain Drops have established communities of artists that are generating pieces directly onto the Arweave and Ethereum blockchains, respectively.[6] Many of the pieces are attractive, if otherworldly—enough so to be widely available as nonfungible tokens—the currency of the emerging metaverse. Existing within a blockchain, a piece's ownership can always be verified or transferred (sometimes for a price).

While some generative artists are expert programmers who can modify the code of algorithms to achieve desired effects, one doesn't have to have such skills to synthesize compelling art. Platforms for algorithmic art have lowered the bar to entry by wrapping very complicated algorithms with simple-to-use interfaces. Another platform in this mode is Artbreeder, which implores users to extend their imaginations to "change anything about an image just by modifying its 'genes.' "[7] Genes in this case are parameters sent to a generative algorithm to change some aspect of a given image (for example, the color palette). Content on the platform is meant to evolve over time, as users within its community collectively alter various genes and share the results, which are then remixed by others. Posted works on content aggregators like Artbreeder are now an indication of what happens when AI hallucinations are united with human ingenuity.

Perhaps more important than the ability to synthesize wholly new images is the capacity to intentionally stylize existing images in new and sometimes radical ways. For instance, imagine restyling the human subject in Johannes Vermeer's famous painting *Girl with a Pearl Earing* to resemble the look of a character in the popular Netflix animated television series *Arcane*, thus putting the image in an entirely different milieu (fig. 8.1). In 2019, NVIDIA announced the release of StyleGAN (Karras 2019), a generative adversarial network that embedded this concept of style transfer in the generative framework of deep learning. While it was not the first algorithm to perform this trick, the quality of the images it produced was excellent, drawing the attention of multiple communities on the Internet.

Shortly after its release, newly trained models for StyleGAN began to appear that were tied to specific *fandoms*, particularly anime franchises. A fandom is a subculture usually attached to an established work of fiction (e.g., a book, movie, television show, or video game), where fans closely identify with its universe and characters in a virtual context, but sometimes also in real life (Gray et al. 2017). This is the twenty-first century way of living out a myth cycle. While the phenomenon might seem whimsical, media franchises, even underground ones, have enormous followings, meaning there are large monetary incentives for keeping fans engaged.[8] And the ability to bring one's immediate environment into a specific fandom is an irresistible avenue to engagement for many. However, money isn't everything. Recontextualization is key to broadening the reach of a subculture, helping to build bridges to others and strengthen the community. ArtStation and other platforms that showcase original visual art are now filled with restyled images and are being used as repositories of source data for further generative algorithm experimentation.[9]

A challenge for the present state of content synthesis is the pressing need, if the metaverse is to become operational, for a procedure for generating avatars that can interact naturally in a virtual environment. Efforts will initially be focused on gaming but then shift into other forms of immersive space that will be of broader interest, eventually replicating the physical world, as Maçães has suggested. Generative algorithms are already being used to synthesize and animate both faces and bodies.[10] Similarly to how one chooses a new handle on the conventional Internet, one could choose an entirely new body in the metaverse, facilitating a more complete alternate persona. Such avatars need to be animated realistically, in a novel context and on the fly. This can be achieved using the same neural networks used to create deepfakes. But here, the algorithms are applied in a socially constructive way, reflecting the primary focus of creators and users of this technology. And there are few constraints on the types of figures that can be animated, bringing more traditional 2-D animation into the set of alternate existences into which one can be inserted (Siyao et al. 2021).

Text will not go away in the metaverse, but how it is produced and consumed will change. Large language models, exemplified by OpenAI's GPT-3 (Brown et al. 2020), are being used to automatically write long passages of highly readable text (fig. 8.4). The purpose of a language model is to learn the probabilistic relationship between linguistic elements like words, and then harness that knowledge to organize information in a novel way that is interpretable by people. When provided a prompt, GPT-3 and related models do their best to generate new corresponding text. A relentless stream of critiques of large language models have emanated from journalists, established writers, and the general public, all alleging that the generated text is far from what a human would write. But maybe that human quality isn't desirable in all cases—a more nuanced assessment might be warranted. In a piece that appeared in the literary magazine *n+1*, writer Meghan O'Gieblyn argues that the human mind and generative algorithms are both channels through which creativity flows from a mysterious source to an output that we appreciate:

Here is an award winning short story:

They Come From The Earth
By John Vickersonik

1. They come from the earth. They crawl through cracks in the sidewalks and find their way into basements, between walls and into all manner of dark places. They come from the earth when we open up the ground to dig a new foundation or plant a tree. They come from the earth when we disturb the dirt. They can't wait to get out.

FIGURE 8.4. Text generated by OpenAI's GPT-3 language model. This example was guided by a prompt provided by Silicon Valley entrepreneur Arram Sabeti in his investigations into the quality of algorithmic writing (Sabeti 2020).

Just as algorithms manipulate discrete symbols, creating new lines of code via endless combinations of os and 1s, so writers build stories by reassembling the basic tropes and structures that are encoded in the world's earliest myths, often—when things are going well—without fully realizing what they are doing. The most fertile creative states, like the most transcendent spiritual experiences, dissolve consciousness and turn the artist into an inanimate tool—a channel, a conduit. (O'Gieblyn 2021)

Large language models used to be the exclusive domain of the powerful technology companies that invented them, because of the enormous computational resources required for training. GPT-3, for instance, has 175 billion trainable parameters and was created using 45 terabytes of text (representing *billions* of pages) from the Internet. In the spirit of open-source development, the playing field has leveled with the appearance of communities of volunteer programmers who pool their coding abilities and cobble together freely available cloud infrastructure to match the level of technical sophistication found at major tech companies. In this mode, the EleutherAI project has produced a model with 6 billion parameters, and its members are optimistic that they will be able to match GPT-3's 175 billion parameters in the near future.[11] The major impetus has been the desire to put the technology under greater scrutiny, as concerns have surfaced about the lack of transparency in OpenAI's corporate development process. However, volunteer initiative also opens up possibilities for tailoring language models to fandoms and other virtualized communities for the generation of new writing that the textfile creators of the 1980s could only dream of.

How will all of these things come together in the metaverse? The practical scenario laid out by Silicon Valley is the virtual meeting space, where people in different geographic locations can interact in a way that is more natural and not as exhausting as what we currently experience using videoconferencing software like Zoom. While useful, this is rather boring and underestimates the potential of these technologies. Throughout this book we have seen grassroots efforts that exploit technologies in ways that the original creators did not anticipate. Clever programmers are waiting in the wings to reengineer the components of the metaverse to suit their needs. This, no doubt, will entail more expansive creative projects, from AI authored novels that reside in virtual libraries to virtual lives within the universe of a fandom. In general, users will experience myth cycles in new and highly imaginative ways. The most important piece in all of this may be the next generation of memes, which will not only be the product of AI (as some already are today) but also contain encapsulated AI systems that will make them autonomous agents. The 2-D static image is an inherently constraining medium, much as the pottery format was in ancient Greece. What could be more fun than passing around quirky virtual objects that can interact with the receiver?

Tempering the Problems That Inevitably Come Along for the Ride

Let's conclude this book with a few realistic recommendations for how to negotiate the fine line between creativity and destruction in a technological landscape where fake things abound. A forensic analysis of content, as noted in chapter 5, can detect manipulation, but the technique is a tool rather than a policy. When pressed to provide a response to the influx of invented information on the Internet, technologists are surprisingly inclined to want to "burn it all down," recommending extreme measures such as abandoning social media (Lanier 2018); tagging all content with badges reflecting "truthfulness" (Rosenthol et al. 2020); and even incarcerating the producers of fake content (Funke and Flamini 2020). This is silly. Nobody really wants these measures, and they're ripe for abuse by authoritarian governments and corporations—entities with a vested interest in controlling speech on the Internet. But neither can the creative communities be left to their own devices. Sometimes they go too far with their activities, reaching unintended audiences who misunderstand what is happening, or letting fiction drive their behavior, to the detriment of themselves and others.

Perhaps then we should first ask whether a specific technology associated with the creation of fake content can contribute to the common good of humanity in some way before reacting unthoughtfully to a perceived use. A sober voice in this context has been the philosopher Shannon Vallor, who has promoted a framework that places the notion of virtue at the center of any ethical assessment of a technology. Virtue, it can be argued, transcends specific problems, allowing one to gauge whether a technology promotes good, within a community and beyond, as an overarching effect. Vallor makes a powerful pitch in her book *Technology and the Virtues*:

A contemporary theory of ethics—that is, a theory of what counts as a good life for human beings—must include an explicit conception of how to live well with technologies, especially those which are still emerging and have yet to become settled, seamlessly embedded features of the human environment. Robotics and artificial intelligence, new social media and communications technologies, digital surveillance, and biomedical enhancement technologies are among those emerging innovations that will radically change the kinds of lives from which humans are able to choose in the 21st century and beyond. How can we choose wisely from the apparently endless options that emerging technologies offer? The choices we make will shape the future for our children, our societies, our species, and others who share our planet, in ways never before possible. Are we prepared to choose well? (Vallor 2016)

Apart from the question of the common good, some things appear inherently bad based on incidental evidence. For instance, it is a fact that in certain circumstances, political disinformation spread through social media has been used by political parties to target their opponents for their own gain. This action is not virtuous, because it exploits an out-group for the benefit of an in-group instead of providing a common good to both. But overgeneralizing from specific bad actions undermines other uses of such content and pulls us away from settings where we can indeed live well with a maligned technology. Following Vallor's advice in this case conjures what initially appears to be a radical question: Can disinformation ever be used for good? The answer, as it turns out, is yes.

Satire is an essential component of several of the escapades chronicled in this book. And much of the political disinformation found online—especially that which appears particularly deranged—is wholly satirical (fig. 8.5). Importantly, people are turning to alternative forms of expression like memes to make legitimate critiques that they no longer can in public spaces in the physical world. These critiques, one can argue, are virtuous, because they help effect corrections that push society back toward the good life. The point of satire has always been to expose folly in environments where speaking bluntly is problematic, as it is in most contemporary political forums. Similar conditions prevailed in Jonathan Swift's time, when he was writing about aristocrats feasting on Irish babies. A compelling case can be made that critics, especially the media, need to stop pedantically decrying all fake content on the Internet based on su-

Anonymous 12/15/20(Tue)16:15:36 No.842400478 ▶

>be beta virus
>have only a 0.02% mortality rate
>can only kill sickly old people (if lucky)
>get made fun of by more deadly viruses
>reluctantly decide to expose myself to the public anyway
>humans hide from me and change their entire lifestyles because of me
>virus bullies see
>mfw no longer beta thanks to cuck humans
Feel good man

FIGURE 8.5. A satirical "green text story" about the COVID-19 pandemic posted to the image board 4chan. Green text stories are brief anecdotes that leverage absurdity to make humorous commentary on contemporary social issues. Frequently transgressive, the writing found on 4chan is akin to much of the writing found in textfiles in the BBS and early Internet eras of computing (Coleman 2012). Superficial readings often lead to misunderstandings. For instance, based on the Pepe the Frog image and a literal reading of the text, this post appears to be far-right disinformation downplaying the severity of SARS-CoV-2, the virus that causes COVID-19. However, 4chan regulars might instead recognize this post as a cathartic story juxtaposing frustration with the ongoing pandemic and attitudes toward contemporary gender relations.

perficial interpretations of specific messaging. Easing up on how we talk about fake content in general can defuse some of the harsh rhetoric being thrown around by political parties as they take misinterpretations as the basis for arguments against their opponents.

There are two key problems associated with fakery on the Internet that we should worry about, because they can lead to bad actions in the real world. Both need to be addressed in a serious manner but haven't been adequately considered in the context of an effective response to the social problems associated with fake things. The first is related to the psychology of mistaking the fake for the real. Why do some people take drastic action based on obviously false information? While possibly rarer than commonly believed, cases are not difficult to find—the Wolverine Watchmen, for instance, a militia group that hatched a credible plot to kidnap the governor of Michigan based on Internet conspiracy theories related to the COVID-19 pandemic (Elinson et al. 2020). Millions of people were exposed to those same conspiracy theories—many obvious satires reflecting the frustration around confusing pandemic policies—but did not act on them. It remains a conundrum to social scientists why exactly this happens, but there is a straightforward mechanism to intervene when it does, before things get bad.

This involves improved in-group/out-group communication when an in-group is manufacturing fake content for an audience that can correctly interpret it, but an out-group that is not the intended audience is also consuming it and misunderstanding what it means. In a better world, the in-group corrects the out-group where appropriate, pointing out in clear language that something is not meant in a literal sense when it becomes apparent that trouble may be afoot. Crucially, the in-group should not antagonize a confused out-group by reinforcing bogus beliefs—a common trolling technique of no social value. In the case of the Wolverine Watchmen, federal investigators allegedly antagonized the group's members by reinforcing the conspiracy theories instead of steering them away from trouble (Garrison and Bensinger 2021).[12] Of course, one may have serious trouble if the common good is not on the mind of a content creator.

The second key problem is the psychology of actually becoming the character one plays online. This has some interplay with the problem above, in that it involves mistaking the fake for the real. But here, in a twist, the fake material is generated by the same person who becomes duped by it. This is a longstanding concern associated with mass media and one that predates the Internet. A notable example is the journalist Hunter S. Thompson, who gradually turned into the fictionalized, exaggerated version of himself found in his writing—much to the delight of his fans but at the expense of his sanity (Klein 2007). In essence, Thompson became his own brand. The more his real life resembled his drug fueled gonzo persona in *Fear and Loathing in Las Vegas*, the more engagement his professional career garnered. Needless to say, this did not end well for Thompson, yet the template persists for others to exploit.

While it is cliché to say that thanks to the reach of the Internet, *everyone* is now creating a personal brand to build an audience, there is nevertheless some truth to this. Recall the computer scientists from the University of Montreal who adopted guru-like personas after gaining notoriety on the Internet for their legitimate breakthroughs in artificial neural-network research. By leveraging that one success, they marketed themselves as experts who could solve any problem. A belief in the ability to tackle the impossible made them unlikely promoters of clairvoyance—a paranormal phenomenon that does not exist—as a mechanism to address climate change. The ethical problem in this instance is the drift away from the common good (addressing climate change in a serious way) and toward an activity that can do no more than elicit a superficial reaction (a generative algorithm producing sensational futures). There is a distinct potential for such tendencies to be exacerbated in the metaverse, as new identities are adopted more completely and aggressively. The solution here is to stay true to oneself when something serious is on the line.

Considering both of these problems, it would help if we could realize a cleaner distinction between what is true and what is false when it really matters. Complications in problem solving can arise when challenges are oversimplified in the context of a myth. Contemporary American politics is plagued by this. From the "stolen 2020 election" to "Russiagate," both political parties are expending tremendous amounts of time and energy on the construction of elaborate fictions that wholly subsume real challenges like the COVID-19 pandemic and an assertive Russian foreign policy. While this may make these problems perfectly manipulable, the wholly virtualized solutions that come out of such political mythology are not particularly helpful as policy.

Moreover, there is a troubling entanglement of celebrity and fantasy in government when one's political fortunes are tied to maximizing public engagement. This has led to a lack of problem-solving skill, policy experience, and overall seriousness in a sphere that sorely needs them at the moment. None of these are new concerns, but the Internet is essential to their visibility in the twenty-first century, where nearly all aspects of public life are channeled through platforms, apps, and algorithms. The choices we make about how these technologies are used to communicate with others are consequential for activities in a reality that is simultaneously physical and virtual. As Vallor urges, we must choose well for a successful future.

Converging on a Global Village

In considering the vast sea of fictions available on the Internet, it's time to leave the excessive pessimism of current discourse behind. McLuhan ended *The Medium is the Massage*, his manifesto for a radical transformation of the media, with these words from the mathematician and philosopher Alfred North Whitehead: "It is the business of the future to be dangerous." That is to say, risk is always present in the unknown, but we mustn't fold at the mere suggestion of a problem. Living dangerously keeps things interesting. The problems we have traced above are certainly manageable. We have norms for behavior, and we've had functional politics in the past; there is no good reason why we can't have them again. Instead of scolding the creators of fake content on the Internet, we must put what they are doing in proper context.

This book has made the case that the interested observer can better interpret what a digital fake represents through an understanding of the media that supports it. Indeed, McLuhan has asserted that "it is impossible to understand social and cultural changes without a knowledge of the workings of media" (McLuhan and Fiore 1967). Fake content on the Internet is intimately tied to broader social and cultural change. It is the expression of myth cycles propagating through communication technologies that are relatively new yet were widely adopted at the moment of their release. McLuhan believed that with the introduction of interactive media in the twentieth century, a "global village" was constituted, whereby the synthesis and exchange of information tightened the interconnectedness of previously dispersed villagers. This is a reframing of the socially binding nature of a myth cycle in technological terms, with a projected outcome that is far from pessimistic. As McLuhan maintains, "Electric technology fosters and encourages unification and involvement." Yet the excessive optimism of technologists in the twentieth century misaligned our expectations of what we might see on the Internet of the future. As we know from chapter 6, the global village needs its dark alleys to capture the full range of human experience. The ambiguities require us to think deeply about what is put in front of us.

Where does this leave the historian of technology faced with the project of the metaverse, which will be built on top of so much that is not true? Lévi-Strauss reminded us that history and mythology share a common cause in providing temporal continuity, if not the precise truth:

> I am not far from believing that, in our own societies, history has replaced mythology and fulfils the same function, that for societies without writing and without archives the aim of mythology is to ensure that as closely as possible—complete closeness is obviously impossible—the future will remain faithful to the present and to the past. (Lévi-Strauss 2017)

Thus even the historian finds himself out to sea, floating in a narrative of his own making.

NOTES

Chapter 1

1. This argument was made famous in the twentieth century by the classicist Milman Parry (Parry 1971). More recent scholarship has analyzed how this process itself has evolved over time to influence modern content (Frosio 2013).

2. While the discussion here is situated in the West, the phenomenon can be observed in Eastern pottery as well (Wells 1971).

3. Athenian vases were mass-produced in the hundreds of thousands in the sixth and fifth centuries BCE. Because of these enormous production runs, a trove of pottery has survived into the present (Mitchell 2009).

4. The Doge is a self-confident appearing Shiba Inu invoked to make light-hearted social commentary; see https://knowyourmeme.com/memes/doge. Wojak is a stock meme character that works in humorously tragic circumstances; see: https://knowyourmeme.com/memes/wojak.

5. https://knowyourmeme.com/memes/meme-man.

6. Neil deGrasse Tyson is one of the most prominent scientists promoting this misrepresentation of history, under the pretense of his rationally grounded expertise: https://www.youtube.com/watch?v=xRx6f8lv6qc.

Chapter 2

1. Lecture given at the University of Notre Dame, 4.11.19.

2. "Robert Osband" is possibly a pseudonym; Bootleg's real name is unrecorded, but he retains legendary status within the computing world to this day for his knowledge of the phone system, thirst for strong drink, and many (alleged) brushes with the law.

3. The name blends the terms *phreak* and *hack*.

4. Interview with Adam O'Donnell, 10.21.20.

5. The science-fiction writer Bruce Sterling chronicled this case in his book *The Hacker Crackdown* (Sterling, 1992). The severity of Grant's crimes was vastly overstated by federal prosecutors.

6. Interview with Chris Goggans, 10.23.20.

7. The Legion of Doom's feud with rival hacking group Masters of Decep-

tion was unfolding at the same time the *Dateline* episode aired (Slatalla and Quittner 1995).

8. Under the guidance of its older members like Chris Tucker, the Cult of the Dead Cow adapted the street theater and pranks of the yippies and other counterculture groups of the 1960s and 1970s to cyberspace (Menn 2020). This group is still active, and it maintains a web presence at https://cultdeadcow .com/.

9. The *Phrack* report on HoHoCon 1992 records that event's mayhem, including the hackers tapping into the radio frequencies of the hotel security staff, ordering sex workers using stolen credit card numbers, launching a drunken raid on the hotel kitchen, and receiving tips on life from Bootleg, the biker, who had parked himself at the hotel's bar. While some of this material is certainly embellished, it's probably not too far from the truth.

10. The very beginning of the HoHoCon 1992 report (fig. 2.1) alludes to the undue attention ("turbulence from the authorities") that the hacker scene was receiving from federal law enforcement. Overzealous prosecution of computer crime was common in this period, with the government using exaggerated claims to pursue cases. Information asymmetry was a large part of this, because federal law enforcement and government lawyers lacked in-depth technical knowledge of computer security and could not, in many cases, determine what was and was not possible.

11. A reverse WHOIS lookup of the IP addresses provided in the HoHoCon 1992 report reveals that as of this writing they are still owned by the Department of Defense.

12. Adam Curtis's 2016 film *HyperNormalization* describes the government's actions here as a primary example of "perception management," the practice of distracting people from the complexities of the real world.

13. Interview with Jason Scott, 10.2.20.

14. Authorship attributed to the "Legion of Doom EFT Division."

15. War dialing is an old technique, used by computer hackers in the 1980s and 1990s, whereby a computer's modem is instructed to dial many thousands of phone numbers, in an attempt to find other computers connected to the phone system. In some cases, computers that were discovered could be used as gateways to larger computer networks.

16. Source: http://www.hpmuseum.net/display_item.php?hw=106.

17. No record of this investigation exists publicly. This account is based solely on the interview with Goggans.

18. Interview with Margaret DeFleur, 11.17.20.

19. Among the authors of these textfiles were renowned computer-security expert and former DARPA program manager Peiter Zatko (aka Mudge) and former US Congressional representative and presidential candidate Beto O'Rourke (aka Psychedelic Warlord).

20. Interview with Joseph Menn, 10.6.20.

21. Interview with Michael Kubecka, 9.18.20.

22. A notable example is an urban legend that UPC barcodes were supposedly encoded with the number 666, the mark of the beast (Metz 2012), the source of which is the 1972 evangelical Christian film *A Thief in the Night* (directed by Donald W. Thompson), which popularized the notion of a rapture of the faithful during the end times among evangelical church groups.

23. "Foo fighter" is synonymous with "UFO." "Foo" is a nonsense term common in the 1940s that was popularized by the comic *Smokey Stover*. Incidentally, the term was in widespread use by computer programmers in the 1990s as a placeholder for various (often unimportant) constructs in code.

24. Jason Scott has compiled an extensive archive of UFO textfiles from the 1980s and 1980s on his website textfiles.com: http://textfiles.com/ufo/.

25. Video recording of HoHoCon 1993 provided by Michael Kubecka.

26. Cult of the Dead Cow Textfile #253 "Better, Stronger, Faster" (http://textfiles.com/groups/CDC/cDc-0253.txt) Published 5/1/1994. The file was also published in issue 45 of *Phrack*, released 3/30/1994. Note that these publication dates are well after HoHoCon 1993, which was held in December of the preceding year. One can assume that the textfile went through further rounds of editing before its official release. Most hackers would have encountered the file in this final published form.

27. Kubecka was referring to the appointment of Admiral Bobby Ray Inman by President Bill Clinton in December of 1993 (the same month HoHoCon 1993 was held). Inman held a string of influential posts within the US intelligence community from the 1970s through the 1990s. Coincidental to our story, he withdrew his nomination for secretary of defense in January 1994 in one of the most baffling political displays of the Clinton administration, blaming attacks from the news media on a sudden reluctance to continue serving the government. (Devroy 1994). The exact circumstances of the withdrawal were never explained.

28. A classic example is the apocryphal story *The Scariest Number in the World*, which appeared in the December 1984 issue of *2600* magazine (Goldstein 2009).

29. This incident is fake, but Grissom was injured in a serious accident during the *Mercury-Redstone 4* mission when the hatch to his spacecraft opened prematurely after landing in the ocean, flooding the capsule and nearly drowning him.

30. This quote is attributed to "Samuel Butler." Whether this is supposed to be the poet, novelist, or somebody else is unclear. A source outside the textfile cannot be located.

31. Kubecka remembered Goggans appearing in the *Dateline* episode. The *Phrack* report on HoHoCon 1992 indicated that only Chasin appeared. In their talk at HoHoCon 1993, Chasin mentioned that both he and Goggans appeared in the episode, while Goggans acknowledged only Chasin's appearance. The introduction to "Better, Stronger, Faster" stated that Goggans was interviewed in the episode. In the footage of the episode obtained during re-

search for this book, no person identifiable as Goggans appears. When interviewed for this book, Goggans provided a longer explanation of what happened to him during the filming of the episode (see the next section).

32. The Cult of the Dead Cow mocked this practice by creating a Mad Libs–style template for lazy journalists who wanted to write pieces on hackers: http://textfiles.com/groups/CDC/cDc-0360.html.

33. Particularly stinging was an episode of *The Geraldo Rivera Show* that aired September 30, 1991. Rivera interviewed Craig Neidorf (aka Knight Lightning), a hacker who had been raided and charged under the Computer Fraud and Abuse Act after he published a technical manual detailing the operation of the 911 system in *Phrack*. This document had been recovered by Legion of Doom members during their exploration of BellSouth computer systems. BellSouth claimed massive damages associated with the publication of the document, which was later determined to contain publicly available information, thus undermining the government's case. Throughout the interview, Rivera described Neidorf variously as a "mad hacker" and "America's most wanted computer hacker" and accused him of crimes that he did not commit, including breaking into the 911 system. This interview was conducted after Neidorf had been acquitted of any wrongdoing. A partial transcript is available here: http://computer-underground-digest.org/CUDS3/cud 337.txt.

34. In the footage obtained for this book, Phillips appears only in his capacity as anchor and does not interview Quentin, Grant, or Chasin. Those interviews are conducted by Jon Scott.

35. The *Los Angeles Times*, however, took the bait (Farley 1999). The persistence of this satellite myth eventually caused some hackers to speak out against it. One notable skeptical voice was Cris Thomas (aka Space Rogue) https://www.spacerogue.net/wordpress/?p=223.

36. Interview with Luke Benfey, 9.18.20. This story is also related in the book *Cult of the Dead Cow* (Menn 2020).

37. GO-FORCE! existed on the Internet as a parody website maintained by Anthony: https://web.archive.org/web/19970609030115/lopht.com/~tfish/go -force.html.

38. Interview with Sam Anthony, 9.18.20.

39. Interview with Sean Lawson, 12.4.20. This concept is drawn from the Nobel Prize–winning work of the Icelandic novelist Halldór Laxness and has been applied to ethnography (Fortun 2011).

Chapter 3

1. "To let everyone become beautiful easily" is the English tagline of the company: https://www.meitu.com/en/.

2. But not all. While the Internet is heavily surveilled by the state in the United States (Greenwald 2014), strong protections for speech are guaranteed by the Free Speech Clause of the First Amendment, especially for political

speech. This is an accelerant to creativity. The Chinese Internet is heavily censored, which is a limiting factor for what it can achieve culturally.

3. The historian and curator Gao Chu and the photographer Fu Yu discussed similar ideas with respect to twentieth-century Chinese photo manipulation in their conversation published in the *Trans Asia Photography Review* (Chu and Yu 2015).

4. An analogous observation was made by Rebecca L. Stein in reference to the paradox of increasing human rights abuses in the midst of so much photographic evidence of them. There is never a guarantee of a single, truthful, interpretation of a photo (Stein 2017).

5. Andrew Davidhazy, a professor at the Rochester Institute of Technology (a school tightly linked to the Eastman Kodak Company), provides a more exhaustive catalog of techniques in his report "Special Effects Photography" (Davidhazy 1993), which appeared near the end of the film era of photography.

6. Photography handbooks from the nineteenth and early twentieth centuries provide instructions and advice for retouching. These include *Photographic Mosaics*, as well as the 1898 volume *On the Art of Retouching Photographic Negatives* (Johnson 1898) and the 1901 volume *Finishing the Negative* (Brown 1901). Jocelyn Sears has written an excellent introduction to this form of photo retouching for the modern reader (Sears 2016).

7. A tagline on the company's website: https://gradient.photo/.

8. The photographer William H. Mulmer pioneered both the technique and the supernatural sales pitch (Waldorf 2021).

9. Interview with Edward Delp, 10.7.20.

10. Rocha et al. have enumerated the different techniques available for digital photo manipulation (Rocha et al. 2011).

11. Still in widespread use today and available at https://imagemagick.org.

12. John Knoll's Industrial Light & Magic biography chronicles his early life: https://web.archive.org/web/20201001120441/https://www.lucasfilm.com/leadership/john-knoll/.

13. John Knoll recreated this demo in a 2010 video produced by Adobe and released on YouTube: https://www.youtube.com/watch?v=Tda7jCwvSzg.

14. Comparisons can be drawn to the famous "Lena" test image that depicted the November 1972 *Playboy* centerfold, Swedish model Lena Forsén. Use of the Lena image within computer science has ceased due to its blatantly sexist overtones (Eismann 2018).

15. https://www.somethingawful.com/photoshop-phriday/.

16. Several meme histories have been published over the past decade, including Limor Shifman's *Memes in Digital Culture* (Shifman 2013), Ryan M. Milner's *The World Made Meme: Public Conversations and Participatory Media* (Milner 2018), and An Xiao Mina's *Memes to Movements: How the World's Most Viral Media is Changing Social Protest and Power* (Mina 2019).

Chapter 4

1. As a sequence of button presses on a video game controller: Up, Up, Down, Down, Left, Right, Left, Right, B, A. This cheat code is so well known that it persists to this day as a meme within the gamer and retrocomputing communities.

2. Interview with Jason Scott, 10.2.20.

3. Scott discussed the handoff of the board to Dave Ferret in this message about the state of The Works from the mid-1990s, which provides historical context on the way underground infrastructure was managed: http://textfiles .com/bbs/works.phk. Testimonials by various Boston-area hackers about their time on The Works in the early 1990s also mentioned the management of the board (Fisher 2018).

4. According to former members, it remains somewhat unclear how exactly the government discovered the Lopht. The office of Senator Fred Thompson was confirmed to have been involved, yet rumors circulated that it was Richard Clarke, a senior national-security figure who served in both Bush administrations and the Clinton administration, who first identified the group (Fisher 2018). Several Lopht members were involved in work supported by the federal government in their day jobs, according to their own testimony— meaning they were likely known quantities to several agencies charged with computer security. These included Brian Hassick (aka Brian Oblivion), Peiter Zatko (aka Mudge), Paul Nash (aka Silicosis), and Chris Wysopal (aka Weld Pond); all did stints at the Boston-area defense contractor BBN (now Raytheon BBN Technologies). Nash noted the BBN connection in a post on *Hacker News*: https://news.ycombinator.com/item?id=17170095.

5. Interview with Cris Thomas, 1.14.21.

6. Stack Overflow is a popular software development community for programming questions and answers: https://stackoverflow.com/.

7. Textfiles were formatted using the American Standard Code for Information Interchange (ASCII), more commonly known as "plaintext." Nothing was available in these files except for the characters found on a keyboard.

8. According to the anthropologist Gabriella Coleman, as late as the early 2000s, the know-how for exploiting security vulnerabilities at federal agencies was coming not from within the government but from textfiles produced by the hacking scene. Famed computer-security expert and ex-NSA hacker Charlie Miller (Bogan 2012) told Coleman that he gained his knowledge by reading the underground hacking zine *Phrack*. (Interview with Gabriella Coleman, 11.20.20.)

9. Kicking this off was Comsec Data Security, one of the earliest computer-security firms, which was cofounded by members of the hacking group Legion of Doom and was a direct outgrowth of the textfile scene (New York Times News Service 1992).

10. Scott has archived a significant number of textfiles on hacking and phreaking on his website: http://textfiles.com.

11. Commenting on BBS and early Internet textfile pranks, Jason Scott noted, "You can see so much of Abbie Hoffman in these things." The idea that any serious topic could easily be rendered a joke—one that shrewd observers would recognize as social commentary but would be mischaracterized by those with a superficial understanding—was very intriguing to hackers and phreaks.

12. The number 2600, the frequency in hertz that the blue box operated at, carries particular weight in underground writing about technology up to the present day.

13. Five versions of the Blotto box instructions can be found in Scott's phone-phreaking box archive (http://textfiles.com/phreak/BOXES/) and another in his directory of files associated with the classic counterculture text *The Anarchist Cookbook* (http://cd.textfiles.com/group42/ANARCHY/COOK BOOK/). The urine box, which reportedly could induce seizures in somebody answering their phone, is a variation on the same theme and is often mentioned alongside the Blotto box when phreaks and hackers recall notable early textfiles. It is unclear which box came first. Luke Benfey (aka Deth Vegetable) remembered Tom Dell (aka Soylent), a textfile writer associated with the group Anarchy Incorporated and founder of the shock-content website rotten .com, as having something to do with the creation of the urine box. Scott also suspected that some part of the prank was the product of Anarchy Incorporated.

14. The longform version of the textfile credits a phreak using the handle "The Traveler" (http://textfiles.com/phreak/BOXES/blotto), while an apocryphal addition to *The Anarchist Cookbook* credits "The Jolly Roger," the handle that replaced true author William Powell on the digital edition of that famous text.

15. The Blotto box was mentioned as one of the most interesting examples of a fake textfile in interviews conducted for this book with Scott, Benfey, and Michael Kubecka (aka Omega).

16. Examples include using the letters "ph" (representing phreak / hack) instead of the letter "f," using "warez" for software, and the number 31337, which is a rough numeric transliteration of the word "elite." For a nonexhaustive yet still extensive catalog of various hacking terms from the era, see the *Hacker's Encyclopedia*, by Andy Ryder (aka Logik Bomb): https://insecure .org/stf/HackersEncyclope2.0.html.

17. http://www.textfiles.com/groups/METALCOMMUNICATIONS.

18. http://textfiles.com/magazines/HOE.

19. The blueprints for such attacks were first published as textfiles by the Lopht (Zatko 1995) and *Phrack* (Levy 1996).

20. In the 1990s, Levy was outspoken about the emerging security threat of disinformation on the Internet, making prescient comments on the matter in a profile that was published in *Phrack* (Levy 1997). This was likely galvanized by his experience moderating Bugtraq.

21. In 1998, *Phrack* editor-in-chief Mike Schiffman (aka route) temporarily took over moderation duties of Bugtraq while Levy was away on vacation. The list received a sudden influx of bogus posts from false email addresses, which Schiffman inadvertently believed were legitimate. Schiffman was an expert programmer and was widely regarded as one of the planet's top hackers. In his apology to the list's subscribers, he declared, "I am like a substitute teacher and the kids aren't being very nice." See the following posts: https://seclists.org/bugtraq/1998/Aug/197 and https://seclists.org/bugtraq/1998/Aug/202.

22. The database went offline when the project ended in 2016. Brian Martin relayed the information on OSVDB found in this chapter when interviewed on 1.5.21.

23. File transfer protocol: a now mostly obsolete way to transfer files on the Internet. It used to be possible for anyone to connect to public FTP servers and browse the files that were stored on them; Internet relay chat: a text-based message transfer system that was popular before multimedia chat systems like Slack and Discord were developed. Following the BBS era, IRC became the primary gathering place for hackers to socialize online.

24. https://seclists.org/bugtraq/1998/Aug/166.

25. Given the ease with which an email address can be spoofed (a security weakness that was well documented in early textfiles: http://textfiles.com/hacking/INTERNET/smtp.txt), it's quite possible this address is not real.

26. https://seclists.org/bugtraq/1998/Aug/168.

27. Matt Goerzen and Gabriella Coleman have traced the evolution of the computer hacking scene in this period, specifically focusing on the pivot from underground hacking to business (Goerzen and Coleman 2022).

28. Security expert Bruce Schneier was an early skeptic concerning the claims made by the nascent computer-security industry and advocated for a more measured approach that acknowledged the pervasive risk of attack (Schneier 2004).

29. Representative of this type of activity were attacks against *Phrack* editor Schiffman, one of the first whitehat hackers to join the corporate world in the 1990s. In his words, he "got owned a few times." In one particularly embarrassing incident, which he noted upset his girlfriend, the blackhat group H4GiS hacked into his phone company and proxied his phone number, redirecting calls to a number they controlled. For a period, Schiffman's friends and family reached a voicemail message saying that he had died of AIDS when they attempted to call him. His SoldierX (a website that archives information about the hacker scene) biography alludes to this incident (https://www.soldierx.com/hdb/route-daemon9-ms). Interview with Mike Schiffman, 10.10.20.

30. Interview with representative from Gobbles Security, 10.19.20. This subject requested to remain anonymous while speaking on the record.

31. While these hackers were technically underground, they often made

appearances at hacker meet-ups and conferences, and the scene was small enough that whitehat and blackhat hackers often knew each other in real life.

32. Watt and a representative from Gobbles Security shared critical thoughts on the growing commercialization of the hacking scene in a panel held at DEF CON 10: https://www.youtube.com/watch?v=DAJSxOzrD1g&t=254s.

33. Interview with Stephen Watt, 10.15.20.

34. The Lopht sustained itself in its early years by selling old computers and parts at the MIT flea market in Cambridge, MA (Fisher 2018).

35. For instance, the blackhat hacker turned neo-Nazi Andrew Auernheimer (aka Weev) helped convert blackhat communication strategies into more coordinated political campaigns for the far right. In addition to trolling activities such as sending white supremacist flyers to unsecured printers at various universities, Auernheimer was a system administrator for *The Daily Stormer*, a now dark-web-only outlet that blended noxious humor with racist content (Gutman 2018).

36. http://web.textfiles.com/ezines/BoG/; http://web.textfiles.com/ezines /EL8/el8.0.txt; https://elly.town/m/zines/hono; https://www.exploit-db.com/e zines/kr5hou2zh4qtebqk.onion/b4bo; http://textfiles.com/magazines/BOW; http://web.textfiles.com/ezines/HAXoR; https://web.archive.org/web/201205 12133929http://gonullyourself.org/ezines/ZFo.

37. https://web.archive.org/web/20120512133929/http://gonullyourself .org/ezines/ZFo.

38. A mirror of the Phrack High Council Website (phrack.ru) is still online via the Internet Archive: https://web.archive.org/web/20060813105812/http: //phrack.ru.

39. http://lists.jammed.com/vuln-dev/2001/11/0129.html.

40. Scriptkids: unskilled neophyte hackers who did not understand how the hacking tools they would run worked.

41. Interview with Adam O'Donnell, 10.21.20.

42. https://seclists.org/bugtraq/2003/Jan/173.

43. The RIAA released a statement characterizing the Gobbles advisory and the supposed involvement of the industry organization as a hoax (Lemos 2003).

44. Both Julian Assange and Snowden had ties to the computer underground. The former was active in the Australian hacking scene in 1980s and 1990s under the handle "Mendax" (Wattercutter 2012), and the latter as an avid user of the tools that came out of the hacking scene to securely transmit information point-to-point, which would be essential for communicating with journalists (Hruska 2015).

45. https://seclists.org/bugtraq/2002/Apr/429.

46. https://seclists.org/bugtraq/2002/Jun/282.

47. https://www.exploit-db.com/ezines/kr5hou2zh4qtebqk.onion/GoD/GoD .txt.

Chapter 5

1. Farid's long career in media forensics was chronicled in the *New Yorker* (Rothman 2018).

2. Interview with Nasir Memon, 10.18.20.

3. The Melissa virus was a fairly benign macro virus targeting Microsoft Windows users via email. David L. Smith, its author, claimed that he intended the virus to be a "harmless joke" in tribute to a Florida-based exotic dancer that he knew. Prosecutors alleged that the virus had caused $80 million in damages. Smith ended up serving twenty months in prison for his joke (Gibian 2019).

4. Many of those videos were pornographic, but occasionally a more interesting political deepfake would surface—for instance, this video where comedian Jordan Peele took over Barack Obama's face and voice: https://www.youtube.com/watch?v=bE1KWpoX9Hk.

5. Both Memon and Farid had attempted to commercialize their research before the deepfake problem emerged. Memon formed the company Digital Assembly in 2006, which ceased operations in 2015. Farid founded Fourandsix Technologies in 2014; its technology was acquired by Truepic in 2018. He currently serves as an adviser to the company.

6. Pushing back against this hysteria, technology ethicists Britt Paris and Joan Donovan have noted, "The high-profile deepfakes cases . . . are just a fraction of the examples that exist." Crude manipulations, or "cheap fakes," are a bigger threat (Paris and Donovan 2019).

7. Google Scholar searches using the query "image forensics" (the term used before "media forensics" entered common use around 2015).

8. Google Scholar search using the query "media forensics".

9. The journal: https://signalprocessingsociety.org/publications-resources/ieee-transactions-information-forensics-and-security. Meetings include the IEEE Workshop on Information Forensics and Security (https://wifs2021.lirmm.fr), the IEEE International Workshop on Biometrics and Forensics (https://www.iwbf2021.com), the Workshop on Image and Video Forensics (http://users.cs.cf.ac.uk/Paul.Rosin/IVF2019), and the Workshop on Media Forensics (https://sites.google.com/view/mediaforensics2021).

10. https://knowyourmeme.com/memes/911-tourist-guy.

11. Now known as the Committee for Skeptical Inquiry, which publishes the magazine *Skeptical Inquirer.*

12. Interview with Jessica Fridrich, 10.29.20.

13. Interview with Edward Delp, 10.7.20.

14. See the Crunchbase business profile for Rhoads: https://www.crunchbase.com/person/geoff-rhoads.

15. See Digimarc's self-published history: https://www.digimarc.com/about/history-of-digimarc.

16. Interview with Min Wu, 11.17.20.

17. Interview with Hany Farid, 11.5.20.

18. Interview with Siwei Lyu, 11.18.20.

19.. Farid served as an expert witness for the state in one of these cases (Court of Appeals of Ohio, Eleventh District 2007). In a separate child pornography case, Boland, acting in the capacity of an attorney for the defendant, filed a memorandum in the Supreme Court of Ohio intended to undermine Farid's credibility as a witness under the Frye and Daubert standards (Supreme Court of Ohio 2008).

20. But PRNU wasn't a perfect indicator. Lukáš et al. conceded that if the person creating an image "possesses enough skill in signal processing," they could intentionally remove or change the pattern noise in an image, making identification impossible.

21. Cole's investigative strategy was covered by CNN in 2013 (Coutlim 2013).

22. https://retractionwatch.com/retracted-coronavirus-covid-19-papers.

23. Yet even this scenario, which appears clear-cut, can be subject to multiple modes of interpretation. Perceived instances of scientific misconduct can be intentional acts of social critique, not altogether different from the actions taken against NBC News by the computer hackers featured in chapter 2 (Mody et al. 2020).

Chapter 6

1. The film is frequently referenced in textfiles from the 1980s and 1990s, and various elements from the film surface in the computer hacking subculture. For instance, a member of Lopht Heavy Industries adopted the handle "Brian Oblivion," which he used as his official identifier when testifying before Congress in 1998.

2. https://web.archive.org/web/20151107203215/http://www.rotten.com/diana/di-acc.html.

3. https://web.archive.org/web/20150317050619/http://www.rotten.com/about/press.html.

4. https://web.archive.org/web/20050516235424/http://www.rotten.com/FAQ/.

5. This statement wasn't just posturing. Dell was so familiar with fake content that it became possible for him to call out other outlets for publishing it as if it were real. Shortly after the 9/11 attacks in the United States the *Times* and the BBC published bogus nuclear weapons plans purportedly compiled by Al-Qaeda. Dell correctly identified the plans as having originally been published as an article in a satirical magazine, *Annals of Improbable Research*, in 1979. That article was reworked over the years into various textfiles that circulated around BBSs and the Internet (Hari 2001).

6. As remarked in the notes to chapter 4, Luke Benfey and Jason Scott both believed that Dell played some role in the creation of the urine box parody phreaking file—one of the most notable textfiles ever.

7. Interview with Samuel Anthony 9.18.20; interview with Luke Benfey 9.18.20.

8. http://software.bbsdocumentary.com/IBM/DOS/WAFFLE.

9. http://protovision.textfiles.com/groups/ANARCHYINC.

10. https://textfiles.meulie.net/groups/ANARCHYINC/300murdr.hum.

11. http://protovision.textfiles.com/groups/ANARCHYINC/reality!.hum.

12. While at Netscape, Dell invented the popular Java Archive (JAR) file format used to distribute Java programs (https://www-archive.mozilla.org/projects/security/pki/nss/contributors).

13. Interview with Samuel Anthony, 9.18.20.

14. In 2015 Poole sold 4chan to 2channel, the Japanese site that originally inspired him to create his own. While the sum was not disclosed, the *New York Times* reported that Poole "has treated the message board more as a hobby than a business." He then decamped for Google, where he made contributions to that company's social media efforts (Isaac 2015).

15. Troubling human rights abuses from around the globe can be summoned in an instant, from torture perpetrated in Kazakh prisons (Radio Free Europe/Radio Liberty 2019) to gruesome acts committed during Syria's civil war (Ana Press 2013). By policy, such videos may be in violation of YouTube's content guidelines (Google 2022). In practice, the platform is well stocked with depictions of violence—possibly because it is very difficult to ascertain whether a video depicts a real incident.

16. See (Moretta and Buodo 2021). Compulsive porn viewership is commonly assumed to be largely relegated to adolescent males, yet it is actually a universal phenomenon consistent with McLuhan's theory of communications mediums (Schofield 2021).

17. The cover (https://vhscollector.com/movie/faces-death-0) of the *Faces of Death* VHS tape claimed that the film was "Banned in 46 Countries." This was not true, but after a dismal box office showing, the forbidden aura around *Faces of Death* gave the film new life as a popular rental title.

Chapter 7

1. For instance, the film *Jurassic Park* is nearly thirty years old, but its special effects still look good.

2. They aren't very accurate, according to National Public Radio (Neuman 2012).

3. A reliable model for this exists in computational neuroscience (Lotter et al. 2017).

4. Aquinas addresses superstition in divinations in Question 95 of his *Summa Theologica* (Freddoso 2018).

5. Following the publication of their papers, the authors created a website, https://thisclimatedoesnotexist.com, which allowed users to upload their own photos for a glimpse into the future. Rhetorically, this site is reminiscent of rotten.com (chapter 6), with ambiguous and conflicting language found throughout. For instance, the site's introduction states, "The following experience gives you a window into the current effects of climate change on the

lives of millions of people around the world, except that window looks out onto your street and the places you love to frequent." Yet browsing deeper into the site, one can find an acknowledgement that the images created by the AI "are not real." Importantly, the generated climates do exist, but as digital artifacts, not manifestations of the earth's atmosphere.

Chapter 8

1. Google Books Ngram Viewer search using the query "imagination".

2. "Metaverse" is a term borrowed from the science fiction writer Neal Stephenson's thriller *Snow Crash*.

3. https://obvious-art.com/.

4. https://sites.google.com/zalando.de/cvfad2021/home?authuser=0.

5. Parikh's work is primarily released via Twitter: https://twitter.com/devi parikh/status/1017213261765230593.

6. https://www.artblocks.io; https://braindrops.cloud.

7. https://www.artbreeder.com.

8. For example, consider *Star Wars*, a franchise valued at $68 billion (Morris 2019).

9. https://www.artstation.com.

10. An idea promoted early on by the Brown Pattern Theory group (Mumford and Desolneux 2010), and then taken up by the likes of NVIDIA with their StyleGAN work (Karras 2019).

11. https://www.eleuther.ai.

12. This is not altogether dissimilar to what unfolded in the Bennewitz affair covered in chapter 2, or the many cases of government entrapment in suspected terror plots that occurred after the 9/11 attacks on the United States.

BIBLIOGRAPHY

Abad-Santos, Alex. 2018. "Why People Are (Mostly) Joking about Eating Tide Pods." *Vox*, Jan. 19. https://www.vox.com/2018/1/4/16841674/tide-pods-eating-meme-tide-pod-challenge.

Adlington, William, and Stephen Gaselee, eds. 1922. *The Golden Ass*. London: Heinemann.

Ai4. 2020. "Media Integrity in a Post-Truth World: Seeing Is Believing?" Jan. 27. https://www.youtube.com/watch?v=aAAn5pdoojw.

Allison, Graham. 2017. "What Xi Jinping Wants." *Atlantic*, May 31.

Amaral, Kimberly. 1999. "The Digital Imaging Revolution: Legal Implications and Possible Solutions." https://www.whoi.edu/science/B/people/kamaral/digitalimaging.html.

Ana Press. 2013. "Leaked Video Shows Alawite Officers Being Tortured by Syrian Forces." Apr. 18. https://www.youtube.com/watch?v=zGmVWJmzEQE.

Anderson, Janna, and Lee Rainie. 2017. "The Future of Truth and Misinformation Online." *Pew Research Center*, Oct. 19. https://www.pewresearch.org/internet/2017/10/19/the-future-of-truth-and-misinformation-online/.

Anderson, Lessley. 2012. "Snuff: Murder and Torture on the Internet, and the People Who Watch It." *The Verge*, June 13. https://www.theverge.com/2012/6/13/3076557/snuff-murder-torture-internet-people-who-watch-it.

Andreessen, Marc. 2007. "Pmarca Guide to Career Planning: Opportunity." *Pmarca Blog*, Sept. 30. https://fictivekin.github.io/pmarchive-jekyll//guide_to_career_planning_part1.html.

——. 2011. "Why Software Is Eating the World." *Wall Street Journal*, Aug. 20.

Arendt, Hannah, 1967. "Truth and Politics." *New Yorker*, Feb. 25.

Aristotle. 1938. *Aristotle: Categories. On Interpretation. Prior Analytics*. Trans. H. P. Cooke and Hugh Tredennick. Loeb Classical Library No. 325. Cambridge, MA: Harvard Univ. Press.

Atwood, Jeff. 2008. "Our Hacker Odyssey." *Coding Horror*, Dec. 7. https://blog.codinghorror.com/our-hacker-odyssey.

——. 2012. "I Was a Teenage Hacker." *Coding Horror*, Aug. 8. https://blog.codinghorror.com/i-was-a-teenage-hacker.

Ball-Rokeach, Sandra, and Melvin DeFleur. 1976. "A Dependency Model of

Mass-media Effects." *Communication Research* 3 (1): 3–21.

Banerji, Gunjan, Juliet Chung, and Caitlin McCabe. 2021. "GameStop Mania Reveals Power Shift on Wall Street, and the Pros Are Reeling." *Wall Street Journal*, Jan. 27.

Barkun, Michael. 2013. *A Culture of Conspiracy*. Berkeley: Univ. of California Press.

Barlow, John Perry. 1990. "Being in Nothingness." *Mondo 2000* (2).

———. 2007. "Is There a There in Cyberspace?" *UTNE Reader*, Oct. 9. https://www.utne.com/community/isthereathereincyberspace.

Beckett, Lois. 2021. "The Misogynist Incel Movement Is Spreading. Should It Be Classified as a Terror Threat?" *Guardian*, Mar. 3. https://www.theguardian.com/lifeandstyle/2021/mar/03/incel-movement-terror-threat-canada.

Beran, Dale. 2019. *It Came from Something Awful*. New York: All Points.

Beuken, W. A. 1978. "I Samuel 28: The Prophet as 'Hammer of Witches.'" *Journal for the Study of the Old Testament* 3 (6): 3–17.

Blankenship, Lloyd. 1986. "The Conscience of a Hacker." *Phrack*, Sept. 25. http://phrack.org/issues/7/3.html.

Blanz, Volker, Kristina Scherbaum, Thomas Vetter, and Hans-Peter Seidel. 2004. "Exchanging Faces in Images." *Computer Graphics Forum* 23 (3): 669–76.

Bogan, Jesse. 2012. "Wildwood Man Is Renowned for Hacking, Cybersecurity Skills." *St. Louis Post-Dispatch*, June 18.

Bonderud, Doug. 2020. "Zipping Past the Zettabyte Era: What's Next for the Internet and Digital Technology?" *Now*, Oct. 14. https://now.northropgrumman.com/zipping-past-the-zettabyte-era-whats-next-for-the-internet/.

Bosker, Bianca. 2020. "Why Witchcraft Is on the Rise." *Atlantic*, Mar. 15.

Bostock, John, ed. 1855. *The Natural History*. London: Taylor and Francis.

Bowyer, Kevin W., Michael C. King, Walter J. Scheirer, and Kushal Vangara. 2020. "The 'Criminality From Face' Illusion." *IEEE Transactions on Technology and Society* 1 (4): 175–83.

Breen, Benjamin. 2015. "Into the Mystic. From Stonehenge to Silicon Valley: How Technology Nurtured New Age Ideas in a World Supposedly Stripped of Its Magic." *Aeon*, Apr. 7. https://aeon.co/essays/will-new-age-ideas-help-us-in-the-high-tech-future.

Brown, George. 1901. *Finishing the Negative*. New York: Tennant and Ward.

Brown, Janelle. 2001. "The Internet's Public Enema No. 1." *Salon*, Mar. 5. https://www.salon.com/2001/03/05/rotten_2/.

Brown, Tom, Benjamin Mann, Nick Ryder, Melanie Subbiah, Jared D. Kaplan, Prafulla Dhariwal, Arvind Neelakantan, et al. 2020. "Language Models Are Few-Shot Learners." *Advances in Neural Information Processing Systems*.

Bruenig, Elizabeth. 2021. "Modern Porn Education Is Totally Unprepared for Modern Porn." *Atlantic*, July 18.

Brugioni, Dino A. 1999. *Photo Fakery*. Dulles, VA: Brassey's.

Bump, Philip. 2020. "Trumpworld's Latest Effort to Undermine the Russia

Probe May Be Even Less Substantive Than Prior Attempts." *Washington Post*, Oct. 7.

———. 2021. "A Year After Trump Said Coronavirus Was 'Under Control,' a Look Back at the First News Stories." *Washington Post*, Feb. 24.

Burke, Lilah. 2019. "Your Interview with AI." *Inside Higher Ed*, Nov. 4. https://www.insidehighered.com/news/2019/11/04/ai-assessed-job-interviewing-grows-colleges-try-prepare-students.

Burton, Tara Isabella. 2019. "The Rise of Progressive Occultism." *American Interest*, June 7. https://www.the american-interest.com/2019/06/07/the-rise-of-progressive-occultism/.

Campbell, Joseph. 2008. *The Hero with a Thousand Faces*. Novato: New World Library.

Carroll, Noël. 1987. "The Nature of Horror." *Journal of Aesthetics and Art Criticism* 46 (1): 51–59.

Chayka, Kyle. 2022. "Have iPhone Cameras Become Too Smart?" *New Yorker*, Mar. 18.

Christie's. 2018. "Is Artificial Intelligence Set to Become Art's Next Medium?" Christies.com, Dec. 12. https://www.christies.com/features/a-collaboration-between-two-artists-one-human-one-a-machine-9332-1.aspx.

Chu, Gao, and Yu Fu. 2015. "Photographic Manipulation in China: A Conversation between Fu Yu and Gao Chu." *Trans Asia Photography* 6 (1).

Chun, Wendy Hui Kyong. 2014. "Marshall McLuhan: The First Cyberpunk Author?" *Journal of Visual Culture* 13 (1): 36–38.

Cimpanu, Catalin. 2021. "Iconic BugTraq Security Mailing List Shuts Down After 27 Years." *ZDNet*, Jan. 15. https://www.zdnet.com/article/iconic-bugtraq-security-mailing-list-shuts-down-after-27-years/.

Clark, Mitchell. 2021. "NFTs, Explained." *The Verge*, Aug. 18. https://www.theverge.com/22310188/nft-explainer-what-is-blockchain-crypto-art-faq.

Cole, Samantha. 2018. "We Are Truly Fucked: Everyone Is Making AI-Generated Fake Porn Now." *Vice*, Jan. 24. https://www.vice.com/en/article/bjye8a/reddit-fake-porn-app-daisy-ridley.

Coleman, Gabriella. 2012. "Phreaks, Hackers, and Trolls and the Politics of Transgression and Spectacle." In *The Social Media Reader*, ed. Michael Mandiberg. New York: NYU Press.

———. 2014. *Hacker, Hoaxer, Whistleblower, Spy*. New York: Verso Books.

———. 2016. "Hacker." In *Digital Keywords*, 158–72. Princeton, NJ: Princeton Univ. Press.

Collman, Ashley. 2020. "Brazilian President Bolsonaro Suggested His People Are Naturally Immune to the Coronavirus, Claiming They Can Swim in Sewage and 'Nothing Happens.'" *Business Insider*, Mar. 27. https://www.businessinsider.com/coronavirus-jair-bolsonaro-suggests-brazilians-immune-to-disease-baseless-2020-3.

Comstock, Gordon. 2014. "Jennifer in Paradise: The Story of the First Photoshopped Image." *Guardian*, June 13. https://www.theguardian.com/art

anddesign/photography-blog/2014/jun/13/photoshop-first-image-jennifer
-in-paradise-photography-artefact-knoll-dullaart.

Cooper, Helene, Ralph Blumenthal, and Leslie Kean. 2019. " 'Wow, What Is
That?' Navy Pilots Report Unexplained Flying Objects." *New York Times*,
May 26.

Coorlim, Leif. 2013. "Agents Racing to Save Girl Had One Blurred Clue."
CNN, June 20. https://www.cnn.com/2013/06/19/us/cfp-us-race-against
-time/index.html.

Cosne, Gautier, Adrien Juraver, Mélisande Teng, Victor Schmidt, Vahe
Vardanyan, Alexandra Luccioni, and Yoshua Bengio. 2020. "Using Simulated Data to Generate Images of Climate Change." *ICLR Machine Learning in Real Life Workshop*.

Court of Appeals of Ohio, Eleventh District, Ashtabula County. 2007. "State
v. Brady, 2007 Ohio 1779 (Ohio Ct. App. 2007)."

Craddock, David L. 2016. "How Cheat Codes Vanished from Video Games."
Vice, Dec. 21. https://www.vice.com/en/article/8qg7gk/how-cheat-codes
-vanished-from-video-games.

Crawford, Blyth, Florence Keen, and Guillermo Suarez-Tangil. 2021. "Memes,
Radicalisation, and the Promotion of Violence on Chan Sites." *International AAAI Conference on Web and Social Media*.

Crichton, Michael. 1992. *Rising Sun*. New York: Knopf.

Crossley, Rob. 2014. "Mortal Kombat: Violent Game That Changed Video
Games Industry." BBC News Services, Jun 2. https://www.bbc.com/news/
technology-27620071.

CSPAN. 1998. "Lopht Heavy Industries Testifying before the United States
Senate Committee on Governmental Affairs." May 19. https://www.you
tube.com/watch?v=VVJldn_MmMY.

Curtis, Adam. 2016. *HyperNormalisation*. Sandra Gorel, prod. BBC, Oct. 16.

Da, Nan Z. 2020. "Disambiguation, a Tragedy." *n+1*, no. 38, Fall.

Dateline. 1992. "Are Your Secrets Safe?" Susan Adams, prod. Mary Ann Martin, ed. NBC, Oct. 27. https://www.youtube.com/watch?v=NoQflNaPi7A&
t=99s.

Davidhazy, Andrew. 1993. "Special Effects Photography." In *The Focal Encyclopedia*, 3rd ed., ed. Leslie Stroebel and Richard Zakia, 389–95. Waltham,
MA: Focal Press.

Davis, Vincy. 2019. "Now There's a CycleGAN to Visualize the Effects of
Climate Change. But Is This Enough to Mobilize Action?" *Pakt*, May 20.
https://hub.packtpub.com/now-theres-a-cyclegan-to-visualize-the-effects
-of-climate-change-but-is-this-enough-to-mobilize-action/.

Dawkins, Richard. 2016. *The Selfish Gene: 40th Anniversary Edition*. Oxford: Oxford Univ. Press.

de Leusse, Constance Bommelaer, and Carl Gahnberg. 2019. "Consolidation in
the Internet Economy." *Internet Society*. https://future.internetsociety.org
/2019/.

Delp, Edward, Jiwu Huang, Nasir Memon, Anderson Rocha, Matt Turek, and Luisa Verdoliva. 2020. "Media Authentication and Forensics: New Solutions and Research Opportunities." *IEEE Journal of Selected Topics in Signal Processing* 14 (5): 906–9.

Dennett, Daniel C. 2010. "Memes and the Exploitation of Imagination." In *Philosophy After Darwin: Classic and Contemporary Readings*, ed. Michael Ruse. Princeton, NJ: Princeton Univ. Press.

Devroy, Ann. 1994. "Inman Quits, Leveling Charges." *Washington Post*, Jan. 19.

Domo. 2017. "Data Never Sleeps 6.0." https://www.domo.com/learn/infogra phic/data-never-sleeps-6.

Douthat, Ross. 2021a. "Memes Against Decadence." *Reactions Substack*, Mar. 12. https://douthat.substack.com/p/memes-against-decadence.

———. 2021b. "A Guide to Finding Faith." *New York Times*, Aug. 14.

Downey, Greg. 2009. "Thinking Through Claude Lévi-Strauss." *Neuroanthropology*, Nov. 8. https://neuroanthropology.net/2009/11/08/thinking-through -claude-levi-strauss/.

Durbach, Nadja. 2009. *Spectacle of Deformity*. Berkeley: Univ. of California Press.

Dyson, Esther. 1995. "Digital Watermarks." *Wired*, July 1.

Economist. 2017. "A Plan to Build a City from Scratch That Will Dwarf New York." *Economist,* Apr. 6. https://medium.economist.com/a-plan-to-build -a-city-from-scratch-that-will-dwarf-new-york-d0b63ab88646.

Edwards, Benj. 2020. "Fake Video Threatens to Rewrite History. Here's How to Protect It." *Fast Company*, Oct. 3. https://www.fastcompany.com/905 49441/how-to-prevent-deepfakes.

Eismann, Michael T. 2018. "Farewell, Lena." *Optical Engineering* 57 (12): 120101.

Elinson, Zusha, Erin Ailworth, and Rachael Levy. 2020. "In Michigan Plot to Kidnap Governor, Informants Were Key." *Wall Street Journal*, Oct. 18.

Else, Holly. 2021. "Publishers Unite to Tackle Doctored Images in Research Papers." *Nature*, Sept. 28. https://www.nature.com/articles/d41586-021 -02610-7.

Emba, Christine. 2022. *Rethinking Sex*. New York: Sentinel.

Eveleth, Rose. 2015. "How Many Photographs of You Are out There in the World?" *Atlantic*, Nov. 2.

Ewalt, David M. 2013. "The Tale of Captain Midnight, TV Hacker and Folk Hero." *Forbes*, Mar. 18. https://www.forbes.com/sites/davidewalt/2013/03/18 /the-tale-of-captain-midnight-tv-hacker-and-folk-hero/?sh=1c6012111053.

Fadilpašić, Sead. 2019. "12 Billion Devices Will Be Internet-Connected by 2022." *ITProPortal*, Feb. 20. https://www.itproportal.com/news/12 -billion-devices-will-be-internet-connected-by-2022/.

Farid, Hany. 1999. "Detecting Digital Forgeries Using Bispectral Analysis." *MIT AI Memo*, Dec. 1.

———. 2003. "A Picture Tells a Thousand Lies." *New Scientist* 179 (2411): 38–41.

———. 2009. "Image Forgery Detection." *IEEE Signal Processing* 26 (2): 16–25.

———. 2016. *Photo Forensics*. Cambridge, MA: MIT Press.

———. 2018. "Digital Forensics in a Post-Truth Age." *Forensic Science International* 289: 268–69.

Farley, Maggie. 1999. "Dissidents Hack Holes in China's New Wall." *Los Angeles Times*, Jan. 4.

Fisher, Dennis. 2018. "An Oral History of the Lopht." *Decipher*, Mar. 6. https://duo.com/decipher/an-oral-history-of-the-lopht.

Folha de S.Paulo. 2009. "Dilma contrata laudos que negam autenticidade de ficha." June 28. https://www1.folha.uol.com.br/fsp/brasil/fc2806200911 .htm.

Fonseca, Brian. 2000. "Odd Coupling Links Hackers with Security Firm." *InfoWorld*, Jan. 7. https://web.archive.org/web/20041116162703/http://www.info world.com/articles/ic/xml/00/01/07/000107icstake.html.

Fortun, Mike. 2008. *Promising Genomics*. Berkeley: Univ. of California Press.

Frankfurt, Harry G. 2009. *On Bullshit*. Princeton, NJ: Princeton Univ. Press.

Freddoso, Alfred J. 2018. *New English Translation of St. Thomas Aquinas's "Summa Theologiae" (Summa Theologica)*. https://www3.nd.edu/~afred dos/summa-translation/Part%202-2/st2-2-ques95.pdf.

Frosio, Giancarlo F. 2013. "Rediscovering Cumulative Creativity from the Oral Formulaic Tradition to Digital Remix: Can I Get a Witness." *John Marshall Review of Intellectual Property Law* 13 (2).

Funke, Daniel, and Daniela Flamini. 2020. "A Guide to Anti-Misinformation Actions around the World." *Poynter*, Mar. 3. https://www.poynter.org/ifcn /anti-misinformation-actions/.

Galston, William A. 2020. "Is Seeing Still Believing? The Deepfake Challenge to Truth in Politics." Brookings Institution, Jan. 8. https://www.brookings .edu/research/is-seeing-still-believing-the-deepfake-challenge-to-truth-in -politics/.

Gardner, Dan. 2010. *Future Babble*. Toronto: McClelland & Stewart Limited.

Garrison, Jessica, and Ken Bensinger. 2021. "The FBI Allegedly Used at Least 12 Informants in the Michigan Kidnapping Case." *BuzzFeed News*, July 12. https://www.buzzfeednews.com/article/jessicagarrison/fbi-informants -in-michigan-kidnap-plot.

Gaylord, Chris. 2007. "Digital Detectives Discern Photoshop Fakery" *Christian Science Monitor*, Aug. 29. https://www.csmonitor.com/2007/0829/p1 3s02-stct.html.

Gehl, Robert W., and Sean T. Lawson. 2022. *Social Engineering*. Cambridge, MA: MIT Press.

Gershgorn, Dave. 2020. "How Instagram's Viral Face Filters Work." *OneZero*, Jan. 24. https://onezero.medium.com/how-instagrams-viral-face-filters-work -5c98ba05122f.

Gertner, Jon. 2012. *The Idea Factory*. New York: Penguin.

Gibian, Rebecca. 2019. "How the Melissa Virus Changed the Internet." *Inside Hook*, Mar. 26. https://www.insidehook.com/article/history/melissa-virus -changed-internet.

Gibson, William. 1986. *Count Zero*. London: Victor Gollancz.

Godley, Alfred Denis, ed. 1920a. *Histories Book III*. London: Heinemann.

Goerzen, Matt, and Gabriella Coleman. 2022. "Wearing Many Hats: The Rise of the Professional Security Hacker." *Data & Society*, Jan. 14. https:// datasociety.net/library/wearing-many-hats-the-rise-of-the-professional-se curity-hacker/.

Goggans, Chris. 1989. "How We Got Rich through Electronic Fund Transfers." *Phrack*, Nov. 17. http://phrack.org/issues/29/7.html.

———. 1993. "HoHoCon 1992 Miscellany." *Phrack*, March 1. http://phrack .org/issues/42/13.html.

Goldberg, Michelle. 2021. "Why Sex-Positive Feminism Is Falling Out of Fashion." *New York Times*, Sept. 24.

Goldstein, Emmanuel. 2009. *The Best of 2600, Collector's Edition*. Hoboken, NJ: John Wiley & Sons.

Goodfellow, I., Jean Pouget-Abadie, Mehdi Mirza, Bing Xu, David Warde-Farley, Sherjil Ozair, Aaron Courville, and Yoshua Bengio. 2014. "Generative Adversarial Nets." *Advances in Neural Information Processing Systems*.

Goodfellow, Ian, Yosgua Bengio, and Aaron Courville. 2016. *Deep Learning*. Cambridge, MA: MIT Press.

Goodin, Dan. 2008. "Security Researchers' Accounts Ransacked in Embarrassing Hacklash." *The Register*, Aug. 13. https://www.theregister.com/2008/08 /13/security_researchers_targeted/.

Google. 2022. "Violent or Graphic Content Policies." https://support.google .com/youtube/answer/2802008?hl=en&ref_topic=9282436.

Graham, Paul. 2016. "The Refragmentation." Jan. http://www.paulgraham .com/re.html.

Gray, Jonathon, C. Lee Harrington, and Cornel Sandvoss. eds., 2017. *Fandom*. New York: NYU Press.

Greene, Thomas C. 2001. "Dead-Baby Muncher Pic Spawns Police Inquiry." *The Register*, Feb. 22. https://www.theregister.com/2001/02/22/deadbaby_ muncher_pic_spawns_police/.

Greenwald, Glenn. 2014. *No Place to Hide*. New York: Macmillan.

Grinter, Beki. 2022. "Photo Tampering Throughout History." Georgia Institute of Technology. Accessed Jan. 17, 2022. https://web.archive.org/web/202111 20133432/https://www.cc.gatech.edu/~beki/cs4001/history.pdf.

Gutman, Rachel. 2018. "Who Is Weev, and Why Did He Derail a Journalist's Career?" *Atlantic*, Feb. 14.

Han, Byung-Chul. 2020. *The Burnout Society*. Redwood City, CA: Stanford Univ. Press.

Hari, Johann. 2001. "Did the Newspaper Miss the Joke?" *New Statesman* 14 (687): 41.

Harmon, Amy. 1997. "Phony Diana Photo Reignites Debate on Internet Postings." *New York Times*, Sept. 22.

Hankins, James. 2020. "Imprudent Expertise: Science Alone Cannot Guide Our Moral and Political Lives." *First Things*, June.

Harrison, Phil. 2016. "HyperNormalisation: Is Adam Curtis, Like Trump, Just a Master Manipulator?" *The Quietus*, Oct. 6. https://thequietus.com/arti cles/21077-adam-curtis-hypernormalisation-review-bbc-politics-doom.

Hashemi, Mahdi, and Margaret Hall. 2020. "Criminal Tendency Detection from Facial Images and the Gender Bias Effect." *Journal of Big Data* 7 (1): 1–16.

Heaven, Will Douglas. 2021. "Hundreds of AI Tools Have Been Built to Catch COVID. None of Them Helped." *MIT Technology Review*, July 30. https://www.technologyreview.com/2021/07/30/1030329/machine -learning-ai-failed-covid-hospital-diagnosis-pandemic/.

Heisig, Eric. 2019. "Court Says Broadview Heights Attorney Who Created Fake Child Porn for Expert Witness Work Must Pay $300,000 to Victims Despite Bankruptcy." Cleveland.com, Feb. 14. https://www.cleveland.com /court-justice/2019/02/court-says-lakewood-attorney-who-created-fake -child-porn-for-expert-witness-work-must-pay-300000-to-victims-despite -bankruptcy.html.

Henderson, Jeffrey, ed. 2009. *Longus: Daphnis and Chloe. Xenophon of Ephesus. Anthia and Habrocomes*. Cambridge, MA: Harvard Univ. Press.

Hesseldahl, Arik. 2015. "Famed Security Researcher Mudge Leaves Google." *Vox*, June 29. https://www.vox.com/2015/6/29/11563960/famed-security -researcher-mudge-leaves-google-for-white-house-gig.

Holden, Madeleine. 2021. "These Gen Z Women Think Sex Positivity Is Overrated." *BuzzFeed.News*, July 29. https://www.buzzfeednews.com/arti cle/madeleineholden/gen-z-sex-positivity.

Holland, Tom. 2017. "A 2,500th Birthday for the Father of History—and Fake News." *Wall Street Journal*, Mar. 30.

Holzmann, Gerard J. 1988. *Beyond Photography*. Hoboken, NJ: Prentice Hall.

Hruska, Joel. 2015. "Snowden-Approved: The 'Citzenfour' Hacker's Toolkit." *ExtremeTech*, Mar. 20. https://www.extremetech.com/extreme/201636 -snowden-approved-the-citizenfour-hackers-toolkit.

Hubbard, Ruth. 2003. "Have Only Men Evolved?" In *Discovering Reality*, ed. Sandra Harding and Merrill B. Hintikka, 45–69. Dordrecht, Netherlands: Springer.

Humphrey, Samuel D. 1858. *The American Hand Book of the Daguerreotype*. 5th ed. New York: S. D. Humphrey.

International Telecommunications Union. 2007. "Global ICT developments." https://www.itu.int/ITU-D/ict/statistics/ict/.

Isaac, Mike. 2015. "4chan Message Board Sold to Founder of 2Channel, a Japanese Web Culture Pioneer." *New York Times*, Sept. 21.

Jaubert, Alain. 1989. *Making People Disappear*. Mclean: Pergamon-Brassey's International Defense Publishers.

Jeffries, Stuart. 2019. "Is Standup Comedy Doomed? The Future of Funny Post Kevin Hart, Louis CK and Nanette." *Guardian*, Jan. 19. https://www .theguardian.com/culture/2019/jan/19/is-standup-comedy-doomed-future -of-funny-kevin-hart-louis-ck-nanette.

Jenkins, David. 2016. "The Dirty Tricks and Shady Tactics of Adam Curtis." *Little White Lies*, Oct. 27. https://lwlies.com/articles/adam-curtis -hypernormalisation-tricks-and-tactics/.

Johnson, Khari. 2019. "Nvidia's Business Model Is Blurring the Lines of Reality." *VentureBeat*, Mar. 22. https://venturebeat.com/2019/03/22/ai-weekly -nvidias-business-model-is-blurring-the-lines-of-reality/.

Johnson, Robert. 1898. *On the Art of Retouching Photographic Negatives*. London: Marion and Co.

Kantilaftis, Helen. 2014. "Double Exposure Photography." *New York Film Academy*, Nov. 3. https://www.nyfa.edu/student-resources/double-expo sure-photography/.

Karras, Tero, Samuli Laine, and Timo Aila. 2019. "A Style-Based Generator Architecture for Generative Adversarial Networks," *IEEE/CVF Conference on Computer Vision and Pattern Recognition*.

Katz, Josh. 2016. "Who Will Be President?" *The Upshot*, Nov. 8. https://www .nytimes.com/interactive/2016/upshot/presidential-polls-forecast.html.

Kessler, Glenn, Salvador Rizzo, and Meg Kelly. 2021. "In Four Years, President Trump Made 30,573 False or Misleading Claims." *Washington Post*, Jan. 20.

Khaliq, Ahsen. 2022. "ArcaneGAN." Hugging Face Spaces. https://hugging face.co/spaces/akhaliq/ArcaneGAN.

Kirk, Nigel. 2020. "A History of Video Game Cheats." *LevelSkip*, Dec. 22. https://levelskip.com/community/A-History-of-Video-Game-Cheats.

Kirn, Walter. 2016. "The Improbability Party." *Harper's*, June.

Klein, Joe. 2007. "Forever Weird." *New York Times*, Nov. 18.

Knappenberger, Brian. 2012. "We Are Legion: The Story of the Hacktivists." https://www.youtube.com/watch?v=-zwDhoXpk9o&t=699s.

Knowable Magazine. 2020. "Information Apocalypse: All about Deepfakes." Mar. 17. https://knowablemagazine.org/article/technology/2020/informa tion-apocalypse-the-problem-with-deepfakes.

Kolata, Gina, and Roni Caryn Rabin. 2020. "'Don't Be Afraid of Covid,' Trump Says, Undermining Public Health Messages." *New York Times*, Oct. 5.

Kristof, Nicholas. 2020. "The Children of Pornhub." *New York Times*, Dec. 4.

Lagorio-Chafkin, Christine. 2018. *We Are the Nerds*. Paris: Hachette.

Lajka, Arijeta. 2020. "Trump Campaign Ad Used Altered Photos to Make Biden Appear to Be 'Alone' When He Wasn't." Associated Press, Aug. 5.

Lamoureux, Mack. 2015. "This Group of Straight Men Is Swearing Off Women." *Vice*, Sept. 24. https://www.vice.com/en/article/7bdwyx/inside-the-global-collective-of-straight-male-separatists.

Lanier, Jaron. 2018. *Ten Arguments for Deleting Your Social Media Accounts Right Now*. New York: Random House.

Lapsley, Phil. 2014. *Exploding the Phone*. New York: Grove.

Larkin, Daniel. 2017. "Laughing at the Jokes on Ancient Greek Vases." *Hyperallergic*, June 2. https://hyperallergic.com/382118/laughing-at-the-jokes-on-ancient-greek-vases/.

Lerner, Jillian. 2014. "The Drowned Inventor: Bayard, Daguerre, and the Curious Attractions of Early Photography." *History of Photography* 38 (3): 218–32.

Lévi-Strauss, Claude. 1955. "The Structural Study of Myth." *Journal of American Folklore* 68 (270): 428–44.

———. 1969. *Le cru et le cuit. (Mythologiques, vol. I)*. Paris: Plon. Eng. trans. John Weightman and Doreen Weightman. *The Raw and the Cooked*. New York: Harper and Row.

———. 1981. *L'homme nu (Mythologiques, vol. IV)*. Paris: Plon. Eng. trans. John Weightman and Doreen Weightman. *The Naked Man*. New York: Harper and Row.

———. 2017. *Myth and Meaning*. Toronto: Univ. of Toronto Press.

Levy, Elias. 1996. "Smashing the Stack for Fun and Profit." *Phrack*, Nov. 8. http://www.phrack.com/issues/49/14.html#article.

———. 1997. "Phrack Prophile on Aleph1." *Phrack*, Apr. 9. http://phrack.org/issues/50/4.html.

Lemos, Robert. 2003. "RIAA Calls Hacking Claim a Hoax." CNET, Jan. 15. https://www.cnet.com/tech/services-and-software/riaa-calls-hacking-claim-a-hoax/.

Liao, Rita. 2019. "Report: Chinese Spend Nearly 5 Hours on Entertainment Apps Daily." *TechCrunch*, June 12. https://techcrunch.com/2019/06/12/china-entertainment-apps-2019/.

Liao, Shen-yi, and Tamar Gendler. 2020. "Imagination." *Stanford Encyclopedia of Philosophy*. Edward N. Zalta ed. https://plato.stanford.edu/archives/sum2020/entries/imagination/.

Light, Ken. 2004. "Fonda, Kerry and Photo Fakery." *Washington Post*, Feb. 28.

Lin, Tao. 2021. *Leave Society*. New York: Vintage Books.

Liu, Zhiye, and Jarred Walton. 2021. "Nvidia Reveals GeForce RTX 3080 Ti: A 3090 With Half the VRAM." *Tom's Hardware*, June 1. https://www.tomshardware.com/news/nvidia-rtx-3080-ti-3070-ti-reveal.

Livingstone, Rob. 2017. "The Future of Online Advertising Is Big Data and Algorithms." *The Conversation*. Mar. 13. https://theconversation.com/the-future-of-online-advertising-is-big-data-and-algorithms-69297.

Londoño, Ernesto, Manuela Andreoni, and Letícia Casado. 2020. "As Brazil's Covid Crisis Eases, Bolsonaro Sees Rising Popularity." *New York Times*, Nov. 16.

Lotter, William, Gabriel Kreiman, and David D. Cox, 2017. "Deep Predictive Coding Networks for Video Prediction and Unsupervised Learning." *International Conference on Learning Representations*.

Lukáš, Jan, Jessica Fridrich, and Miroslav Goljan. 2006. "Digital Camera Identification From Sensor Pattern Noise." *IEEE Transactions on Information Forensics and Security* 1 (2): 205–14.

Maçães, Bruno. 2020a. *History Has Begun*. Oxford: Oxford Univ. Press.

———. 2020b. *Belt and Road*. London: C. Hurst.

———. 2021a. "The Metaverse Is Here." *World Game Substack*, July 25. https://brunomacaes.substack.com/p/the-metaverse-is-here.

———. 2021b. "Launching the Manifesto of Virtualism." Nov. 3. https://brunomacaes.substack.com/p/launching-the-manifesto-of-virtualism.

Macworld Staff. 2000. "Photoshop through the Years." *Macworld*, Aug. 1.

Maddox, Teena. 2018. "The Internet Will Add 1.4 Billion New Users by 2022 as the World Enters the Multi-Zettabyte Era." *TechRepublic*, Nov. 27. https://www.techrepublic.com/article/the-internet-will-add-1-4-billion-new-users-by-2022-as-the-world-enters-the-multi-zettabyte-era/.

Mao Zedong. 1996. *On Practice*. New York: International Publishers.

Marcus, Gary, and Ernest Davis. 2019. *Rebooting AI*. New York: Vintage Books.

Masson, Terrence. 1999. *CG 101*. San Francisco: New Riders.

Matousek, Mark. 2019. "Elon Musk Contradicted a Bold Claim He Made Last Year about Autopilot." *Business Insider*, Jan. 30. https://www.businessinsider.com/elon-musk-contradicts-2019-prediction-about-tesla-autopilot-2020-1.

Mayer-Schönberger, Viktor, and Kenneth Cukier. 2013. *Big Data*. Boston: Houghton Mifflin Harcourt.

Mayor, Adrienne, John Colarusso, and David Saunders. 2014. "Making Sense of Nonsense Inscriptions Associated with Amazons and Scythians on Athenian Vases." *Hesperia: The Journal of the American School of Classical Studies at Athens* 83 (3): 447–93.

McCabe, David. 2021. "TikTok Is Poised to Outlast Trump, and to Test Biden." *New York Times*, Jan. 15.

McGraw, Gary. 2015. "Silver Bullet Talks with Katie Moussouris." *IEEE Security & Privacy* 13 (4): 7–9.

McLeod, Kembrew. 2014. *Pranksters*. New York: New York Univ. Press.

McLuhan, Marshall. 1967. "McLuhan: Now the Medium is the Massage." *New York Times*, Mar. 19.

———. 1994. *Understanding Media*. Cambridge, MA: MIT Press.

McLuhan, Marshall, and Quentin Fiore. 1967. *The Medium Is the Massage*. New York: Random House.

McMillan, Robert. 2015. "Amazon to Offer Window into Web Services Business." *Wall Street Journal*, Apr. 22.

Meier, Allison. 2018. "How a Fake Monster Creeped into Our Museums." *Hyperallergic*, Jan. 15. https://hyperallergic.com/421405/how-a-fake-monster-creeped-into-our-museums/.

Mendoza, Jessica. 2015. "ISIS Video: Is This Japanese Beheading Real or Fake?" *Christian Science Monitor*, Jan. 24. https://www.csmonitor.com/World/Global-News/2015/0124/ISIS-video-Is-this-Japanese-beheading-real-or-fake.

Menn, Joseph. 2014. "Elite Security Posse Fostered Founders of WhatsApp, Napster." Reuters, Mar. 17. https://www.reuters.com/article/us-whatsapp-woowoo/elite-security-posse-fostered-founders-of-whatsapp-napster-id USBREA260KF20140307.

——. 2020. *Cult of the Dead Cow*. New York: Public Affairs.

Metz, Cade. 2012. "Why the Barcode Will Always Be the Mark of the Beast." *Wired*, Dec. 28.

——. 2021. *Genius Makers*. New York: Dutton.

Milner, Ryan M. 2018. *The World Made Meme*. Cambridge, MA: MIT Press.

Mina, An Xiao. 2019. *Memes to Movements*. Boston: Beacon Press.

Mitchell, Alexandre G. 2009. *Greek Vase-Painting and the Origins of Visual Humour*. Cambridge: Cambridge Univ. Press.

Mody, Cyrus CM, H. Otto Sibum, and Lissa L. Roberts. 2020. "Integrating Research Integrity into the History of Science." *History of Science* 58 (4): 369–85.

Moore, Talia Y., Kimberly L. Cooper, Andrew A. Biewener, and Ramanarayan Vasudevan. 2017. "Unpredictability of Escape Trajectory Explains Predator Evasion Ability and Microhabitat Preference of Desert Rodents." *Nature Communications* 8 (1): 1–9.

Moretta, Tania, and Guilia Buodo. 2021. "The Relationship between Affective and Obsessive-Compulsive Symptoms in Internet Use Disorder." *Frontiers in Psychology* 12.

Morris, Errol. 2007. "Liar, Liar, Pants on Fire." *New York Times*, July 10. https://opinionator.blogs.nytimes.com/2007/07/10/pictures-are-supposed-to-be-worth-a-thousand-words/.

Morris, Tom. 2019. "The Fandom Menace: Profiling Star Wars' Influential Fanbase." *GWI*, Dec. 3. https://blog.gwi.com/chart-of-the-week/star-wars-influential-fanbase/.

Mumford, David, and Desolneux, Agnès. 2010. *Pattern Theory*. Boca Raton, FL: CRC Press.

Murillo, Luis Felipe R. 2020. "Complément du n°56 : Magie et/comme hacking." *Revue du MAUSS permanente*, Nov. 27.

Murphy, Graham J. 2010. "Angel (LINK) of Harlem: Techno-Spirituality in the Cyberpunk Tradition." In *Beyond Cyberpunk*, 229–45. Abingdon-on-Thames, UK: Routledge.

National Academies Press. 2016. "Glenn F. Knoll." *Memorial Tributes* 20: 148–55.

National Science Board. 2018. "Science & Engineering Indicators 2018." National Science Foundation. Jan. https://www.nsf.gov/statistics/2018/nsb 20181/report.

Nerdy Rodent. 2021. "VQGAN-CLIP." GitHub Repository. https://github.com /nerdyrodent/VQGAN-CLIP.

Net Cafe. 1997. "Weird Web." Cheifet, Stewart, Sara O'Brien, and Annaliza Savage. KTEH, Apr. 25 https://www.youtube.com/watch?v=Yf-1_d63Nbo.

Neuman, Scott. 2012. "Decoding the Allure of the Almanac." National Public Radio, Mar. 2. https://www.npr.org/2012/03/02/147810046/decoding-the -allure-of-the-almanac.

Newton, Casey. 2021. "Mark in the Metaverse." *The Verge*, July 22. https:// www.theverge.com/22588022/mark-zuckerberg-facebook-ceo-metaverse-in terview.

New York Times News Service. 1992. "Computer Hackers Put New Twist on 'West Side Story.'" *Chicago Tribune*, July 24.

Newzoo. 2020. "Newzoo Global Mobile Market Report 2020." Sept. 24. https://newzoo.com/insights/trend-reports/newzoo-global-mobile-market -report-2020-free-version/.

Nilsson, Patricia. 2020. "MindGeek: The Secretive Owner of Pornhub and RedTube." *Financial Times*, Dec. 17. https://www.ft.com/content/b50dcoa 4-54a3-4ef6-88e0-3187511a67a2.

Niture, Suryakant K., Abhinav K. Jain, Phillip M. Shelton, and Anil K. Jaiswal. 2011. "Src Subfamily Kinases Regulate Nuclear Export and Degradation of Transcription Factor Nrf2 to Switch off Nrf2-Mediated Antioxidant Activation of Cytoprotective Gene Expression." *Journal of Biological Chemistry* 286 (33): 28821–34.

Olson, Parmy. 2012. *We Are Anonymous*. New York: Random House.

O'Gieblyn, Meghan. 2021. "Babel." *n+1*, no. 40: 37–58.

Ord, Toby. 2020. *The Precipice*. Paris: Hachette.

Ostroff, Caitlin, and Caitlin McCabe. 2021. "What Is Dogecoin, How to Say It, and Why It's No Longer a Joke." *Wall Street Journal*, June 2.

Owens, Jeremy C. 2017. "CA Bids $614 Million for Veracode." *MarketWatch*, Mar. 6. https://www.marketwatch.com/story/ca-bids-614-million-for-vera code-2017-03-06.

Paglen, Trevor. 2010. *I Could Tell You but Then You Would Have to be Destroyed by Me*. Brooklyn, NY: Melville House.

Paraguassu, Lisandra, and Ricardo Brito. 2021. "After Record COVID-19 Deaths, Bolsonaro Tells Brazilians to Stop 'Whining'." *Reuters*, Mar. 5. https: //www.reuters.com/article/us-health-coronavirus-brazil/after-record-covid -19-deaths-bolsonaro-tells-brazilians-to-stop-whining-idUSKBN2AX114.

Paris, Britt, and Joan Donovan. 2019. "Deepfakes and Cheap Fakes." *Data & Society*, Sept. 18. https://datasociety.net/library/deepfakes-and-cheap-fakes/.

Parks, Bob. 1997. "Leave Your Marc." *Wired*. Sept. 1.

Parrish, Michael, and Donald W. Nauss. 1993. "NBC Admits It Rigged Crash, Settles GM Suit." *Los Angeles Times*, Feb. 10.

Parry, Milman. 1971. *The Making of Homeric Verse*. Adam Parry ed. Oxford: Oxford Univ. Press.

Pengelly, Martin. 2020. "Trump Condemned for Retweeting Fake Islamophobic Image Featuring Pelosi." *Guardian*, Jan. 14. https://www.theguardian.com/us-news/2020/jan/14/trump-retweet-fake-islamophobic-image-pelosi-schumer.

Perez, Sarah. 2021. "Consumers Now Average 4.2 Hours per Day in Apps, up 30% from 2019." *TechCrunch*, Apr. 8. https://techcrunch.com/2021/04/08/consumers-now-average-4-2-hours-per-day-in-apps-up-30-from-2019/.

Pew Research Center. 2019. "In U.S., Decline of Christianity Continues at Rapid Pace." Oct. 17. https://www.pewforum.org/2019/10/17/in-u-s-decline-of-christianity-continues-at-rapid-pace/.

———. 2021. "Social Media Fact Sheet." Apr. 7. https://www.pewresearch.org/internet/fact-sheet/social-media/.

Phrack Editorial Staff. 1996. "Introduction by the Editorial Staff." *Phrack*, Sept. 1. http://www.phrack.com/archives/issues/48/1.txt.

Phrack High Council. 2002. "Stop Posting, Stop Helping the Security Industry, or Get Owned. THIS IS WAR." *pHC Phrack*. https://web.archive.org/web/20060512090505/http://phrack.ru/59/p59-0x01.txt.

———. 2003a. "New Hacking Manifesto." *pHC Phrack*. https://web.archive.org/web/20060508224330/http://phrack.ru/62/p62-0x0b.txt.

———. 2003b. "Crucial LKMs for All Hackers." *pHC Phrack*. https://web.archive.org/web/20060508224323/http://phrack.ru/62/p62-0x0a.txt.

———. 2003c. "Sneeze: Wreaking Havoc upon Snort." *pHC Phrack*. https://web.archive.org/web/20060508224342/http://phrack.ru/62/p62-0x0d.txt.

Piketty, Thomas. 2020. *Capital and Ideology*. Cambridge, MA: Harvard Univ. Press.

Podoshen, Jeffrey S. 2020. "Reconceptualizing David Cronenberg's Videodrome in the Age of Social Media." *Quarterly Review of Film and Video* 37 (3): 275–83.

Pollantz, Katelyn, and Stephen Collinson. 2018. "12 Russians Indicted in Mueller Investigation." CNN, July 14. https://www.cnn.com/2018/07/13/politics/russia-investigation-indictments/index.html.

Popescu, Alin C. 2004. *Statistical Tools for Digital Image Forensics*. PhD diss., Dartmouth College. https://digitalcommons.dartmouth.edu/cgi/viewcontent.cgi?article=1009&context=dissertations.

Radio Free Europe/Radio Liberty. 2019. "Videos Show Apparent Torture in Kazakh Prison." July 30. https://www.youtube.com/watch?v=TEMCqAI_gdE).

Rajalingham, Rishi, Elias B. Issa, Pouya Bashivan, Kohitij Kar, Kailyn Schmidt, and James J. DiCarlo. 2018. "Large-scale, High-resolution Comparison of the Core Visual Object Recognition Behavior of Humans, Monkeys, and State-of-the-art Deep Artificial Neural Networks." *Journal of Neuroscience* 38 (33): 7255–69.

Randall, Eric. 2012. "Really, No One Supports Photoshopped Porn of Female Pundits." *Atlantic*, May 23.

Read, Max. 2018. "How Much of the Internet Is Fake? Turns Out, a Lot of It, Actually." *New York*, Dec. 26. https://nymag.com/intelligencer/2018/12/how -much-of-the-internet-is-fake.html.

Ren, Yuan. 2018. "Know Your Chinese Social Media." *New York Times*, Nov. 19.

Reynolds, Matt. 2020. "The Judicial System Needs to Learn How to Combat the Threat of 'Deepfake' Evidence." *American Bar Association Journal*, Feb. 28. https://www.abajournal.com/news/article/aba-techshow-experts-warn -of-deepfake-threats-to-justice-system.

Rid, Thomas. 2020. *Active Measures*. New York: Farrar, Straus and Giroux.

Ripatrazone, Nick. 2017. "The Video Word Made Flesh: 'Videodrome' and Marshall McLuhan." *The Millions*, Apr. 2017. https://themillions.com/20 17/04/the-video-word-made-flesh-videodrome-and-marshall-mcluhan .html.

Roane, Kit R., and Sarah Weiser. 2019. "Population Bomb: The Overpopulation Theory That Fell Flat." *Retro Report*, Oct. 22. https://www.retrore port.org/video/the-population-bomb/.

Rocha, Anderson, Walter J. Scheirer, Terrance Boult, and Siome Goldenstein. 2011. "Vision of the Unseen: Current Trends and Challenges in Digital Image and Video Forensics." *ACM Computing Surveys* 43 (4): 1–42.

Romano, Aja. 2019. "Deepfakes Are a Real Political Threat. For Now, Though, They're Mainly Used to Degrade Women." *Vox*, Oct. 7. https:// www.vox.com/2019/10/7/20902215/deepfakes-usage-youtube-2019-deep trace-research-report.

Romm, James. 1998. *Herodotus*. New Haven, CT: Yale Univ. Press.

Rose, Steve. 2014. "The Real Men in Black, Hollywood and the Great UFO Cover-Up." *Guardian*, Aug. 14. https://www.theguardian.com/film/2014/ aug/14/men-in-black-ufo-sightings-mirage-makers-movie.

Rosencrance, Linda. 2004. "Brief: Vulnerability Database Goes Live." *Computerworld*, Apr. 16. https://www.computerworld.com/article/2563666/ brief--vulnerability-database-goes-live.html.

Rosenthol, Leonard, Andy Parsons, Eric Scouten, Jatin Aythora, Bruce MacCormack, Paul England, Marc Levallee, et al. 2020. "The Content Authenticity Initiative: Setting the Standard for Digital Content Attribution." Adobe Whitepaper, Aug. 4.

Rothman, Joshua. 2018. "In the Age of A.I., Is Seeing Still Believing?" *New Yorker*, Nov. 5.

Rumsfeld, Donald. 2002. "DoD News Briefing Addressing Unknown Unknowns." United States Department of Defense, Feb. 12. https://web.archive

.org/web/20191206110743/https://archive.defense.gov/transcripts/transcript
.aspx?transcriptid=2636.

Russakovsky, Olga, Jia Deng, Hao Su, Jonathan Krause, Sanjeev Satheesh, Sean Ma, Zhiheng Huang, Andrej Karpathy, Aditya Khosla, Michael Bernstein, Alexander C. Berg, and Li Fei-Fei. 2015. "Imagenet Large Scale Visual Recognition Challenge." *International Journal of Computer Vision* 115 (3): 211–52.

Sabeti, Arram. 2020. "GPT-3: Using Fiction to Demonstrate How Prompts Impact Output Quality." July 31. https://arr.am/2020/07/31/gpt-3-using-fiction -to-demonstrate-how-prompts-impact-output-quality/.

Salus, Peter H. 1994. *A Quarter Century of UNIX*. Boston: ACM Press.

———. 1995. *Casting the Net*. Boston: Addison-Wesley.

Salganik, Matthew J., et al. 2020. "Measuring the Predictability of Life Outcomes with a Scientific Mass Collaboration." *Proceedings of the National Academy of Sciences* 117 (15): 8398–8403.

Sankin, Aaron. 2015. " 'The Anarchist Cookbook' and the Rise of DIY Terrorism." *The Kernel*, Mar. 22. https://web.archive.org/web/201701091838 16/http://kernelmag.dailydot.com/issue-sections/headline-story/12210/an archist-cookbook-history-usenet/.

Scharf, Aaron. 1965. *Creative Photography*. London: Studio Vista.

Schiffman, Mike. 1996. "Project Neptune." *Phrack*, Sept. 1. http://www.phrack .com/archives/issues/48/13.txt.

Schewe, Jeff. 2000. "Thomas & John Knoll." *PEI*, Feb.

Schmidt, Victor, Alexandra Luccioni, S. Karthik Mukkavilli, Narmada Balasooriya, Kris Sankaran, Jennifer Chayes, and Yoshia Bengio. 2019. "Visualizing the Consequences of Climate Change Using Cycle-Consistent Adversarial Networks." *ICLR AI for Social Good Workshop*.

Schneier, Bruce. 2000. "The Process of Security." *Schneier on Security*, Apr. 2000. https://www.schneier.com/essays/archives/2000/04/the_process_of _secur.html.

Schofield, Daisy. 2021. "The Young Women Struggling with Porn Addiction." *Refinery29*, Sept. 27. https://www.refinery29.com/en-gb/2021/09/106665 72/porn-addiction-women.

Schroeder, Audra. 2014. "The Legacy of Rotten.com" *The Kernel*, Oct. 26. https ://web.archive.org/web/20191005094145/https://kernelmag.dailydot.com/ issue-sections/features-issue-sections/10700/rotten-history-shock-site/.

Searle, John R. 1995. *The Construction of Social Reality*. New York: Simon and Schuster.

Sears, Jocelyn. 2016. "How Photo Retouching Worked before Photoshop." *Mental Floss*, July 28. https://www.mentalfloss.com/article/83262/how -photo-retouching-worked-photoshop.

Sencar, Husrev T., and Nasir Memon. 2009. "Overview of State-of-the-Art in Digital Image Forensics." *Algorithms, Architectures and Information Systems Security*: 325–47.

Shen, Bingyu, Brandon RichardWebster, Alice O'Toole, Kevin Bowyer, and Walter J. Scheirer. 2021. "A Study of the Human Perception of Synthetic Faces." *IEEE International Conference on Automatic Face and Gesture Recognition.*

Shifman, Limor. 2013. *Memes in Digital Culture.* Cambridge< MA: MIT Press.

Shreve, Jenn. 2001. "Photoshop: It's All the Rage." *Wired*, Nov. 19.

Silver, Nate. 2012. *The Signal and the Noise.* New York: Penguin.

———, 2016. "Final Election Update: There's a Wide Range of Outcomes, and Most of Them Come up Clinton." *FiveThirtyEight*, Nov. 8. https://five thirtyeight.com/features/final-election-update-theres-a-wide-range-of-out comes-and-most-of-them-come-up-clinton/.

Simonite, Tom. 2017. "Nvidia CEO: Software Is Eating the World, but AI Is Going to Eat Software." *MIT Technology Review*, May 12. https://www .technologyreview.com/2017/05/12/151722/nvidia-ceo-software-is-eating -the-world-but-ai-is-going-to-eat-software/.

Siyao, Li, Shiyu Zhao, Weijiang Yu, Wenxiu Sun, Dimitris Metaxas, Chen Change Loy, and Ziwei Liu. 2021. "Deep Animation Video Interpolation in the Wild." In *IEEE/CVF Conference on Computer Vision and Pattern Recognition.*

Slatalla, Michelle, and Joshua Quittner. 1995. *Masters of Deception.* New York: HarperCollins.

Smith, Allan. 2021. "Trump Declares Himself 'Immune' to Covid-19. His Doctors Won't Say When He Last Tested Negative." *NBC News*, Oct. 1. https://www.nbcnews.com/politics/2020-election/trump-declares-himself -immune-covid-19-his-doctors-won-t-n1242851.

Spitzner, Lance. 2003. "The Honeynet Project: Trapping the Hackers." *IEEE Security & Privacy* 1 (2): 15–23.

Srinivasan, Amia. 2021. *The Right to Sex.* London: Bloomsbury Publishing.

Stein, Rebecca L. 2017. "GoPro Occupation: Networked Cameras, Israeli Military Rule, and the Digital Promise." *Current Anthropology* 58 (S15): S56-S64.

Sterling, Bruce. 1992. *The Hacker Crackdown.* New York: Bantam.

Stetler, Brian. 2008. "NBC Settles with Family That Blamed a TV Investigation for a Man's Suicide." *New York Times*, June 26.

Stoll, Clifford. 1989. *The Cuckoo's Egg.* New York: Doubleday.

Story, Derrick. 2000. "From Darkroom to Desktop: How Photoshop Came to Light." *Story Photography*, Feb. 18. https://web.archive.org/web/200706 26182822/http://www.storyphoto.com/multimedia/multimedia_photo shop.html.

Stylianou, Abby, Jessica Schreier, Richard Souvenir, and Robert Pless. 2017. "Traffickcam: Crowdsourced and Computer Vision Based Approaches to Fighting Sex Trafficking." *IEEE Applied Imagery Pattern Recognition Workshop.*

Syrian Arab News Agency. 2017. "Syrian President Bashar al-Assad Responds to Grilling by US Reporter over Allegations of Human Rights Violations in Syria." https://www.youtube.com/watch?v=qImp9HAsac4&t=342s.

Supreme Court of Ohio. 2008. "State v. Harrison, Appellant's Memorandum in Support of Jurisdiction." Feb 1.

Supreme Court of the United States. 2002. ASHCROFT V. FREE SPEECH COALITION (00–795) 535 U.S. 234 198 F.3d 1083, affirmed.

Sutherland, Ivan. 1965. "The Ultimate Display." *International Federation of Information Processing Congress.*

Szabo, Sarah. 2021. "The Untold Truth of Faces of Death." *Looper*, Feb. 1. https://www.looper.com/86648/untold-truth-faces-death/.

Thomas, Jim. 1992. "Some Comments on NBC Dateline's 'Hacker' Segment." *Computer Underground Digest*, Oct. 31. https://www.ripco.com/download/info/CuD/cud4.54.

Tranchese, Alessia, and Lisa Sugiura. 2021. " 'I Don't Hate All Women, Just Those Stuck-Up Bitches': How Incels and Mainstream Pornography Speak the Same Extreme Language of Misogyny." *Violence Against Women* 27 (14): 2709–34.

Trenholm, Richard. 2021. "Nvidia Faked Part of a Press Conference with a CGI CEO." CNET, Aug. 12. https://www.cnet.com/news/nvidia-faked-part-of-a-press-conference-with-a-cgi-ceo/.

Tufekci, Zeynep. 2020. "Can We Finally Agree to Ignore Election Forecasts?" *New York Times*, Nov. 1.

Turek, Matt. 2022a. "Media Forensics: MediFor." DARPA. Accessed Jan. 17, 2022. https://www.darpa.mil/program/media-forensics.

———. 2022b. "Semantic Forensics: SemaFor." DARPA. Accessed Jan. 17, 2022. https://www.darpa.mil/program/semantic-forensics.

United States Court of Appeals, Sixth Circuit. 2011. "Doe v. Boland, 630 F.3d 491 (6th Cir. 2011)".

United States District Court, N. D. Oklahoma. 2006. "U.S. v. Shreck, Case No. 03-CR-0043-CVE."

United States Securities and Exchange Commission. 2020. "Alphabet Inc. Form 10-K." Dec. 31. https://www.sec.gov/Archives/edgar/data/1652044/000165204421000010/goog-20201231.htm.

Vallor, Shannon. 2016. *Technology and the Virtues.* Oxford: Oxford Univ. Press.

Verdoliva, Luisa. 2020. "Media Forensics and Deepfakes: An Overview." *IEEE Journal of Selected Topics in Signal Processing* 14 (5): 910–32.

Waldorf, Sarah. 2021. "The Man Who Photographed Ghosts." *Getty*, Oct. 27. http://blogs.getty.edu/iris/the-man-who-photographed-ghosts/.

Wang, Sam. 2016a. "All Estimates Point Toward HRC>50% Probability. What Determines the Exact Number?" Princeton Election Consortium, Nov. 6. https://election.princeton.edu/2016/11/06/is-99-a-reasonable_probability/.

———. 2016b. "Why I Had to Eat a Bug on CNN." *New York Times*, Nov. 18.

Wattercutter, Angela. 2012. "*Underground* Brings Drama to Julian Assange's Teenage Hacker Days." *Wired*, Sept. 7.

Wells, Henry W. 1971. *Traditional Chinese Humor*. Bloomington: Indiana Univ. Press.

West, Mick. 2015. "Debunked: The Latest ISIS Video of Two Japanese Men Is a Fake, Shadows Wrong [Perspective]." *Metabunk*, Jan. 22. https://www.metabunk.org/threads/debunked-the-latest-isis-video-of-two-japanese-men-is-a-fake-shadows-wrong-perspective.5614/.

Wilbur, Josh. 2020. "America Needs a Ministry of (Actual) Truth." *Wired*, Feb. 4.

Williams, Jordan. 2020. "Eric Trump Shares Manipulated Photo of Ice Cube and 50 Cent in Trump Hats." *The Hill*, Oct. 20. https://thehill.com/blogs/in-the-know/in-the-know/521898-eric-trump-shares-manipulated-photo-of-ice-cube-and-50-cent-in.

Wilson, Edward L. 1890. *Photographic Mosaics*. New York: Edward L. Wilson.

Witness Media Lab. 2021. "Backgrounder: DeepFakes in 2021." WITNESS. March 1. https://lab.witness.org/backgrounder-deepfakes-in-2021/.

Wood, Michal. 1998. *In Search of the Trojan War*. Berkeley: Univ. of California Press.

Woolf, Nicky. 2018. "QAnon: Inside the 4Chan Conspiracy That Suggests Donald Trump Is a Secret Genius." *New Statesman*, Aug. 10. https://www.newstatesman.com/uncategorized/2018/08/qanon-inside-4chan-conspiracy-suggests-donald-trump-secret-genius.

Wu, Min, and Bede Liu. 1998. "Watermarking for Image Authentication." *IEEE International Conference on Image Processing* 2: 437–41.

Xiang, Ziyue, and Daniel E. Acuna. 2020. "Scientific Image Tampering Detection Based on Noise Inconsistencies: A Method and Datasets." arXiv preprint arXiv:2001.07799.

Yeung, Minerva M., and Fred Mintzer. 1997. "An Invisible Watermarking Technique for Image Verification." *IEEE International Conference on Image Processing*.

Yuan, Yuan. 2020. "Bengio and Mila Researchers Use GAN Images to Illustrate Impact of Climate Change." *Synced AI Technology & Industry Review*, Feb. 24. https://syncedreview.com/2020/02/24/bengio-and-mila-researchers-use-gan-images-to-illustrate-impact-of-climate-change/.

Zatko, Peiter. 1995. "How to Write Buffer Overflows." *Lopht Heavy Industries Technologies*, Oct. 20. https://insecure.org/stf/mudge_buffer_overflow_tutorial.html.

———. 1996. "Sendmail 8.7.5." *Lopht Security Advisory*, Sept. https://insecure.org/sploits/sendmail8.6.12-gecos-overflow.freebsd.html.

Zetter, Kim. 2007. "Dateline Mole Allegedly at DefCon with Hidden Camera." *Wired*, Aug. 3.

Bibliography

Zhang, Daniel, Saurabh Mishra, Erik Brynjolfsson, John Etchemendy, Deep Ganguli, Barbara Grosz, Terah Lyons, James Manyika, Juan Carlos Niebles, Michael Sellitto, Yoav Shoham, Jack Clark, and Raymond Perrault. 2021. "The AI Index 2021 Annual Report." AI Index Steering Committee, Human-Centered AI Institute, Stanford University, Stanford, CA. Mar. https://aiindex.stanford.edu/wp-content/uploads/2021/11/2021-AI-Index-Report_Master.pdf.

Zhang, Michael. 2014. "Beauty Retouching from the Early 1900s: A Portrait of Actress Joan Crawford That's 'Photoshopped.'" *PetaPixel*, Oct. 17. https://petapixel.com/2014/10/17/beauty-retouching-early-1900s-portrait-actress-joan-crawford-thats-photoshopped/.

Zuckerman, Ethan. 2019. "QAnon and the Emergence of the Unreal." *Journal of Design and Science* 6. July 15.

———. 2021. *Mistrust*. New York: W. W. Norton & Company.

INDEX

Page numbers with an "f" refer to figures.

Index